Sport Operations Management and Development

This essential textbook introduces the work of sport management and sport development from the perspective of the day-to-day operational challenges faced by managers and sport development officers. It addresses the practicalities of designing and delivering sport services safely, efficiently and effectively, for profit or in non-profit contexts.

The book covers core topics such as time management, project management, customer care, developing partnerships, fundraising, crisis management and research. It adopts a problem-based learning approach, with a strong, practical focus on putting theory into practice, to illustrate good practice and to help the reader develop sound operational skills, knowledge and decision-making, underpinned by the principles of safety, effectiveness and efficiency. It features a range of diverse international case studies, covering different sports and operational management challenges, including global pandemics and terrorism. Connecting theories, ideas and scientific disciplines, the book helps managers approach operations management more creatively, combining both management and development work to show areas of difference and overlap. It also introduces systems theory and the principles of marginal gains or small wins, to help managers develop working cultures which can be utilised in all areas of management, encouraging a culture of learning, reflection and ethical action.

Sport Operations Management and Development is designed for both practitioners and students working in sport management, development, coaching or aspects of sport science.

Mark Piekarz is Associate Head of School at Coventry University, UK. He has taught and developed courses in sport management and development. Before beginning teaching, he worked as a sport facility manager and community sport development officer.

Sport Operations Management and Development

AN APPLIED APPROACH

Mark Piekarz

Routledge
Taylor & Francis Group

LONDON AND NEW YORK

First published 2021
by Routledge
2 Park Square, Milton Park, Abingdon, Oxon OX14 4RN

and by Routledge
52 Vanderbilt Avenue, New York, NY 10017

Routledge is an imprint of the Taylor & Francis Group, an informa business

© 2021 Mark Piekarz

The right of Mark Piekarz to be identified as author of this work has been asserted by him in accordance with sections 77 and 78 of the Copyright, Designs and Patents Act 1988.

All rights reserved. No part of this book may be reprinted or reproduced or utilised in any form or by any electronic, mechanical, or other means, now known or hereafter invented, including photocopying and recording, or in any information storage or retrieval system, without permission in writing from the publishers.

Trademark notice: Product or corporate names may be trademarks or registered trademarks, and are used only for identification and explanation without intent to infringe.

British Library Cataloguing-in-Publication Data
A catalogue record for this book is available from the British Library

Library of Congress Cataloging-in-Publication Data
Names: Piekarz, Mark, author.
Title: Sport operations management and development:
an applied approach / Mark Piekarz.
Description: First Edition. | New York: Routledge, 2021. |
Includes bibliographical references and index.
Identifiers: LCCN 2020036056 | ISBN 9780367333485 (Hardback) |
ISBN 9780367333492 (Paperback) | ISBN 9780429319327 (eBook)
Subjects: LCSH: Sports administration—Study and teaching. |
Special events—Management—Study and teaching. |
Operations research.
Classification: LCC GV713 .P55 2021 | DDC 796.06/9—dc23
LC record available at https://lccn.loc.gov/2020036056

ISBN: 978-0-367-33348-5 (hbk)
ISBN: 978-0-367-33349-2 (pbk)
ISBN: 978-0-429-31932-7 (ebk)

Typeset in Palatino LT Std
by codeMantra

CONTENTS

List of figures viii
List of tables x
List of case studies xi
List of contributors xiii
Preface xiv

Chapter 1 What is sport service operations management and development? 1
1.1 Introduction 1
1.2 What is sport management and development? 2
1.3 What is sport operations management? 10
1.4 The importance of systems theory and the sport operation system 11
1.5 Understanding the impact of the external business environment on sport operations 21
1.6 What makes sport services different from other services? 23
1.7 Conclusion 28

Chapter 2 Organisational purpose and evaluating service operations 31
2.1 Introduction 31
2.2 The importance of performance evaluation 32
2.3 Overview of the performance evaluation process 32
2.4 Sector rationales and purpose 34
2.5 Writing aims and smart objectives 41
2.6 Targets and PIs 45
2.7 Action plans, implementation and monitoring 52
2.8 Conclusion 52

Chapter 3 Job tasks, scheduling and time management 55
3.1 Introduction 55
3.2 Too many jobs, too little time to do them? 55
3.3 Identifying job tasks 59
3.4 Analysing and prioritising work tasks and jobs 63
3.5 Monitoring, reviewing and adjustment 74
3.6 Conclusion 75

Chapter 4 Creating sport programmes to meet needs and wants   77
    4.1 Introduction   77
    4.2 The importance of marketing theory to service design   77
    4.3 How to create a new sport programme   81
    4.4 Conclusion   96

Chapter 5 Customer care, quality systems and regulatory compliance   98
    5.1 Introduction   98
    5.2 The importance of customer care   98
    5.3 Is the customer always right?   102
    5.4 Quality systems and customer care   104
    5.4 The customer service encounter and journey   106
    5.5 Conclusion   119

Chapter 6 Project sport and event management   121
    6.1 Introduction   121
    6.2 The similarities and differences between operations, project and event management   121
    6.3 The project operations process   126
    6.4 Conclusion   141

Chapter 7 Stakeholders, partnerships and volunteers   143
    7.1 Introduction   143
    7.2 Stakeholder theory   143
    7.3 Networking theories   148
    7.4 Partnerships   152
    7.5 The third sector and volunteers   156
    7.6 Operations management skills and knowledge needed for networking, partnerships and managing volunteers   160
    7.7 Conclusion   162

Chapter 8 Fundraising, sponsorship and digital target marketing   164
    8.1 Introduction   164
    8.2 The funding gap   164
    8.3 Overview of funding techniques and the art of persuasion   167
    8.4 Conclusion   187

Contents **vii**

Chapter 9 Crisis management, risk and dynamic risk assessments 189
    9.1 Introduction 189
    9.2 Defining risk, crisis and dynamic risk assessments 189
    9.3 Overview of the risk and crisis management process 195
    9.4 Developing crisis management plans 197
    9.5 Developing a crisis manual or business continuity plan 204
    9.6 Dealing with the media and the need for integrity 207
    9.7 Dynamic risk management, assessments and crisis management 209
    9.8 Conclusions 209

Chapter 10 Researching and consulting communities 212
    10.1 Introduction 212
    10.2 Researching communities and outcomes 212
    10.3 Overview of data collection methods 214
    10.4 Conclusion 230

Index 233

FIGURES

1.1 Sport Services Composition   2
1.2 The Sport Service Operations System   16
1.3 System Causation Factors for the Bradford Fire   18
1.4 Operations System and Coaching Abuse   20
1.5 Examples of Theoretical Sport Positive Outcomes   24
2.1 The Areas of the Sport Management System Which Can Be Evaluated   33
2.2 Key Attributes of Performance Evaluation Process   33
2.3 Three Critical Areas for Clarifying Organisational Purpose   36
3.1 Sources of Job Tasks   56
3.2 The Classic Four-Point Priority Grid   64
3.3 Example of an Overall To-Do lists   69
3.4 Example of a Daily Plan and To-Do List   71
4.1 Programming Checklist Flow Chart   81
4.2 System Showing the Barriers to Participation for People with Disability   85
4.3 Pricing Calculation Form   89
4.4 Application of the Pricing Calculation Form   91
4.5 Service Market Position Map of Competing Facilities   94
5.1 The Virtuous Customer Care Cycle   99
5.2 Overview of the Service Encounter   107
5.3 Sample Barriers to Women's Participation in Sport   109
6.1 The Operational Project Management System   123
6.2 An Overview of the Key Project and Event Planning Process Phases   127
6.3 Post-it Tab Exercise: Identifying Key Tasks, Resources and Stakeholders   130
6.4 Simplified Gantt Chart and Schedule Using a Sport Building Analogy   134
6.5 Sample Gantt Chart for Homeless Rugby Event (Simplified)   136
7.1 Generic Representation of Different Stakeholders   145
7.2 Three Simple Steps in Stakeholder Analysis   146
7.3 Example of a Stakeholder Paradox for a Fun Run Event   147
7.4 Example of Communication Network   149
8.1 The Foundations of Persuasion   168

8.2 Overview of Funding Sources 170
8.3 Overview of the Types of Sponsorship Relationships and Benefits 178
9.1 Synthesised Risk and Crisis Management Process 196
9.2 Examples of Fault and Event Tree Analysis for Sudden Death of Sport Participants 198
9.3 Sources of Crisis Events and Key Consequences 201
10.1 Overview of Research Process 215
10.2 Why Research and Consult Communities 218
10.3 What Data is Collected? 219
10.4 When Do You Collect Data 222
10.5 Data Collection Techniques Overview 225

TABLES

1.1 The Key Functions of Management and Business   8
1.2 Examples of Operations Management Definitions   11
1.3 Examples of Sport Positive Outcomes, Leverage Mechanisms and Nudges   26
2.1 Examples of Classic PIs Based around the Key Areas of Performance   46
2.2 Facility and Service Annual Comparative Data   48
2.3 Comparative Efficiency Ratios   49
2.4 Annual Expenditure (Input data)   50
2.5 Annual Revenue (Output data)   50
2.6 Annual Usage (Output Data)   51
3.1 Examples of Prioritisation Questions and Categories   64
5.1 Servicescape Dimensions   114
5.2 Example of Maintenance Schedule   116
5.3 Customer Care Tips   118
6.1 Similarities and Differences between Operations and Project Management   122
8.1 Sample Factors Which Can Be Leveraged for Persuasion   169
8.2 Examples of Different Countries Grants Available for Sport   172
8.3 Examples of Different Countries Grants Available for Sport   176
8.4 Key Tasks for Seeking and Winning Potential Sponsors   180
8.5 Key Features of a Successful Crowdfunding Campaigns   183
8.6 Overview of Fundraising Techniques   186
9.1 Comparing Definitions of Risk, Crisis and DRA   190
9.2 Description and Examples of Key Sources of Crisis Events   202

CASE STUDIES

1.1 Changing government policies: 'sport for sport's sake' or 'sport for good' 5
1.2 The global nature of sport development work 6
1.3 Examples of overlapping management and business functions in sport management and development work 8
1.4 Black box thinking and marginal gains (British and Canadian cycling) 13
1.5 Examples of complexity and operational failures 17
1.6 The challenges of the external business environment impacting on sport operations 22
2.1 Examples of clarifying purpose with vision and mission statements 37
2.2 Examples of organisational values which shape working practices and can enhance brand appeal 40
2.3 Identifying the principles of SMART objectives even when they are not always explicitly stated 43
2.4 Illustrative examples of analysing data to evaluate performance 48
3.1 A day in the life of a sport agent 57
3.2 Operationalising a basketball strategic plan in China 61
3.3 How would you prioritise these typical job tasks generated in a day? 65
3.4 How the mind works (Levitin, 2014) 72
4.1 The product lifecycle (PLC) of keep fit services 79
4.2 The rise of social sport enterprise programming 82
4.3 Exploring group needs and barriers for swimming 84
4.4 Pricing strategies 90
4.5 Comparing health and fitness services and market placement 93
5.1 Examples of online customer complaints when reviewing sport services 100
5.2 Testing the loyalty of sport fans and the future of the stadium experience 102
5.3 The service encounter, women and removing barriers 108
5.4 Carrying capacity, queue management and the impact of social distance measures 110
6.1 Applying the project system concepts to a fun run event 124

xii   Case studies

6.2 The triple constraints of event projects and the risks generated   126
6.3 From boiling an egg to organising the Olympics: starting an event project   128
6.4 Example of the preliminary job task identification and scheduling of job tasks: homeless rugby project   135
6.5 Micro-leveraging the impacts from events – an observational study of the 2019 Rugby World Cup   138
7.1 The importance of stakeholder theory and CSR   146
7.2 Example of a communications network   149
7.3 The growing importance of partnership work as discrete areas of operations management   154
7.4 Doha world athletics championship and the night of 10,000 metres personal bests (PBs)   156
7.5 Volunteers and the Japan Rugby World Cup   158
8.1 Completing a grant application: small grant application, Sport England   173
8.2 Examples of sponsorship   181
8.3 Examples of sport crowdfunding campaigns   184
9.1 Applying risk and crisis management concepts to swimming pools and swimming   192
9.2 Contextual variations in risk management   194
9.3 When a bat flaps its wings: crisis management, chaos theory and global pandemics   199
9.4 The operational challenges of managing the risk of concussion in sport   206
10.1 Performance evaluation and data collection for a sport *for* development: slam dunking aids out   215
10.2 Using secondary databases to assess demand   220
10.3 Theoretical modelling   223
10.4 An applied example for researching third age users and their active recreation needs and wants   226

CONTRIBUTORS

Paul Blakey is Senior Lecturer in Sport Business Management at the University of Worcester, UK.

Mandy Newbold is Lecturer in Sport Development and Management at the University of Worcester, UK. She is also Tutor and National Faculty Trainer for the Youth Sport Trust and Sport England.

Gillian Renfree is Senior Lecturer and Course Director in Sport Management at the University of Worcester, UK.

PREFACE

The aim of this book is to explain and illustrate how good quality sport services can be researched, designed and delivered safely, efficiently and effectively. It does this by applying some of the key operation management theories and concepts to relevant sport service operations, using a range of local, national and international case studies, to help illustrate best management practice and the universal challenges faced in sport management and development work. Where this book differs from other books on sport management and operations is its more detailed, applied focus of turning theoretical management concepts, into tangible services.

For those who are familiar with sport development work, this book could initially appear more 'management' orientated than 'development' focused. This is because the 'coaching' elements – which can be a strong feature of sport development work – is not discussed in any detail in this book (this subject is better served by more specialist texts). Our argument for combining 'management' and 'development' in a book on sport operations is that the word 'management' should not simply refer to a type of job; management also describes and encapsulates the process of coordinating resources, such as organising the money, staffing and equipment to deliver sport services. In this sense, all coaches and development offices are sport managers, hence the combination.

Whilst the sport industry includes both the delivery of services (e.g. sport events, coaching programmes, etc.) and the manufacturing of sport goods (e.g. sport equipment, clothing, etc.), this book *only* focuses on the delivery of sport services and the many operational challenges this generates. These sport services can be designed for numerous purposes, occur in a variety of locations or require different types of participant involvement. There is, to say the least, a huge variety in the sport services which managers and sport development officers (SDOs) can design and offer to people, to achieve a variety of purposes.

Whatever the purpose, location or type of involvement in the sport service, a crucial underpinning goal for the organisation designing and delivering the service is that they meet people's needs and wants, safely, effectively and efficiently. Those who are familiar with the business function of marketing will recognise this broad principal as being 'market orientated'; this places the customer and client as the central focus of business activity, in terms of understanding what they *need, want* and *expect* from a service, in order to gain satisfaction.

An important theme throughout this book is to challenge many simplistic assumptions about the virtues and benefits of sport. The playing and watching of sport does not, we argue, automatically mean positive benefits to individuals, communities and countries occur. What needs to be understood are the additional intervening mechanisms and actions which managers and development workers need to implement, in order to leverage sport participation into larger, transformational positive changes. Without this understanding, many of the positive benefits may not accrue, which in worse case scenarios, can mean negative impacts occur instead.

Preface **xv**

A key challenge when writing a book on operations sport management and development is that there is a danger that because a service sector has the word 'sport' in it, that this somehow makes them the same or similar. In fact, the sport industry is far more diverse than many would expect. For example, one could compare a small, local amateur football club, with clubs such as Manchester United or Real Madrid. They may share an involvement with the competitive physical activity of the game of football, which needs management and planning, but the scale of resources and the breadth of issues they face will be very different.

So just how can a book be written which is meaningful for sport managers and SDOs who can work in so many different sports, levels of management, supply sectors and countries? The answer is that whilst some of the technical expertise will vary in different roles or sports, it is still possible to identify some of the universal challenges and areas of best practice, which have relevancy in different countries around the world.

This book has the following structure:

- Chapter 1 defines operational management and looks at the similarities and differences between sport management and development. As part of the introduction, it shows how operations management needs to utilise systems and complexity theory to help ensure sport services are operationalised and delivered safely.
- Chapter 2 examines how sport organisations define their purpose and evaluate their performance, based on the levels of performance. Particular attention is given to how outputs (e.g. sport participation) can be leveraged to achieve outcomes (e.g. health benefits).
- Chapter 3 looks at the practicalities of getting jobs done, on time, to the expected level of quality.
- Chapter 4 gets at the heart of designing a sport service, in terms of generating ideas, costing, pricing and delivering the service. This chapter is intimately related to the business function of marketing.
- Chapter 5 looks at the importance of customer care and how using quality systems can enhance the visitor experience, where a critical underpinning is using systems and complexity theory, discussed in Chapter 1.
- Chapter 6 considers the practicalities of project management and the principals and concepts which overlap with operations management, with a particular focus given to sport event projects.
- Chapter 7 explains the importance of using stakeholder theory, when developing networks and partnerships in the effective and efficient design and delivery of services.
- Chapter 8 looks at the importance of fundraising and sponsorship in the contemporary sport service sector around the world, paying particular attention to new fundraising techniques, such as using social media for crowdfunding campaigns.
- Chapter 9 explores risk and crisis management. It explains how risk and crisis management are linked and some of the practical skills which can be developed to help with effective decision-making.

- Chapter 10 examines the importance of research and some of the practical techniques for collecting data and information, particularly on local communities, in order to make the best management decisions.

1
WHAT IS SPORT SERVICE OPERATIONS MANAGEMENT AND DEVELOPMENT?

Challenges for managers

- What is involved in working at an operations level in sport?
- How does operation service delivery differ from manufacturing operations?
- What are the similarities and differences between sport management and sport development?
- What theoretical concepts can help analyse operations to create, maintain and improve services?

1.1 INTRODUCTION

Just what does a sport manager or a sport development officer (SDO) do in their working day, week or month? For someone unfamiliar with the day-to-day workings of a sport manager or SDO, it can be difficult to envision the sheer variety of job tasks which have to be coordinated and completed: Some can be planned for; some will be a reaction to events and incidents on a day; some may be exciting and be the reason why the person entered into the profession; some may be mundane, dull even, yet still vital to ensure the efficient and safe delivery of services. In this chapter, we introduce the variety of job tasks that a manager or SDO will engage with and how they can be represented and categorised.

This chapter begins by defining what is meant by operations management. It explains the difference between simple sport administration, sport management and sport development. It then moves onto exploring operations management as it relates to sport management and development work. A key part of this discussion will be the representation of an over-arching theoretical operations system model. This model gives the key concepts used in operations management, in *any* working sector, together with giving the foundation concepts for later chapters.

1.2 WHAT IS SPORT MANAGEMENT AND DEVELOPMENT?

It is important to gain an insight into the similarities and differences between sport administration, management and sport development. To begin with, this book *is not* about sport administration. Although it is a term commonly referred to around the world, it is conservative and dated one. In the past, managers of leisure venues would primarily focus on facility maintenance and administration, which was often reflected in the types of qualifications required, such as having pool maintenance certificate. The idea of a manager having a degree in sport management would have been a highly unusual occurrence. Torkildsen was always critical of this unimaginative approach to management, arguing that it could be wasteful, if not negligent (Torkildsen, 2005, p. 553. Today, although this type of sport administrator can still be found, it is an outdated concept, difficult to sustain in the modern, global sport business world. In this book, our preference therefore is to adopt Watt's (1998) view of the modern sport manager and SDO, who needs to be dynamic and outward looking, with skills and knowledge of the key management and business functional areas, who takes the initiative in sport service operations.

It is also important to recognise the full diversity of sport, whereby because a service sector has the word 'sport' in it, then this somehow makes a single homogenous area of management. It does not. Whilst there can be linking strands, the work and challenges between various sports or sport sectors can be very different. To help explain why this is the case, we therefore adapt Wilson and Piekarz (2015, p. 9) sector model and Torkildsen's (2005, p. 451) programme classification which identify the many different elements which can shape sport services, presented in Figure 1.1.

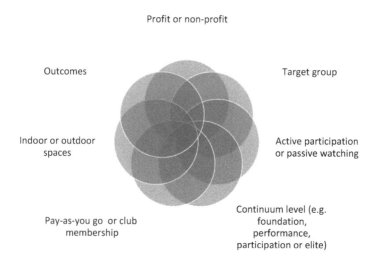

Figure 1.1 Sport Services Composition.
Source: Adapting Wilson and Piekarz (2015) and Torkildsen (2005).

The different elements identified in Figure 1.1 help illustrate variations in service delivery, each presenting their own operational challenges, as the following examples illustrate:

- **Example 1 – Fitness class**: This could take place in an *indoor* gym; runs for *profit* (private sector); can be done as *pay-as-you* go (i.e. you just turn up and pay for the service when you want it); is *non-competitive* and involves *active* participation; and designed to achieve health *outcomes*.
- **Example 2 – A children's community football programme**: This can take place *outdoors*; can be run by a *commercial* football club, but is run on a *non-profit* basis, as children pay a minimal fee to cover just operating costs (called a 'loss-leader' service); it has a small *club* subscriptions for a set number of weeks for the coaching sessions; it is primarily focused on *amateur, foundation level of active* participation, but the club wants to identify future *elite* talent and even encourage the children and their families to attend football games and develop fandom attachment *outcomes*.
- **Example 3 – A sport event in an arena**: This can be done for commercial, *profit* reasons; it can be *ind*oors; it could also be an example of a more complex, large-scale operation, where hundreds of staff may need to be coordinated and thousands of spectators managed; and it involves the *passive* watching of professional athletes, to help achieve inspiration *outcomes*.

One important observation to make is that depending on the combination of elements highlighted in Figure 1.1, this can have profound implications on operational management processes and the risks which need to be managed (e.g. large-scale sport events can carry a higher risk of terrorist attack, or outdoor events can be exposed to weather hazards, which can generate numerous risks, such as extreme weather forcing event closures). These will be elaborated on throughout this book.

Further explanation is needed on the similarities and differences between sport development and sport management jobs. The concept of 'development' in sport can describe a type of job in the sport sector, or be understood as a working philosophy in sport. This becomes clearer when the definition of sport development is explored. Whilst there is no single, agreed definition of sport development, Hylton (2013) gives a useful starting point about some of the challenges and key features of sport development, saying:

> The use – and, some would argue misuse – of the term 'sport(s) development' can be appreciated by a closer look at what each word is describing. Sport has at times been narrowly defined in terms of competitive, rule governed games, involving some degree of physical activity and exercise. Development conjures up ideas of maturation, of education; the gradual consolidation of knowledge; and the teaching of competences and practical skills… Consequently, to develop someone or something suggests a transition through progressive

stages where new and improved outcomes are both possible and desirable. But put the two strange words together, each drawing on different vocabularies, such as sport and development, and what do you get? A new hierarchy or range of meanings emerges.

Hylton (2013, p. 4)

Houlihan (2011, p. 5) notes that sport development is a contested term, observing how it 'starts off apparently simple, but soon becomes mired in ambiguity'. Coalter (2010) also gives an invaluable, critical discussion of how the concept of 'sport development' can be a politically contested term, arguing that the use of sport *for* development has been regularly espoused in public sport policies within westernised societies over the past 20 years. A further illustrative example of this is given in Box 1.1. Exploring these many tensions could be a book in itself, but for now the following key features of development work are focused on here:

- **Sport development is about engagement**: Sport development can describe work which relates to getting more people active or involved with sport in some manner, which often targets particular communities or groups, such as children and the elderly women. At times this can be criticised, particularly if a 'missionary' style of outreach work is adopted, where the sport is 'forced' upon a community whether they want it or not.
- **Sport development is about nurturing**: Sport development can describe the identification and nurturing of sport interest and talent. This is illustrated with the use of the Sport Development Continuum model, which develops the theory that people playing sport go through a pyramid of progression, starting with the foundation level (e.g. getting children to play sport), then moving onto participation (e.g. playing on a regular basis for fun, socialisation or fitness), then performance (e.g. playing on a regular, semi-professional basis) finishing with elite performers (e.g. the small number who perform at the highest competitive level). It is simplistic model, with many limitations, but for now, it offers a basic starting point to explain how people may progress through sport.
- **Sport development is not the same as coaching**: Sport development, whilst often intimately related to sport coaching, should not be used as a synonym or inter-changeable with the term 'coaching'. Whilst all coaches will have a development strand to their role, sport development goes beyond coaching into the sphere of management, as it requires planning and management of resources, hence, the reason it is combined with management in this book.
- **Sport *for* development is different from *sport development***: Coalter (2010) provides a critical discussion of the differences between *sport development* and sport *for* development. Simply put, sport development may focus on expanding participation in a sport, whilst the 'for development' may focus on achieving some other, non-sporting goals, such as trying to improve health or build character traits, such as honesty, teamwork and leadership

(all examples of outputs, explained later). This concept of 'for development' is similar to 'sport plus' arguments, referring to sport being used to achieve goals, such as the claims that it can assist in achieving the UN (United Nations) development goals (UN, 2019), or even with peace and reconciliation projects in war-torn countries.

Box 1.1 Changing government policies: 'sport for sport's sake' or 'sport for good'

The funding of sport by governments has varying rationales, which have reflected the global shifts in political ideologies. For example, in the UK during the 1960s and 1970s, a key rationale for the public funding of sport was based on issues of equity and the idea of 'sport for sport sake' which meant that everyone in society should have the opportunity to access sport and leisure activities, where the intrinsic and personal benefits of sport to the individual were justification enough for the funding.

During the 1980s, there was a global shift in economic and political thinking, where many governments around the world focused on monetarist economic policies, which focused on reducing government expenditure, as this was viewed as a key driver of inflation and poor economic performance. The argument of 'sport for sport sake' as a justification held little sway to the politicians who adopted these neo-liberalist economic policies, so the emphasis by many non-profit sport organisations, who depended on government money to operate, had to change. Steadily, their arguments shifted, focusing on leveraging the externalities of sport (a term from economics, which refers to the potential positive spin-off affects, such as people playing sport becoming healthier, or the claims that it can potentially reduce crime), so sport moved from 'sport for sport sake' to 'sport for good' arguments, which meant that in order to justify public money, sport had to show how it could solve problems or bring benefits. For example, Coalter (1990, p. 16) observed how UK sport funding moved away from general welfare structures (i.e. part of the services that governments support, such as health and education services), to being used *as* welfare, whereby it was seen as a tool to deal with wider social and economic problems.

Around the world, sport policy and funding has continued to move between these philosophies of sport for sport sake and sport for good, reflecting the economic, social and political conditions of the time, as illustrated by Collins (2010) or Green et al. (2018) discussion of sport policy in Scandinavian countries.

Discussion

For a country of your choice, identify the government's current policies towards the funding and support of sport. Is the policy focused more on sport for sport sake or sport for good philosophies?

These key features of sport development highlight two key linking strands between sport development and management, which are:

- **SDOs need to manage resources**: When management is understood in relation to its classic management and business functions, it is clear that SDOs will need to apply the management functions of planning, organising, leading, controlling and communicating in relation to the three key business functional areas of managing staff and volunteers (the HR function), managing money (the finance function) and what services are needed for customers (the marketing function). This is explored in more depth in the next section.
- **Sport managers need to develop sport engagement and participation**: When looking at the key characteristics of sport development, it is clear that most managers of sport services will engage with development-type work, such as how they can get more people involved and engaged with their sport services, whether this is playing, supporting or even to help deliver sport services as volunteers.

Referring back to Figure 1.1 and the different elements of sport services, SDOs can have a preponderance towards the non-profit sector and the active participation of sport. It should, however, be appreciated that there is a continued blurring of the boundaries between the sectors, where development work has increasingly been used on a global scale by *both* commercial and non-commercial purposes, as illustrated in Box 1.2.

Box 1.2 The global nature of sport development work

Here are three examples to illustrate how the boundaries between the profit/non-profit sectors and management/development have become more blurred:

- **Case Study 1 – NFL (National Football League)**: The NFL is the professional American Football League, consisting of 32 teams. It is a league which is constantly seeking to grow its market appeal around the world. In relation to Europe, as part of this strategy, it has developed a variety of activities and events to grow and develop the interest of both playing and watching the sport of American football. As part of this strategy, there has been a growing number of NFL games played in Europe, particularly the UK. There are also strategies for the development of the sport and the leagues to appeal for the lucrative Chinese market. Whilst some of the activities, in the short term, may not generate much profit, the aim is to grow the market interest, which can increase the commercial opportunities for advertising and sponsorship, or selling merchandise.

- **Case Study 2 – World Rugby**: This governing body has developed some particularly ambitious plans for growing women's participation and interest in rugby around the world. As Part of the attempts to operationalise this growth strategy, it appointed ten global leadership scholarships and has held a variety of global forums in Botswana, Madrid and Bangkok. This growth strategy has attempted to strengthen and professionalise the key women's rugby events, such as women's world cup (World Rugby, 2019). Many of the development projects set up to support women's rugby are targeted at the grass roots, foundation level, which are not necessarily designed to generate short-term revenues and profits. The real gains are to be had from growing the popularity of the game, which helps enhance its future commercial appeal and so, it is hoped, helps ensure the sport remains viable in the future.
- **Case Study 3 – UNICEF**: Over the years UNICEF has developed a range of non-profit outreach sport programmes, of the 'Sport *for* Development' type work, where the potential positive outcomes of sport are leveraged to try and deal with a variety of individual and broader political, social and economic problems. For example, there have been initiatives of: encouraging girls to play football, in order to overcome social barriers in education progression; using sport programmes to try and deal with the rehabilitation of child soldiers in Burundi; and using of sport to help educate people about the disease of Aids in African and the Caribbean (UNICEF, 2019).

Discussion

How important is development-type work for the manager who is working in the commercial sector?

How much should SDOs working in the non-profit public or voluntary sectors be concerned with financial management and marketing?

Management has various definitions, where it can be considered in terms of management functions, roles and skills (Wilson & Piekarz, 2015), summarised in Table 1.1. Crucially, all managers in all sectors will need to apply these functions, roles and skills to the three key business functional areas of financial management, human resource management (HRM) and marketing management. Both the management and business functions can also be applied to all the levels of management, which in this work are presented as the strategic, project and operational levels.

In larger organisations, managers and SDOs have the potential to specialise in certain areas, such as working in a HR, marketing or finance department. It is however vital that both managers and SDOs have an insight and understanding of how *all* these areas overlap and interact with each other, if they are to deliver sport services which meet both customers' expectations and the organisations goals, efficiently and safely. Examples of this are given in Box 1.3.

8   Chapter 1

Table 1.1 The Key Functions of Management and Business

Management Functions, Roles and Skills	Business Functions	Levels of Management
All managers and SDOs need to apply the management functions of: - **Planning** (this can relate to goal setting and time management) - **Organising** (who does the what, when, where and how) - **Leading** (giving direction, confidence and energy to drive policies and management initiatives) - **Controlling** (ensuring jobs are kept on track, delegating work and making changes) - **Communicating** (adapts the old command function, but focused on how people are informed and updated on what needs to be done, so there is clarity in their thinking and actions) **Roles of management** relate to interpersonal roles, informational roles and decisional roles **Skills of management** relate to technical skills, human skills and conceptual skills	All managers and SDOs will need to have some understanding and capability to utilise the business functions of: **Human resource management (HRM)** (the capacity to manage staff and volunteers) **Finance** (the capacity to cost out programmes, evaluate performance and control costs) **Marketing** (understand customers' needs and wants and how to communicate your services to target groups) **Risk** (the need to risk assess activities to comply with safety regulations and protect brands)	Both the management and business functions need to be applied to all levels of management of: **Strategic** (this gives the over-arching context of operational plans and involves planning over longer time scales, which can be counted in years, needs to manage a broader range of resources and involves analysing the external business environment) **Project** (this overlaps with both the strategic and operational levels, with one of its key defining features of it having a clear end point) **Operational** (involves more limited time scales of hours, days, weeks and months, and focuses on the actually small details of delivering services to customers)

Source: Adapting Wilson and Piekarz (2015).

Box 1.3 Examples of overlapping management and business functions in sport management and development work

The following examples are based on the job specifications given for three different jobs advertised in the sport of cricket. They help to illustrate how all managers and SDOs will need to utilise the different management functions and skills, summarised in Table 1.1, with the areas between management, development and coaching type work, often blurred.

Case Study 1 – Indoor cricket centre manager for professional cricket club: A top, professional English cricket club in the North of England, built a new indoor cricket facility, to complement its mainstream services of staging cricket matches for people to pay and watch. The new indoor facility has a mixed set of objectives, ranging from traditional facility management and SDO type work, such as:

- Run operations for profit, but with some programmes run as loss-leaders, in order to help achieve other objectives, such as those relating to strengthening community club connections.
- Have active participation programmes for amateurs, foundation level target groups, such as having both boys' and girls' cricket, disability cricket and coaching programmes for talent identification and finally growing interest in the game and affiliation to the club.
- Offer time slots on a pay-as-you go basis for community groups who can hire parts of the facility at their convenience.
- Have time slots for professional players, who would utilise it as a training facility for competitive match games.
- develop partnerships with local amateur clubs, schools, colleges and universities

The role had a requirement of subject expertise to the playing and coaching of cricket, together with a need for experience in the management and business function, such as a capability to manage finances and control costs (the finance function); manage permanent and casual staff (the HR function); develop and promote a range of cricket services or courses, for all abilities, age groups and disabilities (the marketing function); doing risk assessments and ensuring all legal regulations were complied with, ranging from Health and Safety regulations, to child safeguarding (the risk management function).

Case Study 2 – Cricket development officer: A cricket development officer was created by joint funding between Worcestershire Cricket Board and Warwickshire Cricket Board (a professional, commercial club), in partnership with the Lord's Taverners (a charitable organisation). A key part of the job remit was to use the 'power of cricket as a tool for change, social cohesion and make a difference to the lives of people in deprived areas of Birmingham, Dudley & Redditch'. It is an example of cricket being used to generate positive externalities or sport *for* development. In terms of the elements of the service, it was characterised by having non-profit social objectives, focusing on how cricket can be used to tackle social problems, promoting healthy lifestyle choices and developing community inclusivity. It would be a peripatetic role (i.e. they are more mobile, whose remit is to go out into the community, helping to establish various service programmes, in different types of venues), based on setting up programmes in a variety of indoor and outdoor spaces, over a large geographic area. The role also needed to develop partnerships

(continued)

Box 1.3 (continued)

with many key stakeholders, ranging from local cricket clubs, charities and schools (see also Chapter 7).

Whilst this job has many classic sport development-type features and experience needed, it should again be noted that it also required experience of the management and business functions, because the work involved designing new services within specified budgets and compliance with legal regulations.

Case Study 3 – Kooh Sports in India: Kooh Sports describes itself as a sport education and training company primarily based in India and the UAE. It is backed by Gaja Capital, a large domestic private equity fund in India. What is of interest about Kooh is its focus on sport development-type work in a variety of sports, developing partnerships with different sport clubs and educational institutions. The work they do has a strong orientation towards social objectives and trying to achieve positive social outcomes. It is the sort of work which in many countries would be delivered more by the public and voluntary sectors, but in India it is being delivered by a commercial organisation.

Discussion

For a sport you are interested, identify the different types of management and development jobs available, then what are the key management functions, roles and skills needed to perform the job.

1.3 WHAT IS SPORT OPERATIONS MANAGEMENT?

In essence, sport operations is about getting jobs done on time, to the expected level of quality. At an intuitive level, we know the sort of things it should involve, such as opening sport facility doors on time; having qualified/trained staff, coaches and volunteers turn up with the relevant equipment; having facilities which are clean and safe; recruiting and training staff and volunteers; and communicating to staff and customers the *what*, *when* and *where* of sport services.

In Table 1.2, three sample definitions are given in relation to operations management, which can be used to develop a more formal definition of sport operations management. Far more definitions could be used, but these are sufficient to help draw out some of the key features of sport service operations. The first point to focus on is that operations management is about *creating* and *designing* services. The second relates to how some of the definitions require the utilisation of the classic management functions, noted earlier. The third point is the suggestion that operations management can be viewed as part of a *system*, which *transforms* input resources into actual tangible services (the process or throughput part), which when consumed generate *outputs* and potential *outcomes*.

What is sport service operations management

Table 1.2 Examples of Operations Management Definitions

Example 1 Generic Operations Definition	Example 2 Sport Operations Definition	Example 3 Generic Operations Definition
Operations …is 'the part of the organisation where the requirements of the market and the capabilities of organisation's resources have to be reconciled… the reconciliation of market requirements with operations resources is the activity of managing the <u>resources</u> that <u>create</u> and deliver services and products. The operations function is the part of the organisation that is responsible for this activity. <u>Every organisation has an operations function</u> because every organisation <u>creates</u> some type of service and/or products' (Slack et al., 2016, p. 6)	'Operations management for a sport facility is defined as the <u>maintenance, control, and improvement</u> of organisational activities that are required to <u>produce</u> products and services for consumers of the sport facility' (Schwarz et al., 2010, p. 123)	'It is the <u>design</u> and <u>delivery</u> of services. It is about <u>organising</u> <u>resources</u> to <u>produce</u> goods or services, or turning inputs into outputs' (Heizer & Render, 2004)

Our Synthesised Definition

Sport operations management and development is a *transformational process* which *creates*, *maintains* and *improves* the delivery of safe sport services of a consistently high quality

Source: Author.

The synthesising definition of sport operations management presented at the table has three critical features, used throughout this book, relevant for both sport managers and SDOs, which are:

- **Create**: Operations management will often have a focus on designing and creating new services which meet the needs, wants and expectations of clients, customers or stakeholders (see Chapters 4, 6 and 10 for more practical insights).
- **Maintain**: Operations management must always focus on *maintaining* the efficient and safe delivery of services (see Chapters 2 and 5).
- **Improve**: Operational management must always look to *improve* the quality, service experience and safety of services (see Chapters 2, 5 and 7).

1.4 THE IMPORTANCE OF SYSTEMS THEORY AND THE SPORT OPERATION SYSTEM

In this book, systems and complexity theory is a key underpinning for how operations management is approached and used. Systems theory has its roots in understanding how living organisms work, and to do this properly, it is necessary to understand the complex interaction of a living organisms' many parts, whereby if one part was to fail, it can lead to the system impairment or failing (i.e. death of the organism). To use the analogy of the human body, it is about understanding how all the different elements of the body, ranging from the heart, stomach, liver, blood, etc., combine to allow life, whereby if a part is damaged, then it can impair either the quality of life or even lead to death. This provides a useful analogy, which can be adapted not just for sport operations management, but *all* management, as it reminds the manager and SDO that they need to take care of all the different parts of the service to ensure the safe, efficient delivery of services which combine to give customer satisfaction.

What adds to the importance of using systems theory is that the working environment of contemporary sport managers and SDOs is one increasingly characterised by constant change and dynamism. Not only do managers need to consider the complex interaction of all the different business functional areas in order to transform the mix of input resources (e.g. staffing, money, equipment, facilities, etc.) into outputs (e.g. the people coming to watch or participate in the sport service), they also need to consider how external forces, beyond their control, can impact on their operations, such as political events, economic changes and technological developments (i.e. the classic PESTLE factors analysis explained later). Box 1.4 further elaborates on how the theory has been used in practice.

The sheer variety of connecting factors that constantly interact, generating changes or creating crisis events means that the system that the sport manager or SDO operates in is also characterised as being complex, sometimes chaotic. These two concepts have their own theories which are also useful to understand:

- **Complexity theory**: This is rooted in systems theory, which continues with the idea of viewing the organisation and world as operating as part of an interactive, adaptive system. Operations management should try to understand the complex operations systems as best they can. An analogy sometimes used is of a doctor or surgeon who operates on a human body which is considered as a complex system, not (usually) a chaotic one. As part of this surgical operation, the doctor must monitor numerous aspects of the surgical complex, interactive process, such as coordinating team members, monitoring the patients vital signs using a range of technology and operating on the correct part of the body, where even small failures in any of these areas can imperil the patients' health. In business, this theory of complexity can be given further refinement by using the acronym of working in a VUCA world (Gerras, 2004, p. 11), which stands for a business environment which is more:
    - **V**olatile (the speed of unexpected events are generated)
    - **U**ncertain (it is harder to know what will happen in the future, or the repercussions of actions)
    - **C**omplex (managers operate in a complex interactive system)
    - **A**mbiguous (there can be a lack of precedents to know just what issues will be generated in the future and the potential to misread events)

- **Chaos theory**: This relates to how the world is viewed, where small changes or events, which at the time can seem unimportant, can ripple out creating all sorts of unanticipated events and consequences. This is sometimes encapsulated by the analogy of Edward Lorenz's 'butterfly affect', which describes how a butterfly, flapping its wings in Brazil, could create small variations in air currents, which continue to combine and interact, so that eventually a tornado could be created in another part of the world. The difficulty – impossibility even – of trying to predict all these chaotic interactions is why some argue that trying to forecast or anticipate the future will be doomed to fail and businesses will always be operating on the *edge of chaos* (i.e. stable operating conditions which can quickly tip into chaos and a crisis). Our stance in this book is to avoid the fatalistic view of not trying to anticipate the future, as we believe that having a plan that can be adapted is better than not having one at all (see also Chapter 3).

Box 1.4 Black box thinking and marginal gains (British and Canadian cycling)

Syed (2016) discusses complexity theory in his book *Black Box Thinking*. The 'black box' is the analogy used to represent the good practice that the aviation industry has in terms of learning from failure, where blame is avoided in any air crash investigation and where there is a constant desire to make improvements to aviation safety. Black box thinking shows the importance for all organisations of developing cultures which constantly reflect and analyse failure to help improve performance. Syed, as do many others, argues that 'failure is rich in learning opportunities and something which will be inevitable, as the world is complex' (Syed, 2016). The outcomes of these failures will vary from being mildly irritated by poor customer service to catastrophic disasters where people are killed.

An important underpinning theory for Syed's approach is the use of systems theory, which is illustrated through his discussion of the principle of marginal gains: the idea of breaking a complex system down into its many constituent parts, in order to understand how they interact with each other, and examining how small or incremental changes can help improve the performance of the system. Part of the thinking is, as Syed argues, not about making small changes and hoping they fly (Syed, 2015), rather, it is about breaking down a complex issue into smaller parts in order to rigorously establish what works and what does not. To do this requires the use of open system loops, which simply means that each output is reflected on and analysed, where '…every error, every flaw, every failure, however small, is a marginal gain in disguise. The information is regarded not as a threat but as an opportunity' (Syed, 201, p. 196).

(continued)

Box 1.4 (continued)

In truth, the concept of marginal gains are far from a new theory, where the underlying principles can be framed using different terminology. For example, it overlaps with the theories of incrementalism, which refers to how significant changes to an organisation, even a society, should be done gradually, through many smaller actions. Auluck (2001) adapts this principle to develop the *small wins* approach, which examines how a business can become more successful, if they make many small changes and improvements to business practices, as these are both easier to measure and less disruptive. These themes of small improvements and measurement also form a fundamental foundation of total quality management theories, such as Kaizen, discussed in Chapter 5. Another illustration comes from Carlzon (1987), an influential business leader and writer, demonstrates the same points, but without citing systems theory, but it is implicit in his often-quoted point (which also has a number of variations) of:

> You cannot improve one thing by a 100% but you can improve 100 little things by 1%.

One of Syed's case studies used to illustrate his argument was the success of David Brailsford and how he helped transform the competitiveness of UK cycling. It was a system where every aspect of cycling performance was tested, analysed and actioned upon, ranging from cycling positions on a bike, training sessions, diet, etc. Although the system helped deliver fantastic successes, it was also one hit by a variety of controversies, ranging from accusations of bullying and sexism by some of the coaches, and to pushing the limits of how far certain drugs could be used, which has tainted some of the successes. These problems, however, are not necessarily a problem with using the theory of marginal gains or small wins, but how all management also needs to consider its working culture and practices, where there has to be an underpinning consideration of ethics, where the cost of winning should not be at any cost, but what is a right and proper way of behaving.

The influence of these ideas has gained traction in many other countries and sports. For example, Wooles (2018) discusses the importance of the marginal gains concept in relation to Canadian cycling. Crucially, whilst marginal gains are important, Wooles reiterates the importance of not just focusing on the scientific gains made by analysing athlete's performance, but also how it fits in within the whole organisational structure, which should include the operational administration culture which the athletes train within, arguing that 'winning' should not be done at any cost, but must be done legally, safely and ethically.

Discussion

For a sport service which you have used, identify all the key components which helped create the positive or negative experience felt.

When using systems and complexity theory, the following features should therefore be considered in developing an operations management culture that can help guide working practices:

- Sport operations has many different *interconnected* parts.
- The creating, maintaining and improvement of sport services depends on understanding the dynamic interplay of resources, stakeholders and events, which need constant monitoring and management. This is also a vital foundation in management problem-solving.
- Building in points of critical reflection is crucial, because the operations system is a constantly changing one, where management actions will introduce a new dynamic into the system that can potentially generate another set of challenges and problems (explained as the boomerang affect, discussed in Chapter 3).

These theories may initially seem quite complex, but in truth many managers and SDOs may have already used system and complexity-type thinking approaches at an intuitive level, without ever describing or labelling them as such things. For example, a sport coach when trying to improve an athlete's performance may examine different areas of their training, such as diets, working on their strength and conditioning, or even working on their mental strength (see Box 1.4). Alternatively, a sport manager organising an event would identify numerous parts of the event which must be managed, if the event is to be a success, such as organising staff, ensuring the event is promoted and checking that all legal guidelines are adhered to. In both examples, a failure to complete one of these actions can be detrimental to the quality of the outputs and outcomes.

So how should the sport operations system be represented? In Figure 1.2 a representative model is developed which gives a preliminary identification of some of the key concepts of the sport operations system. In this model, it identifies the following key components:

- **Inputs**: There can be two types. Transformed resources, such as the customers entering the venue, or *transforming* inputs, such as the cost of staff and equipment used.
- **Process**: This relates to throughputs, which focuses on the actual programmes and events offered, which transforms the inputs resources into outputs and outcomes.
- **Outputs**: This relates to what the process generates, which can be measured in various ways such as the number of people who attend the event, the revenue generated or the profit or loss made.
- **Outcomes**: These are impacts which are sometimes sought from the outputs, such as behavioural changes, improvements in health or benefits to society. This relates back to the concepts of sport *for* development, sport plus arguments or externalities (i.e. the positive or negative spin-off effects from the production and consumption of the service), discussed earlier.
- **Leverage**: This is used to refer to the intervening actions or policies taken to try and gain the outcomes, from the outputs, whereby a smaller effort

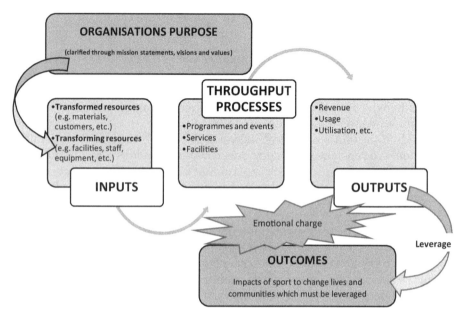

Figure 1.2 The Sport Service Operations System.
Source: Author.

results in a bigger change or impact (e.g. a sporting success at an elite level, such as an athlete winning a gold medal at the Olympics, is leveraged by an SDO who offers some additional taster sessions which gets children involved and active in the relevant sport). Leverage can come in three classic forms (Anderson, 2014): economic (e.g. withholding or awarding grants to sport governing bodies); bargaining (e.g. negotiating actions) and emotional (e.g. inspirational effects of watching elite athletes can be used to encourage others to take up the sport). This latter point is given additional consideration in this model and returned to later in this chapter.

- **Emotional charge**: One of the unique characteristics of sport services is their potential to generate a wide range of emotional experiences (e.g. enjoyment, excitement, relaxation, joy, frustration, etc.), or a strong personal and emotional identification (Blakey, 2011, p. 4), which is as critical resource which can be leveraged to generate action and change behaviour.

Some examples can help to further illustrate what the system concepts are and how they relate to each other. One analogy is to think about how a car is driven. The car can be considered as part as the process stage of the model. To achieve anything however, it needs inputs, which could be the person driving the car (the transformed resource) and fuel to make it go (the transforming resource). With these inputs in place the car can now move and achieve an output, such as getting the person to work. In theory, there may also be some desired outcomes, such as the car being used to feed the persons ego and raise their status by impressing others. However, these outcomes are not automatically achieved by driving from A to B, as they must be leveraged, so consideration must be given to who sees the person driving the car or pictures posted on social media.

A sport example can relate to a SDO with a remit to get more elderly people physically active (the output) in order to improve their health (an outcome). To achieve these things, a sport service or programme is designed to take place in a community hall (the process). To get this process to work, inputs are needed in terms of customers, staff and equipment, which are transformed and generate outputs, such as the number of elderly people who attend. Crucially, having these outputs does not automatically mean the health outcomes are achieved. These must be carefully leveraged, such as ensuring that the activities are done in such a way that injuries do not occur, or additional opportunities are given to help facilitate more social interactions, which contributes towards their mental and social health and well-being.

Adopting systems and complexity theory as part of the managers or SDOs working culture or philosophy encourages a deeper critical analysis of management operations and problems. It does this by examining how service operations and problems exist as part of a dynamic and interactive system, where every set of management decision has the potential to generate another set of issues (what is described later as the boomerang affect, discussed in Chapter 3). It moves away from simple linear cause and affect analysis, looking at how causation factors can depend on the multiple interaction of factors. The importance of using systems theory to explore problem causation is examined in Box 1.5

Box 1.5 Examples of complexity and operational failures

The following examples are used to illustrate how using complexity systems theory can help give a deeper analysis of past crisis events in sport, in order to get a better understanding of the many, *not* the single, operational improvements which need to be made to try and reduce the likelihood of similar risk events occurring again in the future.

Case Study 1 – Bradford fire and operational failures: In 1987, 56 fans died in a fire at the Bradford Valley Parade football stadium, in the UK, whereby in less than five minutes, an old football stand which had thousands of spectators in, was completely ablaze. It is a case which demands analysis because of all the failures in operational practices, which meant people paid with their lives! The causation factors for the stadium catching fire were multiple, which had existed for years, but lying dormant, which just needed a trigger event for the disaster to happen. These factors are represented in Figure 1.3.

The point of this figure is to help illustrate that there are a variety of interaction factors which create the risk probability of a fire occurring in the first instance which needs to be managed (See also Chapter 9). For a fire to

(continued)

Box 1.5 (continued)

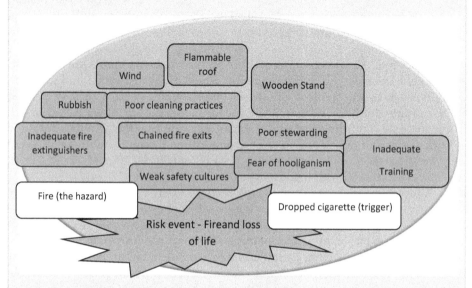

Figure 1.3 System Causation Factors for the Bradford Fire.
Source: Author.

start it needs three things: oxygen (the wind on the day intensified the fire), fuel (the rubbish and wooden stand) and a trigger (the dropped cigarette). These conditions had been there for years, but, on this particular day, they combined with devastating tragic consequences. The Bradford fire illustrates the dangers of having poor operational practices and not understanding the interconnected dynamics of the facility and event. Consider the following points for how different operational practices could have changed the risks of fire occurring or dealing with the severity of the consequences:

- Rubbish had been allowed to collect under seats over a long period of time: if an operations manager had ensured the facility was properly cleaned, the litter hazard would be removed and so the risk of fire starting, reduced.
- The fire was caused by a dropped cigarette smouldering in rubbish which had collected over years: if a no smoking policy been enforced by stewards this could have reduce the risk of a fire starting.
- 27 people died by the fire exits which had been chained closed, to stop people opening them to let other people sneak in: an operations manager should ensure fire exits are checked for *no* obstructions or locks, but using stewards to supervise the exits and aid in evacuations.

Case Study 2 – Coaching abuse in sport: In recent years, there has been greater exposure of the number of sport coaches abusing young athletes around the world. Here are just a few high-profile cases from different countries to show the breadth of the problem, which relate to sexual, physical and mental abuse:

- Larry Nassar, a sport medicine doctor in the USA, was convicted for sexually abusing more than 150 female athletes, over decades, even though the first allegations of abuse were raised in the 1990s. Despite these reports, what was shocking was how much effort went into denying the allegations by the governing body, rather than investigating them, which showed a weakness in the integrity of their working culture.
- In the UK, there has been a spate of convictions of sport coaches, such as Barry Benell who was jailed for 50 cases of child abuse, over twenty years. Another was Bob Higgins who was an influential youth coach at Southampton Football Club (FC), who groomed and abused young boys over a 30-year period, but who was not exposed until former players came forward in 2016. Governing bodies and clubs who could have intervened, frequently failed to investigate allegations or ignored warnings.
- In Australia, a swimming instructor, Kyle Daniels, was arrested and charged with over 30 sexual sex offences, despite complaints made against him months earlier. Scott Volkers was another prominent case, who coached at a national level with the Australian swimming team, who went on trial for child sex offenses with girls, where reports of abuse were ignored as he was considered 'too good a coach to sack.'
- In New Zealand, Alosio Taimo's was a junior rugby coach and was convicted of 95 cases of sexual abuse against young boys, over a 30-year period. Whilst the most prominent case in New Zealand, it was not an isolated one, as many other cases have occurred in New Zealand, such as a football coached grooming and molesting young girls in his care.
- In Canada, the Minister of Sport in the Canadian Federal Government Kirsty Duncan following a CBC investigation revealed more than 200 coaches have been convicted of sexual offences against 600 victims under the age of 18 in the past 20 years (Conversation, 2019).
- In South Korea a speed skating coach, Cho Jae-beom, was convicted of hitting and sexually abusing elite athletes, which also proved a tipping point for more people to come out and reveal instances of coaches who had physical abused, raped or molested athletes going back many years.
- In Japan, the case of the Judo coach Ryuji Sonoda who had brought Olympic success for the women's team, was revealed to have an appalling record of physical and emotional abuses, where he slapped, kicked and even beat athletes with sticks, along with verbally abusing them, calling women pigs and ugly and creating an atmosphere of intimidation and fear. Again, this proved something of a tipping point in Japan, where more cases of abuse were revealed (McNeill, 2013).

Whilst it has been stated that this is not a book about coaching, these cases of coaching abuse illustrate failures in operational practices and ethical

(continued)

Box 1.5 (continued)

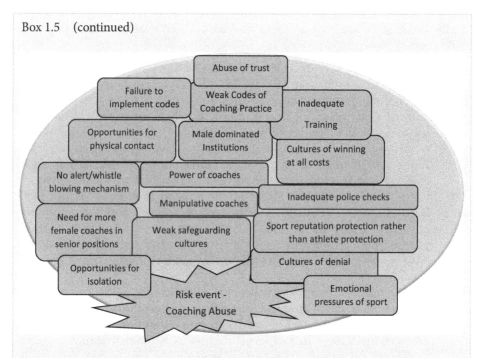

Figure 1.4 Operations System and Coaching Abuse.
Source: Author.

leadership, as it is the managers and SDOs who may employ the coaches or supply the spaces for the sport activities to take place. This means that they have both a moral and legal obligation to ensure the safety and welfare of participants. When analysing the cases and utilising a variety of research journal papers and books, such as the invaluable edited book on *Safeguarding, Child Protection and Abuse in Sport* by Lang and Harthill (2015), it reveals a complex interactive system of factors, represented in the simple operations system in Figure 1.4.

The cases highlighted should also act as a powerful reminder for sport managers and SDOs to always maintain a critical edge about the power of sport to do good. These cases should evoke feelings of anger and frustration and questions of how people could get away with abuse for so long. The cases are particularly revealing about the complacent working cultures of the governing bodies or clubs, where the reputation of the sport was put above the safety of the athletes, sometimes compounded by a 'winning at all cost' culture. Looking at this analysis of factors and how they interact should, however, give the manager or SDO immediate actions to take in service operations, in order to ensure there is greater safety such as:

- Developing codes of good coaching conduct for sport both generic and tailor made for sports-clear protocols of physical contact (e.g. similar to physios and doctors, such as asking people for their permission to examine them), or not working in isolation)

- Challenging traditional male hegemonic institutions and cultures, to help bring longer term organisational cultural changes;
- Challenging cultures of silence and creating opportunities for people to raise areas of concern which are listened and acted on;
- Ensuring any staff in contact with young people have had police checks done and these are checked;
- Ensuring managers and SDOs stay updated of best practice guidelines or regulatory changes.

Discussion

Using a variety of news websites, search for more instances of sport crisis events and distil the key risk causation factors, and what operational practices should have been taken to avoid the crisis?

1.5 UNDERSTANDING THE IMPACT OF THE EXTERNAL BUSINESS ENVIRONMENT ON SPORT OPERATIONS

Sport operation systems not only interact with their many internal constituent parts, but also with many external forces. This is the impact of the external business environment, where perhaps the most common way of representing this is by using the PESTLE framework (or one of its many variations), which can be combined with a SWOT analysis. There are more sophisticated tools, but PESTLE and SWOT are sufficient for our discussion here. These acronyms offer a simple method to analyse both the internal and external business environments and stand for:

PESTLE	*SWOT*
- Political – How do changes in political conditions, such as changes in government, impact on operations - Economic – How the economy is performing can impact on consumer confidence and how much they spend on sport services - Social – How changes in society, such as the age demographics or changing social attitudes, affect sport services - Technological – How new technologies impact on the consumption of sport services, such as the use of social media - Legal – What legal regulations need to applied, such as how new regulations or court rulings can affect safety control measures - Environment/ecological – How natural forces can be positive or negative on services, such as the weather or natural disasters disrupting service operations	- **Strengths** – What is the organisation or business good at - **Weaknesses** – What are the weaknesses or failings of the organisation - **Opportunities** – Where are the opportunities being generated by either competitors' actions, or any of the PESTLE factors - **Threats** – Where are the threats being generated from by competitors' actions or any of the PESTLE factors

The analysis of the external business environment is usually discussed at the strategic level of management and planning, but it is essential that the operations manager or SDO understand the link between strategy and operations, and how the external business environment can impact on day-to-day operations. To reiterate what should be a familiar argument now, sport managers and SDOs who are responsible for the operational delivery or sport services must recognise that their services operate within a complex connected system, where there are numerous external forces which are beyond their control, but which can have profound impacts on the successful delivery of sport services. They should also appreciate that whilst in theory, business strategies feed down and shape sport operations (see Chapter 2), their operational decisions can reverberate back up the chain and have strategic implications (Slack et al., 2016, p. 15). In Box 1.6, a variety of examples are given to illustrate how changes in different environmental factors can impact on their operations.

Box 1.6 The challenges of the external business environment impacting on sport operations

The following examples show how sport managers or SDOs who may be involved with the operational delivery of sport services can have their services disrupted for good or bad, by events beyond their control. The external event which has the largest impact on sport operations around the world was the Covid-19 pandemic which began in China in 2019, which will be returned to in Chapters 4, 5 and 9. For now, here are a couple of other examples to illustrate the VUCA world and how businesses seem to always operate on the edge of chaos.

Case Study 1 – Sport events in Korea: For a sport operations manager in South Korea, when organising any sport events, the political environment and relations with North Korea pose a constant challenge, creating many threats and opportunities. Whilst sport in Korea has often been used as a tool in political diplomacy, to try and improve the relations between the countries, in order to nurture peace and cooperation, the politics of the divided country can also create many operational challenges.

This was keenly felt during the staging of the PyeongChang Winter Olympic games in 2018. For the managers responsible for running the games, they were faced with the constant risk of how tensions between North Korea and other countries would impact on operations. In 2017, for example, tension was particularly high after a spate of North Korea nuclear weapons testing, which had the effect of dampening demand for tickets for the games. The event organisers also had to try and plan for how they would accommodate the North Korean team, where the confirmation that both North and South would march together in the opening ceremony had to be planned for, but having contingencies that this had the potential to be cancelled at any moment. As it was, they did march together, which was all the more remarkable against the backdrop rising political tensions at the time.

Case Study 2 – Volcanic natural disaster: The idea that a volcanic eruption in Iceland impacting on the sport operations around the world might seem a remote idea, but in 2010 that is just what happened. The volcanic ash cloud generated went beyond Iceland, created a hazard for aircraft. The result was a huge disruption to flights, with numerous cancellations. In Europe, it meant that many sport teams had to undertake long coach journeys to attend their fixtures, such as Barcelona FC using a bus/coach to drive to its champion league game in Lyon. Even in Japan, the FIM Moto GP World Championship was cancelled at relatively short notice because of the difficulties created in travel. There was also the move of the Diving World Series, due to be staged in Sheffield, having to be moved to Veracruz in Mexico.

Discussion points
Search the news for more examples of how events in the external and intermediate business environment have changed the operating conditions of sport managers and SDOs.

1.6 WHAT MAKES SPORT SERVICES DIFFERENT FROM OTHER SERVICES?

The subject area of operations management is well served by literature. One criticism, however, is that these many text books can have a bias towards more traditional products and manufacturing operations processes, rather than service delivery. It is worthwhile exploring some of the key differences between products and services, using the four classic attributes of services (there are variations, but these are sufficient for now to convey some core differences), drawn from marketing theory, which are:

- **Intangibility**: Unlike a product, which can be examined, touched or scrutinised, a service is often described as a promise of an experience. In order to try and make a service more tangible to potential customers, managers can use photos, videos or recommendations in leaflets, adverts or websites, to try and give a sense of the experience they may gain (discussed in Chapter 4).
- **Variability (heterogeneity)**: This relates to the challenge of delivering a consistent good quality service experience first time, every time. The problem is that the many variables which go to create a service experience can be prone to variability, such as how staffing behave, the weather and the mood of customers. Utilising quality systems (discussed in Chapter 5) is one method to try and ensure greater service consistency in the customer experience.
- **Inseparability**: Unlike a product which can be bought and used later, for a service, when it is produced, delivered or staged, it is consumed at the time of delivery.
- **Perishability**: With products, if they are not sold on a day, they can be kept, and attempts made to sell them another day. With services, if they cannot

be sold at the time of offering, then they have perished and gone for ever. This is important when analysing performance and utilisation rates of services and spaces (discussed in more detail in Chapter 3).

These service characteristics create different operational challenges in comparison with the manufacturing of products and goods. In addition to these service attributes, it is vital to reiterate the two distinct elements which impact on sport operations and the delivery of services, represented earlier, in Figure 1.1, which are:

- **Outcomes**: The potential positive changes to behaviour involvement in sport can bring, described earlier, with examples given in Table 1.3.
- **Emotion**: The emotional charge and connection that sport involvement can generate can be critical in giving the energy for generating behavioural changes and the achievement of outcomes.

Remember, simply providing sport services *does not* guarantee any positive behaviours or impacts occur. Whilst outputs (e.g. people consuming a service) are a vital condition for achieving outcomes (e.g. leading a healthier lifestyle), this can *only* come about with proper leveraging mechanisms (i.e. the intervening actions). Indeed, we can go further by saying that without proper leveraging mechanisms, there can be the potential for harm to take place or negative

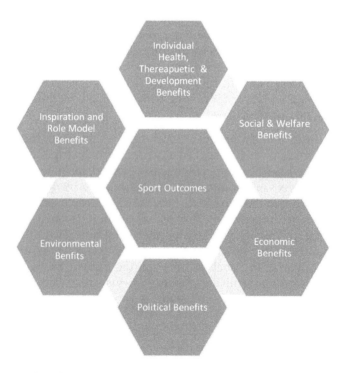

Figure 1.5 Examples of Theoretical Sport Positive Outcomes.
Source: Adapting Wilson and Piekarz (2015).

impacts felt. In Figure 1.5 a range of theoretical positive outcomes often claimed from sport is shown, which adapts and updates Wilson and Piekarz's work (2015, p. 19), who also showed how, for every possible claimed benefit for sport, it is possible to find examples of how sport can be a negative force, such as creating sport injuries, reinforcing prejudice and exclusion, or leaving costly facilities which act as a financial burden on local communities.

One additional theory which can help give more refinement to the critical concept of leverage is to consider it in conjunction with nudge theory. Thaler and Sunstein (2009) developed the theory of 'nudge', which sits in a broader field of behavioural economics. In essence, their work explores, for good or bad, how human behaviour and actions can be altered by different interventions, by focusing on sub-conscious behaviours. Their work has been influential on many government policies around the world, who have looked for ways to try and improve people's behaviour, in terms of welfare and health; rather than trying one bold initiative which tries to illicit a radical change in behaviour, instead, through smaller interactions, people are gradually 'nudged' to different behaviours. It is an important area, which you are encouraged to explore more as it has many interesting possibilities for operations sport managers and SDOs. In Table 1.3, a variety of leverage mechanisms are shown, which can be used to nudge behaviour or generate action, which considers emotional, bargaining and economic leverage mechanisms. Here are a couple of additional innovative examples of leveraging, where people are nudged to encourage different behaviours, which are underpinned by the principles of being fun or engaging and done for good, such as achieving a variety of positive health outcomes:

- To encourage more active recreation in children teachers and SDOs leveraged the children's love (emotional leverage) of the Harry Potter books and films, by adapting the game of Quidditch (Quidditch is the game played by wizards on flying broomstick). Some of the children, who had no interest in playing sports, were, however, delighted to run around on broomsticks playing Quidditch, and so gained the benefits of physical activity and social interaction.
- In the UK, the 'This Girl Can' campaign showed women participating in a variety of sports or active recreation activities, who were of all ages, abilities and ethnicity, whereby the leverage mechanisms were based on showing examples of ordinary women having fun exercising, which could help inspire and build confidence (examples of emotional leveraging) and so nudge women to try new challenges, by conveying a message of 'well if they can do it, so can I'.
- A metro station in Hamburg painted the stairs like a running track, surrounding the dull looking escalator, which looked fun to walk or run up. A variation for encouraging people to use the stairs can be the use of piano steps, or having signs which show how many calories are burnt, or mountains climbed, when the stairs are used.
- There are many interesting operational nudge techniques which can be used to improve the cleanliness and safety of buildings, such as having fun voting bins (e.g. one example is that people put their cigarette butts to

Table 1.3 Examples of Sport Positive Outcomes, Leverage Mechanisms and Nudges

Outcome Category	Examples of the Claimed Benefits	Examples of Leverage Mechanisms to Nudge Changes (Emotional, Economic and Bargaining)
Economic benefits	Improved economic activity; employment opportunities; facilities and stadiums acting as engines to drive regeneration of poor or deprived areas; improvements in health and well-being which in turn can increase productivity; helping poor countries achieve the millennium development goals (MDGs)	- Create opportunities to spend money on local services - Employ local people - Create time and opportunities for workers to be involved with active recreation
Social and welfare benefits	Instilling sense of community and pride; preservation of cultural values; sport and education programmes to reduce crime, instil pride, build community confidence and help integration of groups; education (e.g. the attempts to use sport to educate about diseases, such as the Kick It Out campaign in football); education about issues of racism, sexism and homophobia	- Identify key community stakeholders - Local community engaged with as part of the research process - Facilitate communication and talking between groups to aid in education - Provide opportunities for reflection and transference to other situations - Facilitate empathy and understanding of issues or other groups needs - Act to deal with individuals or groups who do not adhere to visions and values (e.g. dealing with racism, such as bans from participation) - Commitment to human rights and Corporate Social Responsibility (CSR) statements, acting ethical (i.e. practice what is preached in rhetoric and vision statements) - Engage with disaffected youth to provide right services

Political	Peace and reconciliation; opportunity for political leverage to raise issues of human rights abuses or advancements; expressions of liberty; nation building; rebranding and reimaging cities, regions and countries	- Engage community groups to have ownership of projects - Support public spaces to allow people to congregate and share experiences - Reflection and communication to enable transference of wider lessons - Financially reward sport clubs who improve inclusiveness of under-represented groups, or withhold money to sport organisations who refuse to change (e.g. no women represented at a senior level in governance structures)
Environment	Regeneration of poor sites; green agenda promoted; benchmarking of good practice	- Adhere to sustainable practices and guidances, such as reducing CFC (Chlorofluorocarbons) omissions - Signage and bins to encourage recycling in fun ways
Individual health, therapeutic and personal development benefits	Improve physical, mental and social health and well-being; teamwork; development of leadership skills; moral leadership; rehabilitation and healing; courage; good citizenship; confidence building; catharsis (venting of frustrations and anger); self-expression and identity development	- Support, educate and train to ensure sport activity is engaged with properly and safely, which avoids the risk of injury - Coherent, structured training programmes for volunteers - Provide additional support and education on diet and lifestyle, in order to deal with issues of obesity - Therapy and rehabilitation services have a clear mapped out pathway of development - Make it is easy to participate and gain access to help - Provide monetary subsidies and remove barriers to participation - Design spaces to encourage more activity - Signage used to nudge behaviour (e.g. why use stairs and calories used)
Inspiration and role model benefits	Watching high levels of performance inspire people to play (demonstration affect); athletes can act as role models to aspire in moral development and leadership	- Create services for people to try - Provide taster experiences following sport success, to play, support or volunteer - Communicate values and lessons learnt - Celebratory parties

Source: Author.

vote for their favourite football player, rather than just throw them on the floor), or using signs to remind people to wash their hands after visiting the toilet.

When identifying resources to leverage, in order to nudge behaviours, to achieve outcomes, it is vital to build in feedback loops to evaluate effectiveness. How this is done is explored in more detail in Chapters 2 and 10, which also relates back to the principles of black box thinking and marginal gains. Furthermore, aspects of the psychology theories which underpin the theory of 'nudge' are returned to later, in Chapter 7 in relation to new power theories and Chapter 8 and the principles of persuasion. One final consideration to note is that whilst emotions are critical elements for leveraging change and nudging behaviour, they are a fragile resource. The problem is that the strong emotions felt in a sport moment can create a sense that the world could be made better, as people feel good in that sport moment; once these fleeting sport experiences have passed, then it can be harder to actually create lasting changes to behaviour. As will be illustrated later, motivation first needs to be energised (the part which sport can do so well), but the really hard part can be for managers and SDOs to maintain that emotional engagement for new behaviours to be sustained.

1.7 CONCLUSION

This book is not about sport administration and the simple maintaining of systems. It is about the management of complex dynamic sport operations systems, where resources need coordination and controlling in order to produce sport services. This is why systems and complexity theory are used as it shapes the managers and SDOs' working culture, which in turn influences how they approach work and deal with problems when designing, maintaining and delivering sport services.

The term 'management' is used in its broadest sense, to refer to the coordination and control of resources, relating to money (finance), people (HR), customers (marketing) and risk. It should be clear that all SDOs will have a management role to their work. The concept *of* sport development and sport *for* development is a slightly narrower concept, but it is also clear that many sport managers will often have a development strand to their work. Whilst there are some differences in terms of the technical knowledge, skills and to some extent the qualifications, between sport management and SDO work, overall it is felt that the practical process of designing, maintaining and improving on the delivery of sport services needs to utilise some common practices, theories and concepts. Hence the rationale for combining sport management with sport development in a book on sport operations.

Finally, operations management is a discrete level of management and a business management subject area, which is about transforming inputs (staff, money, equipment, etc.) into service processes, which generates outputs (e.g. usage, revenue, etc.). What is unique to sport operations is the frequent desire to try and leverage these outputs into outcomes (e.g. improved health).

References

Anderson, D.M. (ed.) (2014). *Leveraging: A Political, Economic and Societal Framework*. Washington, DC: Springer International.

Blakey, P. (2011). *Sport Marketing*. Exeter: Learning Matters.

Carlzon, J. (1987). *Moments of Truth*. New York: Ballinger.

Coalter, F. (1990). The mixed economy: The historical background to the development of the commercial, voluntary and public sectors of the leisure industries, in Henry, I. (ed.), *Management and Planning in the Leisure Industries*. London: Macmillan, p. 16.

Coalter, F. (2010). The politics of sport for development: Limited focus programmes and broad gauge problems. *International Review for the Sociology of Sport*, 45(3), 295–214.

Collins, M. (2010). From 'sport for good' to 'sport for sport's sake – not a good move for sport development in England? *International Journal of Sport Policy and Politics*, 2(3), 367–379.

Conversation (2019). Protecting young athletes from abusive coaches – Let's get it right, accessed 2 June 2018, available at: http://theconversation.com/protecting-young-athletes-from-abusive-coaches-lets-get-it-right-111950

Gerras, S.J. (ed.) (2004). *Strategic Leadership Primer*, 3rd ed. Carlisle Barracks, PA: U.S. Army War College.

Green, K., Sigurjónsson, T., and Åsrum Skille, E. (2018). *Sport in Scandinavian and the Nordic Countries*. London: Routledge.

Heizer, J., and Render, B. (2004). *Principles of Operations Management*, 5th ed. Upper Saddle River, NJ: Pearson.

Houlihan, B. (2011). The influences on sports development. In Houlinan, B. and Green, M. (eds.), *Routledge Handbook of Sports Development*. London: Routledge, pp. 5–9.

Hylton K. (2013). *Sport Development: Policy, Process and Practice*, 3rd ed. London: Routledge.

Lang, M., and Harthill, L. (ed.) (2015a). *International Perspectives in Research, Policy and Practice*. London: Routledge.

Lang, M., and Harthill, L. (ed.) (2015b). *Safeguarding, Child Protection and Abuse in Sport*. London: Routledge.

McNeill, D. (2013). Judo: Slapped, kicked and beaten with bamboo – The training horros that Japan's women underwent in the run-up to London 2012. *The Independent*, 28th April.

Schwarz, E.C., Hall, S.A., and Shibli, S. (2010). *Sport Facility Operations Management*. London: Routledge.

Slack, N., Brandon-Jones, A., and Johnston, R. (2016). *Operations Management*, 8th ed. London, Pearson.

Syed M. (2016). *Black Box Thinking*. London: John Murray.

Torkildsen, G. (2005). *Sport and Leisure Management*, 5th ed. London: Taylor and Francis.

Thaler, R.H., and Sunstein, C.R. (2009). *Nudge*. London: Penguin.

UN (2019). Sustainable development goals, accessed 2 June 2019, available at: https://sustainabledevelopment.un.org/?menu=1300

UNICEF (2019) Team UNICEF, accessed 6 June 2019, available at: https://www.unicef.org/sports/23619.html

Watt, D.C. (1998). *Event Management in Leisure and Tourism*. Harlow: Addison Wesley Longman.

Wilson, R., and Piekarz, M. (2015). *Sport Management: The Basics*. London: Routledge.

World Rugby (2019). World Rugby women's development action plan 2025 drives global growth in women's participation, Women's Development, accessed 1 June 2019, available at: https://www.world.rugby/news/393705?lang=en

Wooles, A. (2018). Marginal gains reconsidered: How sport organisations hold the key to boosting sport performance. *Sircuit*, 11 July, accessed on June 2019, available at: http://sircuit.ca/marginal-gains-reconsidered/

2 ORGANISATIONAL PURPOSE AND EVALUATING SERVICE OPERATIONS

> **CHALLENGES FOR MANAGERS**
>
> - What is the purpose of the sport operations?
> - How does the manager or sport development officer (SDO) know when they are doing a good job?
> - What methods should be used to evaluate performance?
> - When should performance be reviewed?
> - What actions should be taken in response to poor performance?

2.1 INTRODUCTION

How does a sport manager or SDO know what they should be doing and how well they are doing it? They are simple, important and obvious questions which any manager or SDO needs to ask. The answers, however, can sometimes be complex, multiple and even contradictory. Whist profit may be the key benchmark for success for commercial sport businesses, for many other sport organisations, this is not a suitable measure of success. Indeed, as will be shown, even for commercial businesses, pursuing profit at all cost, which ignores social and environmental objectives, is not one which necessarily ensures long-term viability, where the virtuous rhetoric which often surrounds sport and its potential benefits only serves to accentuate the importance of considering non-profit-related goals because of the impact they can have on the business brand and reputation.

In this chapter, we explore the many ways that operational performance can be measured, which acts as a guide to actions which sport managers and SDOs need to take. It begins by explaining how organisational purpose and performance can be articulated, utilising the concepts of mission statements, aims and objectives. Next, it is explained that in order to answer the question 'how are we performing' it is vital that a variety of performance indicators (PIs) and measures are established. These indicators and measures are based around the operations system model, introduced in Chapter 1, which use the concepts of *inputs, processes* and *outputs*. Crucially, further refinement to performance measures isare given by considering the concepts of *efficiency, economy, equity* and *effectiveness*.

2.2 THE IMPORTANCE OF PERFORMANCE EVALUATION

If operations management is about creating, maintaining and improving the delivery of services, then it is vital that managers and SDOs have methods for evaluating performance or answering the questions 'what should we be doing?' and 'how well are we doing it?' Asking these questions helps to ensure performance evaluation is a constant, active process (Robinson, 2012 citing Anderson *et al.*, 2006, p. 63), offering points for critical reflection to help make decisions which maintain and improve the quality of sport services (see also Box 1.4). It is a process which can be done in a variety of ways, ranging from analysing data generated from services, using creative thinking techniques and simple observations of service delivery, or using surveys and customer reviews (all discussed further in Chapters 4, 5 and 10).

The benefits of engaging in an active learning review process of observation, analysis and assessment are stressed by numerous authors (e.g. Coalter, 2006; Robinson, 2012; Schwartz *et al.*, 2012; Torkildsen, 2005), which can be summarised as follows:

- What gets measured, gets managed (Coalter, 2006; Schwartz *et al.*, 2012)
- Anticipate problems before they become a crisis
- An integral part of quality systems (Chapter 5), such as the Kaizen business philosophy, where a central feature of quality systems is having the capacity to collect data, in order to evaluate performance, using the mantra 'speak with data, manage by facts' (Imai, 1986)
- Give confidence to key stakeholders that services are being managed efficiently and profitably, or public money is effectively spent
- Ensure the long-term viability of the organisation

Leboeuf (2000, p. 3) encapsulates these benefits, based on his experience in sales and research, saying:

> … my years of research and work with organisations have convinced me that the ones that enjoy long-term prosperity do so because they have a consistent willingness to re-examine and improve on basic factors that others regard as obvious.

2.3 OVERVIEW OF THE PERFORMANCE EVALUATION PROCESS

This section gives an overview of what can be evaluated and the process of evaluation. In Figure 2.1, the Operations Management System model, introduced in Chapter 1, is replicated, to show the parts of the system which can be measured. There are three new areas introduced to the system, which are vital for the sport manager and SDO to understand. They are as follows:

- **Efficiency**: This measures how much the input resources, such as staffing, generate outputs, such as usage and revenue. Schwartz *et al.* (2012, p. 226) describe efficiency as being concerned with 'achieving objectives and targets at minimum cost'.

Organisational purpose and service operations 33

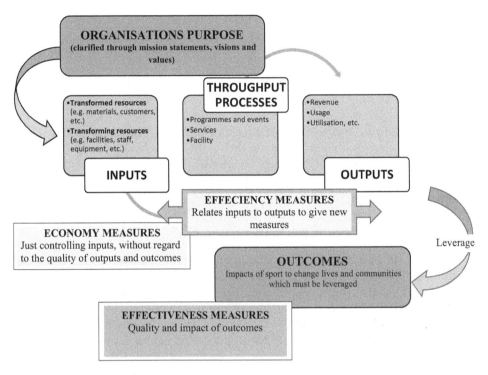

Figure 2.1 The Areas of the Sport Management System Which Can Be Evaluated.
Source: Author.

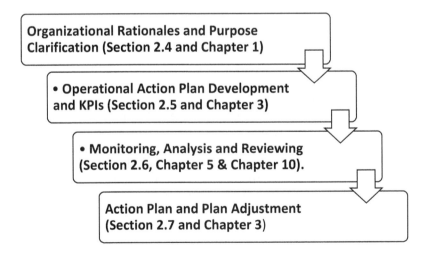

Figure 2.2 Key Attributes of Performance Evaluation Process
Source: Author.

- **Effectiveness**: This measures the quality of achievement and outcomes. Torkildsen (1994, p. 325) gives a useful definition of effectiveness, describing it as 'providing the right service at the right place, and at the right time – in other words, a service that meets the meets the needs of the different sections of the communities'.
- **Economy**: This focuses on simply controlling the inputs, such as reducing staff or cleaning costs.

In terms of turning this systems model in a practical process of performance analysis, there are many variations. To deal with different approaches, we have distilled the key components of performance evaluation from a variety of writers, such as Robinson's (2012) approach, shown in Figure 2.2. Each stage is given subsequent section in this chapter.

2.4 SECTOR RATIONALES AND PURPOSE

Byers (2004, p. 243) argues that a fundamental part of operations management is understanding organisation purpose, as this provides a vital starting point for planning and delivering sport services. This, in turn, provides the fundamental building block for performance evaluation: after all, you have to know what you are trying to achieve, and to know if you are on track to achieving it!

An initial sense of purpose of the organisation can be formed by considering the economic sector it operates in and its organisational classification. As a reminder, broadly speaking, services which are offered in the private or commercial sector are run for profit; the public sector relates to governments, both central and local, who may either directly provide sport services or give subsidies to others, to provide sport and recreation services; finally, the voluntary sector is another non-profit sector which develops to fill a gap in provision where both the private sector (known as market failures) and public sector (known as government failures) fail to provide a service that is needed, or has merit and benefit to individuals and communities. Within these different sectors, there are various ways that organisations can be structured and governed, but which there is not the scope to discuss all the different permeations – to find out more about these different governance structures, it is recommended you read Schwartz *et al.* (2012, p. 7) for fuller discussion.

One of the important trends to occur is the collapsing of the sectors (Wilson and Piekarz, 2015, p. 139), which means that each sector's distinctive features have become more blurred, where non-profit sport service providers have often had to adapt and behave more like commercial providers in terms of operating efficiently and generating revenue; whilst profit-orientated commercial sectors are having to give more attention to non-profit social- and environmental-orientated objectives. For the public and voluntary sectors there are many drivers of this collapse and sector blurring. For example, the growth in Corporate Social Responsibility (CSR) agendas has been an important driver of change, which means that all organisations, in all sectors, have to consider a variety of non-profit objectives, such as acting in an environmentally sensitive manner, and one which considers ethical working practices. For commercial organisations, this is sometimes represented by the three Ps: profit, planet and people. In relation to sport, because it is surrounded by so much virtuous rhetoric about its potential to do good, CSR can be considered as particularly relevant, as will be illustrated later.

The broad sector rationale the sport organisation operates in is useful for giving context to the service purpose. What is needed next are more specific details about the purpose of the organisation, its services and what needs to be achieved by when and by who. A key starting point for capturing and representing these things is a business plan, which (in theory) should clarify the organisational goals and achievements over a specified time period, usually somewhere between three and five years. Whilst the development of business plans is embedded in the strategic and project levels of management, they need to be considered in operations management, because it is the managers and SDOs who turn any stated intentions, aspirations and targets into a reality. In the past, whilst for commercial sport organisations, it would have been the mainstream practice to produce a business plan for public and charitable enterprises, this practice would have been more variable. Today, however, increasingly around the world, for any sport organisation claiming grants or government subsidies, not producing some form of business plan is no longer a realistic option.

There is frequently a difference found between the classic text book template methods of writing strategic business plans and what is actually produced by different sport organisations around the world. The key elements of the 'template' (Rumelt, 2017, p. 67) will usually involve the following concepts:

- Vision, mission and value statements
- Aims, goals or objectives (there can be variations in which terms are used); PIs or key performance indicators (KPIs); and targets
- Lists of actions and strategies

Some organisations will use *all* these concepts in their plans, some none of them, whilst others will use the terms inter-changeably or in contradictory ways compared to other organisations. There is not the scope to explain why these variations exist, but illustrations of the variations are explored in Boxes 2.1 and 2.2. The approach we use here draws on a variety of work, particularly the use of Sondhi (1999) VMOST (Vision, Mission, Objectives, Strategy and Tactics) analysis tool. This is a process which outlines how to develop overall organisational strategies and gives consideration to how they can be implemented. It utilises all the key concepts already discussed. The part of Sondhi's work that we particularly want to emphasise is the importance attached to analysing each component and how they link and flow from or into each other. What we do not use from the VMOST process is the terminology of 'strategies' and 'tactics'; instead, these ideas are represented and captured in our discussion of encouraging managers and SDOs to focus on quite specific tasks, actions or work breakdown structures (WBS), as elaborated on in Chapter 3.

Is this variation in terminology a problem? The key response is to be pragmatic and say that if it helps the organisation stay viable, then how the organisation and service purpose is written and performance evaluated does not really matter. But this does not deal with the difficulty managers and SDOs may have

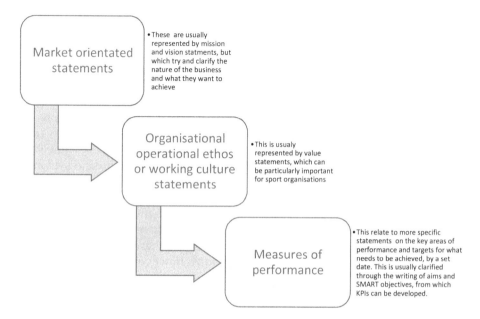

Figure 2.3 Three Critical Areas for Clarifying Organisational Purpose
Source: Author.

when they have to interpret, operationalise and evaluate business plans that have been produced in different ways. To help, in Figure 2.3 a distillation of three core elements which need to be considered when articulating purpose is given, which form the subsequent sub-sections. By understanding these core elements, it can be used to understand the core features of a business plan, not what terminology they use.

2.4.1 Writing market-orientated statements of purpose

Many strategic business plans will begin with a *Vision Statement*. The Australian Sport Commission (2015), for example, describes a vision statement as something which should illustrate what the sporting organisation *wants* to become in the future. It can also be useful to consider how vision statement represents the brand of the organisation (which overlaps with the next section in terms of the businesses values). Some examples of the different approaches and terminology are given in Box 2.2.

Mission statements in theory should have different attributes to visions: in practice, however, when scrutinising different organisational strategic plans, it can sometimes be difficult to tell the difference between the two. The mission statement should in theory attempt to encapsulate the essence of the organisation, its purpose and, even for some, its operational ethos. When examining a variety of definitions of mission statements, the following key features should be considered:

- They should give the organisation its overall purpose or *raison-d'etre*, from which more specific aims and objectives can flow from (see Section 2.5).
- They should be market orientated in approach, which gives an insight into why people need and want to use the sport services, such as the benefits it delivers or the problems it solves, which is relevant for both profit and non-profit sport businesses.

Box 2.1 Examples of clarifying purpose with vision and mission statements

Whilst the importance of mission statements, visions and values is easy to appreciate, writing them can be much harder, with many variations of practice.

Here are a variety of examples to show how different organisations have tried to encapsulate the essence of the business, but who sometimes use different terminologies.

Case Study 1 – Virgin Active: Virgin Active is one of the business strands to Richard Branson's global Virgin brand, which started in music, but which has now leveraged its brand to become involved in airlines, media, trains and health fitness gyms, under the Virgin Active brand. Virgin Active had the following mission and vision statements:

- **Mission**: Our mission is to help bring positive change to peoples' lives (Virgin Active, 2015).
- **Vision**: Very simply, we want to promote wellness by bringing about positive change in your life. We are passionate about wellness and exercise. We invite you to discover your own potential by entering our vibrant health club environment, created with quality, value for money and fun in mind (Virgin Active, 2015).

Richard Branson (2013), the head of the Virgin group, has tried to develop one broad mission statement for the Virgin Group, which includes gyms, travel, banking, etc. Branson recognises that mission statements can be problematic, such as being bland and so vague they are meaningless. He does, however, still believe in them if they are written concisely and with imagination and can encapsulate the purpose of the organisation.

Case Study 2 – Barca Foundation: Barcelona FC (Football Club) is one of the world's largest football clubs, with huge global brand appeal and recognition. As part of their business operations, they have set up a charitable enterprise called the Barca Foundation. This charitable enterprise does not have an explicit vision statement, as such, but they do have an operational credo (their term) of:

More than a club.

(continued)

Box 2.1 (continued)

In essence, although the football club is a commercial enterprise, a key part of its brand appeal is how it links with the community, together with its capacity for using sport and its values to help disadvantaged children and youth. It gives more detail about the mission statement for its charitable enterprise, which is stated as:

> To provide support to the most vulnerable children and youth – through sports and values based education – with the goal of contributing to a more egalitarian and inclusive society

> (Barca Foundation, 2019)

Case Study 3 – World Rugby: World Rugby is the international governing body for the sport of rugby. In their strategic plan, they identify a core mission of:

> creating an environment in which World Rugby and its member unions could flourish in developing and expanding the game globally.

> (World Rugby, 2019)

Interestingly, in their strategic plan which took them to the year 2020, they preferred to have, in their terminology, three broad strategic goals, which were:

- **Protect**: Drive player welfare best practice; protect and promote rugby, its values, spirit and ethos.
- **Grow**: Increase global participation; maximise commercial values and increase the financial sustainability of international rugby.
- **Inspire**: Olympic participate is successful in every way; Provide strong inspirational leadership.

This is another example where the classic strategic planning terminology is planning are still discernable. Looking at the above statements, it is clear that they are in essence trying to articulate what they want to achieve and offer a sense of their operational ethos, which can filter down to help shape different country rugby federation's strategic plans.

Case Study 4 – Australian Rugby: In their five-year plan they also have some variations in their use of terminology compared with the other examples cited here and the classic strategic planning template. In their plan, they have a stated vision statement, which is described as:

> Inspire all Australians to enjoy our great game.

They do not, however, go on to give a mission statement, but state that, in their words, they have 'four additional themes', which are:

1. Make rugby a game for all
2. Ignite Australia's passion for the game
3. Build sustainable elite success
4. Create excellence in how the game is run

(Australian Rugby, 2016)

Examining these themes, they have elements which could be mission statement related, but also drift into aims and objectives. These are returned to later in Box 2.5.

Tasks

Use Rumelt's (2017) criticisms about visions and mission statements often being 'verbiage' and 'empty rhetorical and high-sounding' statements, scrutinise the value of the various statements written in the examples given here, or others you have found.

Rumelt (2017) is critical of the classic template system for producing strategic plans. Based on his years of experience, he makes the observation that these template systems can produce 'verbiage', and creates a lot of 'empty rhetoric' (Rumelt, 2017, p. 67), arguing that these statements are not always particularly useful, describing them as often being 'high-sounding politically correct statements'. More specifically, Rumelt (2017, p. 67) is cynical of some of the attempts to write vision statements, noting how they will often use popular phrases (but ultimately meaningless), such as 'to be the best' or 'the leading'. These critiques can be particularly acute in sport, given that it is surrounded by so much virtuous rhetoric as to the potential benefits of sport. These criticisms do not mean, however, that vision and mission statements should not be written, rather that managers and SDOs should always strive to write for purpose, which helps them design services which are needed and can be critically reviewed.

2.4.2 Operational values and working cultures

A simple way of conveying how the sport organisation wants to operate is to produce value statements. These statements can help set the tone, operational ethos or working culture of the organisation and how it wants to operate, internally with its staff and externally with its customers (see also Chapter 5) and other key stakeholders (see also Chapter 7). The importance of working culture and values cannot be stated enough, particularly if you reflect back to the cases highlighted in Box 1.5 in relation to stadium disasters and coaching abuse, where failures in working cultures and values were key factors in causing the tragedies. The importance of value statements has also been given more impetus because of the growth of CSR agendas, which, as noted earlier, is particularly important for sport because of the many beneficial outcomes claimed. In Box 2.2, a variety of value-type statements are explored based on different sport businesses from around the world.

Box 2.2 Examples of organisational values which shape working practices and can enhance brand appeal

When scrutinising various sport business plans, the notion of 'values' is frequently given a prominent place (although not all will explicitly use the term 'values'). This is perhaps not that surprising as the many virtues attributed to sport can offer powerful messages which can help the brand and reputation of the organisations. Here are a number of examples of how values are written or conveyed, even if they may not explicitly use the term 'values'.

Case Study 1 – Virgin Active: Virgin Active in addition to their mission and vision statements, highlighted in Box 2.1, goes onto utilise the classic strategy template, by giving a value statement, which is:

> Challenging the norm, improving standards and raising the bar. – Having fun – no matter how seriously you may take life, it is vital that you have fun. – Creating a better product through innovation and building closer customer relationships. – Passion and excellence in our people – this is what generates top-quality service. – Adding greater value for money by offering our members great deals through access to other companies in the Virgin Group.

It is a list with many positives and superlatives, with a strong experiential focus. How realistic and measurable these many elements are is another issue, which could be subjected to Rumelt's (2017) criticism of verbiage, noted earlier.

Case Study 2 – Barca Foundation: The Barca Foundation do not necessarily have an explicit value statement, but its values are implicit in its mission statements and how it wants to operate, whereby they use terms such as *respect*, striving for *improvement* and developing *team work*. It goes on to say that they want to build a more *humane* and *altruistic society*, together with having passion, conviction, innovation, desire and enthusiasm wherever they work with conviction, using sport to find game-changing solutions.

Case Study 3 – Australian Rugby: Although they do not have an explicitly stated, single value statement in their plan, their core values are implicitly evident throughout their strategic plan. They state that they want a set of values which everyone can recognise, desiring 'more diversity' in clubs, 'more women involved with the game and in relation to welfare, taking a 'zero tolerance for playing with concussion'. In other documents they give further clarification of their values, which they describe as:

> **Integrity** – A central fabric of the game and is generated through honesty and fair play
> **Passion** – Rugby people have a passionate enthusiasm for game. Rugby generates excitement, emotional attachment and a sense of belonging to the global rugby family

> **Solidarity** – Unifying spirit that leads to lifelong friendships, camaraderie's teamwork and loyalty, which transcends cultural, geographic, political and religious differences
> **Discipline** –Discipline is an integral part of the game both on and off the field and is reflected through adherence to the laws, the regulations and rugby's core values
> **Respect** – Respect for team-mates, opponents, match officials and those involved with the game.
>
> (Australian Rugby, 2019)
>
> These stated values are intimately entwined with the notion of outcomes, explained in Figure 1.2. They also exhibit an attractive positive, virtuous rhetoric which the sport and the governing body can leverage to develop their brand appeal and attract potential sponsors. Sometimes, a criticism can be made that these virtuous statements are often empty rhetoric, but Australian Rugby's dropping of Israel Folau from the national team, before the 2019 rugby world cup, after he had posted what was deemed as homophobic comments on Instagram, would indicate a genuine belief in the value statements to guide actions, describing Folau's comments as 'unacceptable' and 'disrespectful'.
>
> ### Discussion
> How much are value statements used as part of a public relations exercise to simply enhance sport brands, making little difference to how they operate?

2.5 WRITING AIMS AND SMART OBJECTIVES

Mission statements, visions and values (or their variants) are important, but not sufficient or detailed enough to allow for proper performance evaluation. What is needed are concepts and methods which give more detail about what has to be achieved, by who, when and how they can be measured. This is where the concepts of aims, objectives (or their variants) and KPIs or more simply just PIs come into play. Again, as with visions, mission statements and values, there are many variations in terminology, such as using the term 'goals' instead of the term 'aim' or 'objective'. For now however, we will keep it simple and focus on the more common terms of aims and objectives, in order to distil their core underpinning conceptual elements which managers and SDOs can interpret and adapt, depending on the terminology used in their organisation.

As part of the process to give more detail to vision and mission statements, it is usual to develop some broad aims (remember, sometimes in books, they may be described as goals). Aims should, in theory, have the following key features:

- Aims should flow from the mission and vision statements and should be written as broad statements, preferably as a single sentence, which uses active verbs, such as improve, create or transform.

- They offer another way to give more specific direction, acting as a beacon for the organisation to strive towards for different areas of performance.
- Aims are given more refinement by the use of measurable objectives or goals.
- For some smaller-scale projects, such as for a small sport event or funding bid, it can be acceptable to have just one broad aim and a number of more specific objectives.

After writing aims, comes perhaps the most crucial part of the whole planning and evaluation process: writing objectives which can be measured. Over the years, a number of acronyms or mnemonics have been developed in order to try and give more formal structure and detail to objectives. For example, two common approaches are:

SMART objectives, which stand for (including variations):

- **Specific** (is it clear what is being measured, such as income, usage?);
- **Measurable** (is there a numeric value attached?);
- **Attainable/Accurate/Achievable** or even **Attributable** (the variations in the 'A' have been used by different writers to convey different features, such as whether it can actually be achieved, or how accurate the data is in terms of reflecting the objective to be achieved, or can it be attributed to a named person?);
- **Realistic/Relevant** (there can be some variations here in the literature, where it can overlap with attainability, such as whether the target is realistic within the time frame and the resources available, or whether if it is even really wanted?);
- **Time-based** (when should it be achieved by, or what are the key milestones, such as if it needs to be achieved by the end of the month, year, etc.?)

MASTER objectives, which stand for:

- **Measurable** (is it tangible and lends itself for measurement?);
- **Actionable** (can it be done by someone?);
- **Specific** (can a numeric value be attached?);
- **Time-Specified** (when does it need to be achieved by?)
- **Ends** not the means (does it focus on what needs to be achieved, not how it will be done?);
- **Ranked** (is a priority to the objectives? At times objectives can conflict with each other – this also relates to the 'boomerang' affect discussed in Chapters 1 and 3)

There are other variations in acronyms, but some of the core features should be evident, no matter which approach or terms are used, such as writing objectives which are realistic, having time frames and a capacity to be measured in some way by KPIs or just simply PIs. Whilst the MASTER approach has many keen advocates, such as Schawtz *et al.* (2012, p. 225) or Shibli *et al.* (2012), for ease, in this book, we will tend to refer to the more ubiquitous SMART approach (Specific, Measurable, Acceptable, Realistic and Time Bound); we will however, return to the issue of ranking, used in the MASTER approach, in Chapter 3, when the practicalities of prioritising work is considered. In Box 2.3, a number of examples are offered of aims and objectives which can be adapted and made SMART.

Organisational purpose and service operations 43

Box 2.3 Identifying the principles of SMART objectives even when they are not always explicitly stated

When looking at a variety of sport business plans and how they articulate the organisation's purpose and goals, it is again not uncommon to find many variations used in comparison with the classic text book approaches. Despite these variations in terminology, it is still possible to discern some consistency in the underpinning principles relating to aims and SMART objectives, discussed in this chapter.

Case Study 1 – World Rugby: World Rugby use the term 'strategic goals', rather than aims and objectives. For one of their three key 'strategic goals', relating to protect (see back to Box 2.2), they present it as follows:

Protect – Drive player welfare and best practice

1.1 World Rugby recognised as a leader and pioneer of best practices in player welfare. Concussion prevention and management processes are adopted by all member unions and other sports.
1.2 Injury incidence in published injury rates 1,000 hours of playing time in the period 2016–20 remains stable (does not get significantly worse (+ 10 percent)).
1.3 World rugby player welfare standards are adopted by all adult elite competitors.

It is important to examine these strategic goals and how they compare with the classic text book approaches to writing aims and objectives, and the implications for how they could be evaluated at an operational level by managers or SDOs. To begin with, the 'Protect' statement can work well as an aim, as it is a broad statement, where the subsequent bullet points could be read as potential objectives. These three sub-statements vary, however, in their capacity to be made SMART.

The first statement is caught somewhere between a statement of intention and action, which needs some more specific indicators to help inform whether it is on course for being achieved.

The second statement has more of the attributes of a SMART objective, in that it gives some specific indicators which can be measured, although it is within quite a broad time frame. It would be possible to develop a number of PIs, which can be broken down so that they have an operational focus. For example, it would be possible to set targets of injury rates, which can then filter down through the relevant country rugby governing bodies, and out to all the clubs in the countries, who use this to set targets to reduce injury, or to compare or benchmark injury rates between clubs, to help identify best practice.

To try and make these indicators more realistic, they can be informed by additional research. For example, the English RFU, working with its key stakeholders, commissioned research into injury rates in English youth rugby.

(continued)

Box 2.3 (continued)

It examined the rate, severity, type and cause of injuries in English premiership academies and schools, over two seasons. Some of their key findings were that the incidence of match injuries was less than that reported at a senior level, with academies having an injury rate of 44 injuries per 1,000 player hours, whilst schools had 35 injuries per 1,000 hours (Palmer-Green et al. 2009).

Finally, the third stated goal is specific, but it does not have any indicators or targets embedded within it. It could, however, be made SMART, by having a number of KPIs, such as having a percentage take up rate by all national rugby teams by a given year, which can then filter down to the professional clubs. Some questions could however be raised about the 'realism' of it, or a club stating they have adopted it is not the same as *effectively* applying it.

Case Study 2 – Australian Rugby: The Australian Rugby strategic plan shows another example of varied terminology, but discernable underpinning concepts which relate to aims and objectives. Instead of using the terms goals, aims and objectives, they use the terms 'focus area', 'rationale' and 'targets'. To take just one of the themes areas described in Box 2.2, *'Make rugby a game for all'*, this is broken down into the following 'focus areas':

- *Organize Rugby's delivery system through building a high-quality workforce.*
- *Promote the benefits of playing and being involved in Rugby.*
- *Inspire all Australians to enjoy our great game.*

(Australian Rugby, 2016)

In turn, these 'focus areas' were then given 'rationales', which both explained and gave guidance to what actions should be done. Here are three of the targets that they set at the end of the plan:

- *356,500 participants across the three formats of rugby*
- *115,000 Clubs XVs/kids pathway participants*
- *75,000 schools XVs*
- *Increase male population from 4.1% to 4.9%*
- *Increase total female participation rate to 15% of all participation across the three formats*

Looking at these targets, it is clear that what they are in fact doing is developing some SMART objectives, even though they haven't described them as such. These targets would also have the potential to be broken down further, at an operational level, to become PIs or KPIs, such as an SDO having to support and develop a set number of rugby programmes in a month, in a specific location.

Case Study 3 – Barca Foundation: The Barca Foundation do not use the term aims or objectives, but they do list some of their goals, such as:

- *To improve critical aspects affecting children and youth, who are the future of our society*
- *To use the strength and notoriety of sports to raise awareness about issues of equality and to prevent violent behaviour*

- *We want to do it through the leadership of FC Barcelona, a club with the ability to contribute unique solutions to bring about change*

These broad rationales and purposes will ultimately have to be 'operationalised' and measures found to evaluate performance. Examples of sport programmes they offer relate to:

- Refugee program supporting children, using football in refugee camps in Greece, Italy and Lebanon, running programmes to help them integrate in mainstream schools
- Youth Violence Prevention Program, focusing on big cities suffering from a high incident of youth violence and inequality, in countries such as Brazil, Iraq and Columbia

What needs to be considered is just how these could be made SMART? In relation to the first area and refugees, a variety of output data, such as the numbers who participate on the programme, could be used here. What is much harder, however, is trying to gauge if any outcomes are achieved.

Discussion

How much does it matter to have conceptual accuracy for the terms aims and SMART objectives in terms of efficient and effective operational practices and evaluation?

It is worthwhile noting that a common area of confusion relates to the extent that objectives are the *ends*, or should be written to show how they are the *means to the ends*. Coalter (2006, p. 13) is a key critical writer of sport management and policy, but in one of his works, he created some confusion by referring to objectives as the 'the specific actions that will be taken to achieve broad aims'. Both students and practitioners have interpreted this to mean they should elaborate how the objectives achieve the aim, which results in a list of actions (action lists are returned to in Chapter 3). This is wrong. Coalter's definition is simply stating that the objectives, when added together, help achieve the stated aim. In this book, we will therefore use objectives to simply refer to the 'ends', or what has to be achieved by a set date, whereas the practical actions, or the *how*, are written separately. This is discussed partly in Section 2.7 and more fully in Chapter 3.

2.6 TARGETS AND PIs

The types of data that can be used to measure or indicate performance are numerous. For example, Schwartz *et al.* (2012, p. 234) use SIRC (2006, p. 4) four group classification of PIs, based around access, finance, utilisation and satisfaction. Whilst useful, the preference in this work is to keep it simple and give a variety of examples of indicators based around the key areas of performance, presented in Table 2.1, which include and blend in all of SIRC's categories and examples. The variations in the use of PIs, KPIs or even SPIs (Strategic Performance Indicators) can sometimes be a source of confusion, but for ease we will simply use the

Table 2.1 Examples of Classic PIs Based around the Key Areas of Performance

Category	Examples of Measures or Indicators
Input: It is a basic measure and one which in the past was sometimes given too much focus on by sport administrators, who might simply focus on controlling budgets	• Total expenditure • Staffing costs • Energy costs • Number of staff • Cleaning costs • Administration • Capital repayments/loans • Insurance
Output: This is a basic area of operational performance evaluation. Depending on the sector, it can affect the focus of attention, such as commercial organisations may have a stronger focus on revenue and profit, whilst non-profit services may focus more on types of users and overall usage	• Income and revenue • Utilisation as a percentage of total capacity • Total income • Sale of goods and hire charges • Usage by user segment (e.g. pensioners, women, children, etc.) • % of users who are female, low income, disabled, unemployed, etc. • Type of sport and activities participated (compare this with % in community to get a sense of the effectiveness and equity)
Process and programme: This can relate to the type and variety of services offered in a facility or SDO, which can be measured with customer evaluation surveys, or more informal observation of services and how they are running	• Number of sport programs and level • Program and level targeted in terms of the sport development pyramid (foundation, participation, performance and excellence) • Quality of the experience observations
Effectiveness: This focuses more on the quality of achievement and their impacts, which Torkildsen (1994, p. 325) described as 'providing the right service at the right place, and at the right time' such as a service that meets the needs of the different sections of the communities. Crompton and Lamb (1991, p. 171) argues that for many non-profit sport organisations and services, effectiveness indicators should be the primary focus of performance, as they give more attention to customers and how the outputs creates outcomes	• Access by target groups from local community (overlaps with equity) • % visits of target groups (e.g. youths, retired, ethnic group, disability, etc.) • Measures of cleanliness (costs of cleaning as a ratio of complaints) • Satisfaction and quality of the experience surveys and measures (e.g. online rating service operators such as Trip Advisor)
Efficiency: This examines the relationship of a given set of inputs generates in relation to outputs. Schwartz *et al.* (2012, p. 226) describe efficiency as being concerned with 'achieving objectives and targets at minimum cost'. All sport service providers, whatever the sector, must have a variety of efficiency indicators	• Recovery rate = Total income ÷ total expenditure (less loan charges) • Staff productivity = Total income ÷ staff costs • Total income ÷ staff number • Staff costs ÷ operating costs • Net operating costs ÷ total attendance = Subsidy per user • Spend per head • Utilisation • Subsidy per user (total subsidy/loss ÷ by total users)

Organisational purpose and service operations 47

Outcomes: They are a key distinguishing feature of many sport services, which focus on potential positive externalities, or spin-off affects, such as improving health behaviours. The challenge is that these outcomes, whilst of critical importance do not always have direct measures, so a variety of indicators may be looked for. Outcomes are intimately related to the notion of effectiveness measures

- Use output data as proxy indicators
- Secondary data collected by other bodies
- Qualitative follow-up research programmes and testing
- Injury rates to players (see Box 2.5) which can indicate safe operational playing and coaching processes
- Re-offending crime-related outputs
- Health indicators

Equity measures: Schwartz et al. (2012, p. 227) described equity implies fairness of treatment of all customers. Whilst the term may not be as commonly used, the underlying principle still has political resonance, but for convenience, it is possible to blend in equity with the broader effectiveness measures

- % of users and comparison with local community demographics
- Opportunities and services designed for specific segments

Source: Authors adapting a variety of sources (Coalter, 2006; SIRC, 2007).

term PIs, leaving it to managers and SDOs to decide what is 'key' depending on the service operation they have developed.

It is also worthwhile clarifying the difference between an *indicator* and a *measure*. Bryman and Bell (2003, p. 73) argue that a measure is relatively unambiguous and usually quantifiable, whilst indicators are ways to tap into concepts that are less quantifiable. In terms of the model presented in this work, one could say that whilst *outputs* can have direct measures of performance, such as usage and revenue, in relation to evaluating *outcomes*, it is more usual to use indicators, as they often have fewer tangible elements to them, such as the difficulty in measuring if any physical, social or mental health benefits have directly occurred from the consumption of the sport service.

In Table 2.1, a sample of possible measures or indicators are presented around the system model and areas of performance (Figure 2.1). They are by no means exhaustive, and managers and SDOs should always consider how they can find new measures (e.g. Box 2.3 and the use of injury rates). Indeed, for the modern sport manager or SDO, there can be an almost over-whelming amount of data which can potentially be collected from customers; the challenge for the sport manager and SDO is to decide what data to scrutinise, analyse and assess and find the time to do this (returned to in Chapter 3). What can help is that some indicators or measures can feed into multiple objectives, such as considering how effectiveness and outcomes relate to each other.

To help further illustrate the practical process of performance evaluation, in Box 2.4, a variety of input, output and ratio data is presented to illustrate how a manager could analyse data, with the reminder to managers and SDOs that because output targets are met, this does not mean outcomes are achieved.

Box 2.4 Illustrative examples of analysing data to evaluate performance

The following data is taken from a number of real facilities, but has been anonymised. The facilities and SDOs are based in a large town, built and owned by the local council or government, but managed by a separate non-profit trust. The sport and leisure venues vary in terms of their size and the type of facilities. As part of the Council's portfolio of services and facilities, they also employ a number of SDO outreach workers, with the remit of going out into local communities to encourage active recreation in targeted groups. It covers all the areas of performance, highlighted in Figure 2.1.

Performance analysis area 1 – comparative analysis and benchmarking of facilities and services

The sample output and input data presented here compares a number of the facilities and SDO work.

It should be immediately obvious that with the exception of the golf venue (note that the surplus figure appears in brackets which is common accounting practice), all the facilities or services make a loss, and some quite big ones at that. Is this a problem? Not necessarily, as these sport and leisure services are being run and offered to the local community in order to try and achieve a variety of social outcome objectives, rather than profit ones.

This does not mean however that there should be no consideration trying to generate more revenue and be more efficient with resources. To help with this goal, it is worthwhile looking in more detail at some efficiency PI ratios relating to:

Table 2.2 Facility and Service Annual Comparative Data

Facility	Usage	Expenditure	Income	Subsidy	Staffing Expenditure
Community pool	214,596	319,765	214,300	132,300	182,680
Multi-purpose leisure facility (with water flumes)	670,005	2,417,712	1,546,405	871,058	1,261,034
Multi-purpose leisure facility (traditional pool)	618,700	2,619,457	1,214,700	1,410,981	1,307,616
SDO outreach work	45,718	301,697	30,463	277,700	216,236
Golf	14,300	39,958	57,196	8,100	11,106

Table 2.3 Comparative Efficiency Ratios

Facility	Recovery Rate	Staff Productivity	Subsidy per User
Community pool	0.67	0.57	0.77
Multi-purpose leisure facility (with water flumes)	0.63	0.52	1.30
Multi-purpose leisure facility (traditional pool)	0.46	0.49	2.14
SDO outreach work	0.1	0.14	5.79
Golf	1.40	1.30	None

Recovery rate = Total income ÷ total expenditure (how much income is recovered for every £1 spent)
Subsidy per user = Annual total operating costs – annual total income ÷ annual visits (lower score is better for financial performance)
Staff productivity = Total income ÷ staff costs

These ratios are presented in the following table to allow for some comparative analysis.

These simple ratios allow for proper, fairer comparative analysis. For example, if one compared the community pool and the larger multi-purpose facility and the income generated, one might be tempted to think that the larger facility with a traditional pool is the better, as it is generated over £1,214,700 compared with the community facility's £214,300. Yet looking at the ratios, the smaller facility appears to be more efficient, because for every £1 spent it gets back £0.67, whilst for the larger facility this is only £0.46. The smaller facility also requires less subsidy per user, and its staffing ratios are more productive. The golf course has the best efficiency ratio as it actually makes a profit, where for every £1 spent, it gets £1.40 back.

Some of these measures are not necessarily fair to apply to the SDO work, as it is going to be a more heavily subsidised service and has fewer opportunities for income generation. In this instance, various effectiveness measures related to outcomes would be more important and are explored later (see also Table 2.6).

Performance analysis 2 – examples of annual input and output data for an individual facility and SDO work

The above data gives just a small sample of some of the input expenditure items an individual sport facility might incur, which primarily focus on the variable costs (i.e. the costs which vary depending on the services offered and the outputs generated). What is not included are the fixed costs, such as the interest being paid on loan charges which may have been incurred for building the facility. Also some costs, such as energy, might be dependent on the external environment, such as oil price changes impacting on energy costs.

(continued)

Box 2.4 (continued)

Table 2.4 Annual Expenditure (Input data)

	2018 £	2019 £	2020 £
Management	68,500	69,800	78,000
Staff – instructors dry courses	5,114	5,200	5,833
Staff – cleaners	11,300	9,000	8,900
Staff – receptionists	22,00	23,000	22,500
Activity supervisors and assistants	29,000	28,000	31,500
SDOs	28,000	36,000	42,000
Electricity	6,534	7,175	7,030
Gas	7,776	6,000	8,458
Purchase of equipment	2,489	4,863	1,844
Protective clothing/uniforms	259	806	448
Stationary/printing	2,052	2,830	1,395
Advertising	2,621	3,960	4,031

Looking at this data, there are some important observations. There are a number of costs which have increased, particularly the management costs. Whether these trends are a cause for concern depends on other factors and data. If, for example, an increase in some staff costs has resulted in more usage and revenue, then this can be justified.

For the cleaning costs, this has been one of the few areas where costs have been controlled and reduced. If this reduction has resulted in no decline in the number of complaints or quality of cleaning, then efficiency has been gained; if it has resulted in more complaints, then the service has simply become more economic.

The SDO costs have also increased, but again this is not necessarily a problem, provided that this increase in cost is resulting in improved outputs and, crucially, improving outcome effeteness, such as helping people lead more active lives, which can lead to health improvements.

Table 2.5 Annual Revenue (Output data)

Description	2018 £	2019 £	2020 £
Goods for re-sale	8,202	7,509	7,100
Course fees – activity studio	4,612	4,185	2,617
Course fees – dry courses	26,811	32,866	18,853
Course fees – fitness suite	4,333	3,178	1,750
Hire/use of facilities – activity studio	1,025	664	226
Hire/use of facilities – artificial pitch	4,331	3,677	3,300
Hire/use of facilities – fitness suite	12,151	14,000	8,802
Hire/use of facilities – main hall	4,459	8,987	22,861
Outreach community programmes (SDO)	1,200	2,100	4,200

Table 2.6 Annual Usage (Output Data)

Description	2018	2019	2020
Badminton	2,978	3,529	2,202
Table Tennis	180	192	194
Main hall (all activities)	9,100	8,900	7,980
All weather pitch usage	6,422	5,839	5,168
50+ keep fit	2,448	2,500	2,900
Fitness suite	6,164	5,336	2,245
Dance studio	5,547	3,378	1,189
Keep fit classes	3,547	3,378	1,112
Creche (SJ)	250	260	220
Soccer academy SJ	900	950	980
Soft play children's party	225	230	240
SDO outreach community programmes	320	600	1,200

This sample of revenue data has some areas of real concern. Most areas seem to be in decline in revenues, where some of the big income areas, such as dry-course fees, has fluctuated wildly, declining from 32,866 to 18,853. These sorts of declines in income will hurt the facility, and when considered in relation to the output expenditure items, the problems seem to be intensified. The facility is certainly not operating efficiently. The one area which has been improving relates to the outreach SDO work. When compared with the costs of the SDOs in the previous table, it is clear that the revenue does not begin to cover the costs of the workers. Clearly, these are nominal fees being charged, but what is of interest is that the revenue has increased as a proportion to the costs, which shows that the SDOs, although they do not make a profit, appear becoming more efficient with resources. Whether that leads to more effectiveness needs a different set of indicators.

When examining this output data, there are even more causes for concern. So far, in terms of the data, not only are there issues about rising costs and declining revenue, this is being compounded by a decline in usage for many areas, which in turn is likely to impact on the effectiveness of achieving any hoped-for outcomes. There are particular concerns over the fitness and dance programmes, but more positive growth in the development- and outreach-type work, such as for the 50+ keep fit, soccer academies and the SDO community outreach work.

Overall, there are many issues which have to be dealt with. The factors which are causing the decline in usage may be beyond the managers' control, such as the decline of usage because of external competition. There is scope for controlling costs, so this is likely to be a key area of focus for the managers. The SDO work is also to be applauded, but the challenge is just how to expand this if no new subsidies are available, as the opportunities for generating more revenue are limited.

(continued)

Box 2.4 (continued)

Discussion

Reflect back on some of the issues and outline some of the practical actions that could be taken, together with how you would monitor performance using a variety of indicators.

2.7 ACTION PLANS, IMPLEMENTATION AND MONITORING

Ultimately, the whole point of writing all these statements, aims and objectives is to produce services for customers to consume. At some point, the 'what needs to be achieved' needs to be turned into the 'how it will be achieved, by who and when'. These are the practical action points or jobs which must be completed and are explored in more details in all the subsequent chapters of this book, but mostly Chapter 3, hence the lack of discussion here.

One other area which has not been discussed here relates to how these principles of performance management and monitoring relate to individual performance appraisal systems. This is an important area, relating to the HR business function, but for which there is not the scope to fully discuss here. One point to emphasise, however, is that the many targets discussed can potentially be blended into individual manager or SDO's performance appraisal system, whereby by given clear individual attachment, it can help give focus and ownership, which can be of critical importance in the implementation and achievement of the targets.

2.8 CONCLUSION

Performance evaluation of service operations is a vital activity for sport managers and SDOs. Although part of the foundation for performance evaluation begins at the strategic level of management, ultimately, a strategic plan must be operationalised and turned into a reality. The performance evaluation process can be informal, such as simple observations of services, or involve a more systematic analysis of data, which can cover different areas of performance, ranging from inputs, outputs, processes, efficiency and effectiveness. The key foundation for good performance management is the writing of meaningful aims and objectives (or their variations) which have the capacity to be examined with a direct measure or a proxy indicator.

One of the unique challenges for sport organisations is the measurement or identification of a suitable number of indicators that can inform if outcome and social objectives are being met. The problem is that these outcomes can be less tangible or more complex, where the causation factors may be entwined with many other factors. Yet the challenge for managers and SDOs is that they should always strive to try and evaluate them, as it means that outcome moves from being empty virtuous rhetorical statements to actual achievements. The final point to emphasise is that there must be a culture which is open and honest to critical analysis and reflection, because, as Syed (2016, p. 197) argues, 'every error, every flaw, every failure is a marginal gain in disguise'.

References

Australian Rugby (2016). Australian Rugby strategic plan, accessed on 22 June 2018, available at: http://nhru.com.au/wp-content/uploads/2016/04/2016-2020-Australian-Rugby-Strategic-Plan.pdf

Australian Rugby (2019). What is Ruby: Rugby's values, accessed 20 June 2018, available at: https://www.world.rugby/welcome-to-rugby/rugbys-values?lang=en.

Australian Sport Commission (2015). Club development, accessed 20 April 2020, available at: https://www.sportaus.gov.au/club_development/vision_and_mission.

Barca Foundation (2019). Mission, vision, values and principles, accessed 29 April 2019, available at: https://foundation.fcbarcelona.com/missionvisionvalues.

Byers, T. (2004). Managing sport operations, quality and performance. In Beech, J. and Chadwick, S. (eds.), *The Business of Sports Management*. Harlow: Prentice Hall, pp. 240–264.

Branson, R. (2013). Richard Branson on crafting your mission statement. *Entrepreneur Magazine*, July, accessed 2 May 2016, available at: http://www.entrepreneurmag.co.za/advice/starting-a-business/start-up-advice/richard-branson-on-crafting-your-mission-statement/

Bryman, A., and Bell, E. (2003). *Business Research Methods*. Oxford: Oxford University Press.

Coalter, F. (2006). *Sport-in-Development: Monitoring and Evaluation Manual*. Sterling University, available at: http://www.toolkitsportdevelopment.org/html/topic_8A6F8104-DBAD-4F47-927D-3FE9A13B30B4_0D6CC44E-EE2F-480B-B10A-67E11FB997BA_1.htm

Crompton, J.L., and Lamb, C.W. (1991). Effectiveness (not efficiency) is the primary measure of program success in recreation and leisure. In Goodale, L. and Witt, P.A. (eds.), *Recreation and Leisure: Issues in an era of change*. London: Venture.

Imai, M. (1986). *Kaizen: The Key to Japan's Competitive Success*. McGraw-Hill.

Leboeuf, M. (2000). *How to Win Customers and Keep Them for Life*. Berkley Publishing Corporation.

Palmer-Green, D., Trewartha, G., and Stokes, K. (2009). *Sport, Health & Exercise Science, University of Bath*. Report on injury in English Youth rugby union, accessed on 2 July 2018, available at: https://www.englandrugby.com/mm/Document/MyRugby/Headcase/01/30/49/62/110510youthinjurygamewidehighres_Neutral.pdf

Robinson, L. (2012). The management and measurement of organisational performance. In Trenberth, L. and Hassan, D. (eds.), *Managing Sport Business: An Introduction*. London: Routledge.

Rumelt, R. (201). *Good Strategy, Bad Strategy*. London: Profile Books.

Schwartz, E., Hall, S.A., and Shibli, S. (2012). *Sport Facility Operations Management: A Global Perspective*. London: Routledge.

Slack, N., Brandon-Jones, A., and Johnston, R. (2016). *Operations Management*, 8th ed. London: Pearson.

Sondhi, R. (1999). *Total Strategy*. Lancashire: Airworthy Publications.

Sport Industry Research Centre (SIRC) (2006). National benchmarking service for sports and leisure centres, available at: http://www.newforest.gov.uk/media/adobe/d/5/Final_report_-_Lymington.pdf

Sport and Recreation Alliance (2020). The principals of governance for sport and recreation accessed 12 March 2020, available at: https://www.sportandrecreation.org.uk/pages/principles-of-good-governance.

Syed M. (2016). *Black Box Thinking*. London: John Murray.

Torkildsen, G. (1994). *Sport and Leisure Management*, 3rd ed. London: Taylor and Francis.

Torkildsen, G. (2005). *Sport and Leisure Management*, 5th ed. London: Taylor and Francis.

Virgin Active (2015). Commercial fitness organization, accessed 4 May 2017, available at: http://www.aboutus.com/VirginActive.co.uk

Westerbeek, H., Turner, P., Smith, A., Green, C., and Leeuwen, L. (2005). *Managing Sport Facilities and Major Events*. Abington, PA: Allen & Unwin.

Wilson, R., and Piekarz, M. (2015), *Sport Management: The Basics*. London: Routledge.

World Rugby (2019). World Rugby Strategic Plan, accessed on 8 June 2019, available at: https://www.world.rugby/strategic-plan?lang=en

3
JOB TASKS, SCHEDULING AND TIME MANAGEMENT

> **Challenges for managers**
>
> - How do you break down work projects into specific tasks which form part of the daily operational practices?
> - How can you prioritise work effectively?
> - What are the ways you can manage distractions in contemporary working environments?

3.1 INTRODUCTION

What marks out an effective sport manager or sport development officer (SDO)? One simple, but vital benchmark is their capacity to complete jobs or tasks on time, safely, to the expected level of quality. But how is this done? Part of the foundation for effective and efficient operations management is to understand the need to plan, control, coordinate, lead and communicate numerous job tasks or actions, which need good time management practices to be applied. The necessity to adopt a working culture which views operations management existing within a complex, interactive system, where job task are constantly generated which must be managed, is also reiterated.

This chapter begins by looking at the changing business environment and the key drivers of change in modern working environments. It then goes onto examine how job tasks can be identified using a variety of creative thinking techniques. From this preliminary identification stage, it is explained how vital it is to use some form of external memory aid, such as some form of diary systems (electronic or paper based) to help record, prioritise, delegate and plan tasks, in order to ensure job tasks are completed on time, to the expected level of quality.

3.2 TOO MANY JOBS, TOO LITTLE TIME TO DO THEM?

In Chapter 1, systems and complexity theory was discussed. It was explained that operations management is about coordinating and controlling many different input resources (e.g. staffing or equipment), which are transformed through a process (i.e. the throughputs, such as the sport programme, events and activities offered), into an output (e.g. numbers of users, revenue or profit, etc.). What is more, in the context of sport, it was also explained that there is sometimes a desire to turn these outputs into outcomes (e.g. helping people lead a healthier lifestyle).

Every sport manager or SDO will have a constant, ever-changing list of jobs or actions to do, in order to *create*, *maintain* and *improve* the quality of sport services, all of which need to be done *efficiency, effectively* (examined in Chapter 2) and *safely* (looked at in Chapters 5 and 9). These job tasks or actions can be framed as the problem which must be dealt with, requiring different types of decisions, such as whether they are an emergency, routine or debatable decisions (Heller, 1998, cited in Torkildsen, 2005, p. 402). Each type of decision, in turn, will have its own time pressure, such as if they need an immediate response or can be spread out over many weeks. In Figure 3.1 a simple illustration is given of the key categories for where operational job tasks are generated.

The four key categories of jobs referred to in Figure 3.1, are elaborated here:

- **Internally generated by the manager**: This relates to jobs which a manager or SDO initiates, such as designing a new sport service (which may be required in order to meet a strategic plan), or are looking for ways to maintain and improve the quality of services.
- **Externally generated by other external agencies**: This relates to the jobs which are created by intermediate (e.g. competitors) or external (e.g. from PESTLE) forces.
- **Crisis-generated work**: These 'crisis' events vary in seriousness and type (returned to in Chapter 9), ranging from accidents, machinery breaking down or loss of public funding.
- **Boomerang-generated work**: Because operations management is about dealing with an ever-changing, dynamic interactive environment, actions taken to deal with one problem can often come back with a new set of challenges which must be dealt with. This in essence describes the law of

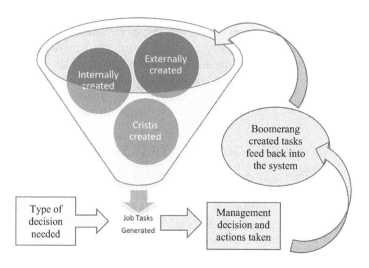

Figure 3.1 Sources of Job Tasks.

unintended consequences, or as Tenner (2003) describes it, 'why things bite back'. In Tenner's book, he gives numerous examples of how actions taken after a crisis or disaster (e.g. how the safety measures put in place after the sinking of the Titanic led to a bigger disaster in Chicago, in 1915) did not in fact lead to more safety, but laid the conditions for future disasters. One of the key arguments he puts forward is the importance of exploring the complex interconnections of causation (i.e. adopting a systems theory approach) to better learn the lessons from disasters.

Some of these tasks or jobs can be simple and quick to do. Others are more complex and can take many hours, days, even months of work to complete, where the job tasks need to be delegated to others and spread out over a longer time period, whereas others can bounce back by generating another set of issues (i.e. the boomerang tasks). Mark and González (2004) and González and Mark (2005) argue that modern working environments with all their potential disruptions and distraction – some from work (e.g. work colleagues chatting), some self-imposed (e.g. getting distracted by social media alerts on phones) – mean that it can sometimes be difficulty to talk of having productive working days or hours, but instead having productive minutes! An illustrative example of this pattern is given in Box 3.1, based on the work day of a sport agent and the operational challenges they face, which can mirror how many managers and SDOs' working day might unfold.

Box 3.1 A day in the life of a sport agent

Eikut Sogut is a sport agent who operates in the UK and has produced a handbook with Pentol-Levy, called *How to become a sport agent* (Sogut & Pentol-Levy, 2019). This book gives many invaluable insights of the operational working environment of an agent. Sogut makes the important observation that:

> It may not be difficult to become a sport agent, but it is difficult to work as a sport agent.

Why is this the case? To begin with, to become a sport agent is not necessarily that hard in the sense that becoming registered as a sport agent can involve relatively little money. In 2019, in the UK, it can take as little as an hour and £500 to register. Other countries, such as in France, have stronger regulations, where an exam needs to be taken. Even, if a person was to do some of the additional agent workshops run by FIFA, this still represents a relatively modest capital investment to become registered as a sport agent.

So, this brings us back to Sogut and Pentol-Levy (2019) point about why *is it difficult to work as a sport agent*. The reasons relate to the operational

(continued)

Box 3.1 (continued)

challenges and the rich mix that the source of the jobs will be generated from, which can at times be characterised by having a high number of crisis and boomerang types of generated tasks which need quick decisions. It means that applying the more traditional parameters of working hours can be difficult, where work and personal leisure time can be blurred. The actual place of work is also more fluid, where it can be characterised by the capacity to be mobile and staying in contact with clients and staff.

For the agent, the working day may not when they enter the office, but when they first look at their phone. To begin with, the agent may have some of the following, internally generated job task which needs to be progressed:

1. To explore new sponsorship deals for a client whose current sponsorship deal is coming to an end. (Internally generated work)
2. To seek more clients to represent. (Internally generated work)
3. To scrutinise and interpret FIFA's (2019) Regulations on the Status and Transfer of Players, paying particular attention to player registration and passports. (Externally generated work)
4. To help support and develop one of your players charities which they have set up, in terms of generating more publicity for their fundraising activities. (Internally generated work)

Each of these jobs whilst having a superficial simplicity to them is in fact highly complex, which will have numerous sub-tasks or nested process attached to them. For example, the nested processes for the new sponsorship task (task 1) could break down into the sub-tasks:

- To research key sponsors who may be interested in sponsoring the client
- To put out some preliminary soundings as to the level of interest of the potential sponsor for their client
- To release stories via social media that the client may be looking for 'new challenges'
- To review and scrutinise any offers that can take place
- To organise meetings with potential sponsors
- To legally inspect all documentation

These tasks can take hours, days or weeks to complete, but which will be competing with a host of other job task which the agent needs to complete. Initially, the time pressure to complete these tasks may be considered as routine (see Section 3.2), but it should be appreciated the longer they are left, the more likely they are to become crisis situations with a pressurised decision-making process occurring.

So already, before the agent has begun their working day, there are a whole set of job tasks waiting for completion, delegation and planning. As the agent switches on their phone and looks at the messages which have arrived, they see one of the following new job tasks being generated by one of their clients whose text message asks:

Hi, can you arrange the transport, accommodation and tickets for my family, for my next game. Thanks.

This immediately creates another set of job task, which will take time to complete, such as searching and booking flights and accommodation, which could be delegated (but still need monitoring), in a day which already has many competing tasks which need completion.

No sooner has this request come in, when it emerges that another player represented has appeared in the newspapers, being photographed going to a nightclub and it is alleged they got involved in a fight with a member of the public. The phone of the agent has already begun to ring from journalists asking for comment. It means that the working day has now switched pace and is working on the crisis-generated work, which needs immediate attention, but will squeeze out all the other jobs which have to be done. What is more, with each response that is given to the story, it may generate a host of other questions and demands (examples of boomerang work).

In very short space of time, the to-do-list of jobs has got a lot longer, whereby the focus of job tasks has changed literally in minutes.

Discussion tasks

What may happen if some of the smaller job tasks, such as returning calls back to journalists and not replying back to potential sponsors, are not completed?

3.3 IDENTIFYING JOB TASKS

What has been presented so far is that there is a constant, dynamic generation of job tasks in the business environment and the operations system, where management decisions can often generate another set of jobs. So how does the manager capture all these job tasks, in order to keep track of them and ensure they are dealt with?

A key part of the answer is to use systems and complexity theory discussed in Chapter 1. Using systems and complexity theory not only helps to analyse problems, but also provides a foundation for managing workloads, as it can help to break down jobs and projects into their smaller, constituent parts, to ensure jobs are completed on time, to the expected level of quality. Systems theory can also be combined with the classic elements of problem-solving (Torkildsen, 2005, pp. 403–404; VanGrundy, 1998). These involve the process elements of identifying the problem or mess (VanGrundy, 1998, p. 15); generating ideas for solutions; consultation with stakeholders; evaluation of solutions; and implementation and evaluation to check the effectiveness of the solutions.

In essence, unless a job or problem is a crisis event which needs immediate attention (see also Chapter 9) or can be done quickly as it is a simple task, what needs to be done is for the job tasks to be visualised or broken down into many smaller job tasks, which have to be completed at different times, with work often delegated to others. This is the same challenges faced in project management, but where this process is sometimes described as identifying the work breakdown structures (WBS) or the nested processes (Nichols, 2001, p. 165).

One common and simply starting point to help break up more complex tasks or identify the WBS is to ask some questions relating to the *what, why, when, how, where* and *who* (see Box 3.2). These simple operational checklist questions can be given further refinement by using a variety of problem-solving or creative thinking tools, such as:

- **Mind-mapping and free association of ideas**: This can be done individually or with a team of people, which can be particularly useful in the early stages of dealing with management problems and project work. There are many variations in the approaches. VanGrundy (1998, p. 71), for example, offers these rules of mind-mapping, which are as follows: defer judgement (in the early stages, rule nothing in or out, which can also be described using the analogies of 'thinking outside of the box' or 'blue sky thinking'); quantity breeds quality (lots of ideas won't work, but the more you have, the greater the potential you may find a good idea); the wider the ideas, the better; take risks with ideas, letting wild ideas flow (sometimes encapsulated by the phrases 'thinking outside the box' or 'blue sky thinking'); and combine and improve ideas (ideas can be selected and further explored).
- **Mind-mapping and the Buzan method**: A variation of these mind-mapping techniques is the Buzan method of mind-mapping (Buzan, 2010), which tries to represent as much information visually, using pictures and symbols. Using this method, they have the following variations of the rules which are as follows: start at the centre of the page with a key word or concept; try and use one-word branches, where other words will flow from them; try and combine using pictures and colours; and have thinker central lines and thinner radial lines.
- **De Bono's lateral thinking**: This relates to De Bono's (1970) work, which also encourages thinking outside of the box. Similar to other techniques, it can begin with defining the problem, but then it looks to bring in more unrelated thoughts to try and stimulate new ideas. This technique can be further refined, by using what De Bono described as different thinking hats, which are: white hats (the facts); yellow hats (brightness and positive attributes); black hats (judgement and looking for the problems); red hats (feelings and emotions of the problem); green hats (creativity and alternatives, or new ideas); and blue hats (control to ensure the others ideas are adhered to). When combined with mind-mapping or the Buzan method, such as using different coloured pens for each hat, some striking information can be captured in a very short space of time.
- **Attribute listing and checklists**: Using this method, all the key attributes of the service or the problem are listed, then questioned and analysed. Using the *what, why, when, how, where* and *who* can also work here. For example, when creating new services, questions or lists might be created, such as asking *how* the service is delivered to a customer? who will deliver it? where will it be delivered? and so on. Indeed, in Chapter 4, you can find an example of this checklist method in Figure 4.1 (Chapter 4), Service Design Planning Checklist.

- **Using stories and analogies**: Using analogies and metaphors (i.e. producing a statement about how objects or person has some similar attributes) can complement the other creative thinking techniques, whilst storytelling techniques can involve, for example, generating ideas by creative and playful writing of stories of around 1,000 words.

Looking at these models one issue which can be considered is the degree that ideas should be challenged in the early stages. Classic mind-mapping theory generally argues that 'anything' goes, but Syed (2016) argues that at times challenging ideas is actually good and healthy and can in the end lead to more creativity. It is one of the reasons why combining the techniques with De Bono's (1985) six hats is encouraged. Syed says:

> The problem with brainstorming is not its insistence on free-wheeling or quick association. Rather, it is that when these ideas are not checked by the feedback of criticism, they have nothing to respond to. Criticism surfaces problems. It brings difficulties to light. This forces us to think afresh.
>
> (Syed, 2016, p. 212)

Box 3.2 Operationalising a basketball strategic plan in China

The National Basketball Association (NBA) is the governing body for the professional basketball league in North America. It is responsible for managing a huge, financially lucrative sport service, worth billions of dollars. It is, however, ambitious to further expand profits by growing its global market appeal. To do this they have engaged in development-type work, in the sense of trying to grow the sport and nurturing talent, which, whilst in the short term, it might be run as a lost leader (i.e. does not make a profit), it offers many long-term benefits as they build the fan base and commercial appeal of the sport.

A key country which has been targeted in their growth and development strategies has been China. According to one headline, in 2018, the NBA has become the most popular online league in China, having received 2.9 billion views for the NBA play-offs (McNicol, 2018). As part of the continued growth strategy, the NBA China chief David Shoemaker has looked to develop a variety of NBA academies in three cities in China (Urumqi, Jinan and Hangzhou), with a key focus on the youth of China (Blinebury, 2018).

This business growth strategy for China needs to be operationalised and broken down into the WBS or sub-tasks. For example, part of the early work required the development of various partnerships with key Chinese organisations, such as the CBA (Chinese Basketball Association), who were looking to develop their elite players, which can compete at the national level (See Chapter 7 for further discussions on partnerships). Here is an illustration of

(continued)

Box 3.2 (continued)

some of the preliminary tasks identified using the classic operational checklist questions noted earlier, such as:

- **Who**: Identify and employ a number of coaches, with the positions advertised, recruited and trained
- **When**: Setting dates for the new academy to start, with trials occurring up to four months before the official opening
- **Why**: The need to grow the sport of basketball in China, ensuring a greater number of people participate – source of future elite talent – and promote the NBA brand
- **What**: Offering a variety of services, whereby SMART objectives are set to attract a yet to-be-specified number of players to the academies, in the first year of operations (see Chapter 2 for how this can then become the basis of a KPI)
- **How**: Setting academies up with a variety of male and female participants, focusing on different age groups. Work with local schools and run basketball trials

So just by using a few checklist questions, it is possible to already start formulating an operational plan and to envision how it can be put into practice. With the date set for opening (what in project management would be described as the key milestone), it allows for some backward scheduling to occur. So, for example, a backward schedule could be planned for staff recruitment, such as the following actions needing to occur for recruiting coaches:

- Outline and write job specification for coaches to work in Chinese academies (e.g. qualifications, skills and experience, etc.)
- Draft adverts to be placed a variety of publications (online and hard copies) and job pages;
- Place and pay for adverts
- Coordinate dates for short-listing candidates to be selected for interviews
- Set interview dates
- Organise contractual details and checks of all qualifications claimed

To give a further sense of the scale of the operational challenges this poses, the City of Urumqi has a population of over 3 million people, having hundreds of schools, which would need to be targeted to try to help create a healthy pool of talent identification. The head coach or manager appointed to this academy would also need to work with the local professional basketball team of Xinjiang Flying Tigers, which plays games in its own stadium.

Finally, it should always be appreciated how the smooth operations can easily be disrupted and tipped into crisis, from even the smallest of actions. For example, in October 2019, the general manager for the Houston Rockets basketball team sent out a tweet supporting the Hong Kong anti-government protests; this tweet, which took only minutes to write, sparked a huge political controversy, ultimately resulting in lost Chinese sponsorship deals, cancelled games and suspended partnerships. It is a classic example of how reputations and brands can take years to build (the Rocket's team was hugely popular in

China, after they signed a Chinese player – Yao Ming – in 2002 which they leveraged to develop their brand appeal), but, literally, minutes to destroy. The tweet was eventually deleted, but by then, the damage was done and various officials from the NBA and the club, where in full blown, crisis recovery management (See Chapter 9).

Discussion

What are the cultural challenges for a non-Chinese manager, SDO or coach working in one of the city academies, which could impact on the operations of the academy services?

3.4 ANALYSING AND PRIORITISING WORK TASKS AND JOBS

3.4.1 Prioritising job tasks

What is emerging is that a manager and SDO will have numerous job tasks to complete, generated from a variety of sources, which vary in terms of their complexity, all of which will place different demands on their time. Some of the job tasks generated can at times seem impossible to deal with, where there is the risk that by failing to complete just one job, it can jeopardise the whole operation. What is therefore needed are some practical management tips and tools which can be used to manage and control all these jobs generated. For example, Allen (cited in Levitin, 2014, p. 71) identifies four basic actionable options which are:

- Do it
- Delegate it
- Defer it
- Drop it

In the first instance, if it is possible to do something in under two minutes, then consideration should be given to doing the job there and then (Levitin, 2014, p. 71). Caution, however, is urged about trying to always adopt a 'do-it' now approach as each new job arrives; to try and use this approach all the time can mean the manager or SDO is simply reacting to events and may ultimately struggle to complete larger, more complex or important work on time.

Noon (1989), writing in a general management context, gave an estimation that 15% of top priority work can often arrive on the day, and 50–57% of work is spent dealing with contingencies. Whilst this statistic is difficult to verify, many managers and SDOs would agree with the underlying argument that many jobs arrive on the day. The challenge can be deciding which of these jobs takes priority and needs immediate attention and action, and which ones can be done later or delegated to others. In Table 3.1 a variety of methods which can be used to help prioritise or decide what jobs to do first are outlined.

There are many other variations for prioritising decisions, but the ones shown in Table 3.1 help identify two classic, core themes to prioritisation:

- To what extent is it 'important'?
- To what extent is it 'urgent'?

Table 3.1 Examples of Prioritisation Questions and Categories

Three Basic Questions to Ask	Six Detailed Questions to Ask	Three-Point Simple Categorisation	Four-Point Prioritisation Grid
- Is it urgent? - Is it important? - Is it my job?	- Is it safe? - Does it represent a danger? - What are the financial cost implications of the job? - Could money be lost, wasted or gained? (the opportunity costs) - Is it my job? - Are people being used effectively? - How will it affect staff morale?	1 Is essential (A category) 2 Is desirable (B category) 3 Is nonessential. (C category)	A. High urgency/high importance B. High importance/ low urgency C. High urgency/ low importance D. Low urgency/ low importance

Source: Author.

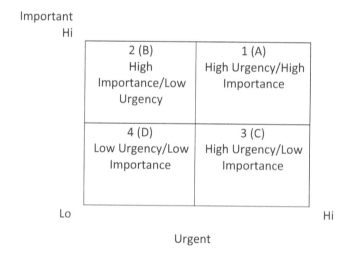

Figure 3.2 The Classic Four-Point Priority Grid.

The difference between importance and urgency is not always understood. This relates to the issue sometimes raised in problem-solving literature, which stresses the importance of understanding the subjectivity of problems, whereby what might be a problem and a priority for one person in an organisation is not for another. The time element when combined with how important a job is allows a simple prioritising matrix of decision-making to be formulated, which is shown in Figure 3.2.

This simple matrix gives a useful conceptual template that can be applied to work, helping managers to decide what they should do and when they should do it, where the questions asked in Table 3.1 can give a sense of how to evaluate the importance of the work task. To help further illustrate how these priorities work in practice, a variety of real-life job tasks are presented in Box 3.3.

Box 3.3 How would you prioritise these typical job tasks generated in a day?

Here is an outline of job tasks based on a real manager's to-do list. As with the sport agent example (Box 3.1), it shows how the working day begins with some job tasks which need to be worked on, but over the morning, additional job tasks are generated from different sources and which will need to be actioned.

To make it more challenging, it is recommended that you read them, then try and apply the four-point A–D Priority Rating (PR), presented in Figure 3.2, to each of the tasks and consider what subsequent actions need to be taken.

Job Task 1 – Working paper – third age users (intended morning work)

You need to draft out a preliminary working paper to outline some different programmes for people in the third age (i.e. the retired and elderly segment) to maximise usage, to fill a market gap and to anticipate future government policies.

Job Task 2 – New legal regulatory compliance (preliminary read in morning if time allows)

You receive an organisational bulletin which states that government legislation has been passed relating to a new set of health and safety regulations, which all organisations need to comply with, but they will not come into force for six months, allowing you the time to prepare your operations to ensure compliance takes place.

Job Task 3 – Working paper – teenagers (intended for afternoon work)

You need to produce a short policy paper about the issue of teenagers who visit the centre, as part of a sport engagement project for young people. The problem is that they often continue to loiter around the centre and can be a nuisance to other customers. The issue has been ongoing for over a year, but it has received more prominence because of an incident three weeks ago, where two members of a sport club were verbally abused by the teenagers in the car park, along with an accusation by the club players that one of the teenagers put a nail in their car tyre.

The paper needs to be presented to the Trustees of the sport centre in a weeks' time.

After sitting at your desk, you begin to read the following messages and emails which have arrived.

(continued)

Box 3.3 (continued)

Job Task 4 (email 1) – This is the email you received from a parent

To whom it may concern

I am writing to inform you that I want to withdraw my child from the Friday junior swimming class.

I have been bringing my child to this coaching class for five weeks. Over the past few weeks I have often thought the coach lacked empathy and their communications skills were something to be desired. But this was nothing in comparison with what took place in last Friday's class.

During one of the training routines a number of children failed to master the swimming drills set (my daughter was one). After a number of mistakes, the coach exploded and began shouting at the children, saying they were still making the mistakes and if they 'couldn't master these basic skills then perhaps they should go back to a beginner's class'. The children and a number of parents were shocked (I'm sure I will not be the only parent to complain).

Please can you organise an immediate refund of the money I paid for the lessons.

Job Task 5 (email 2) – From a manager of another facility

Help! Back in March at a meeting I was asked by our senior manager to prepare a new customer care manual, and talking to you after the meeting, you said you would be happy to share some ideas.

I need to produce a customer care checklist by tomorrow – can you send me a list of points this morning by 10.00, so I can produce my list?

Thanks

Job Task 6 (email 3) – From another facility

We just want to confirm if you are collecting the crash mats you need for your gymnastic event on Wednesday?

It's a busy couple of days and we're short staffed through illness, so we need to make sure the people are available to help load up the mats for you if you still need them?

Job Task 7 – Message from receptionist

Your receptionist has come into your office and given you the following message:

A parent has just come in to complain that the football coach, who was due to run a holiday football camp for juniors, has not turned up.

The parent explained that they think one of the parents has stepped in to do some activities with the children, but they do not appear to be a qualified coach or have a first aid certificate (or, they presume, having a police check).

Job tasks, scheduling and time management 67

Although the parent is reasonably relaxed about the parent stepping in as they are pleased something is being done, the main issue they have complained about is the coach not having turned up, working on the assumption that your centre is running the camp.

The receptionist explained to the parent that it is not in fact a course which your centre manages, as it is run separately by the local football club, who just hire the pitch. The session is still taking place as the receptionist comes in to tell you about the problem.

Before you read what responses could be taken (below), try and prioritise them in terms of the order for completion.

Possible prioritisation and responses to job tasks

Response Job Task 1 (PR B): This does not have an immediate deadline set yet, but it is vital to create some new programmes to help ensure the future viability of the organisation. There is, as a result, some flexibility to move the work, but there is also the danger that by moving it, it fails to be completed properly. As time goes on, your senior managers may begin to ask more pressing questions about what the manager is going to do about the falling usage and revenues.

For today, however, if need be, the work can be delayed.

Response to Job Task 2 (PR B): This will be absolutely vital to comply with as failure to do so could lead to safety being compromised, financial loss and reputational damaged, even imprisonment. There is however time for the implementation, as it will take time to organise the resources, so must be properly planned for, where the work is broken down into smaller work tasks. Failure to comply with it, or to leave it all down to the last moments could be catastrophic and result in legal action, whereby arguments of ignorance or rushing the implementation would not be admissible in court.

For today, it can be moved to a later date.

Response Job Task 3 (PR B): This is an important task, which needs attention. It is vital for both the council members and customers that actions are seen to be done, along with preparing a response to any future media enquiries.

This work would take less time than previous task, so can be returned to later in the day, as the deadline is looming.

Response Job Task 4 (PR A and B): The initial response of acknowledging the issue and the promise of investigating it should be an immediate action, but the full response may take more time. Clearly, this is a worrying issue, and it is vital that a preliminary response is given to acknowledge the message and to ensure that this will be investigated. Consideration can be given to offering the refund.

This work needs an immediate response, but not necessarily an immediate decision (e.g. sacking the coach), as more investigation is needed.

(continued)

68 Chapter 3

> Box 3.4 (continued)
>
> **Response Job Task 5 (PR C)**: Clearly, this is urgent for someone else, but not as important to you, as you have your own priorities. A short reply can be given out of courtesy using the two-minute rule principle, in order to maintain good relations.
>
> For now, there are more pressing tasks which have emerged and need attention.
>
> **Response Job Task 6 (PR A)**: You often share equipment between facilities. This is a task quickly dealt with, but failure to confirm the picking up could mean problems and jeopardise an event which you are running the following day.
>
> This is a classic two-minute task which is in fact both urgent and important to complete.
>
> **Response to Job Task 7 (PR A)**: You do not employ the coach, as the pitch is hired out to one of the local football clubs, who have decided to run some of these taster sessions. However, it needs your urgent attention, as the centre still carries some liability, and it should be assessed in terms of the risks, so you should go outside and check the activities are being run safely.
>
> **Discussion**
>
> Examine the sample responses and consider if you would do anything different and why.

3.4.2 Time management and using diary systems

This section focuses on how to get the job tasks identified and assessed in terms of priorities and completion, to the required standard, or one which exceeds it (see Chapter 5 for more details on quality). To do this requires engagement with the basic principles of time management, which acts as a foundation for effective operations and, indeed, project management (Chapter 6). It can even affect how the manager and SDO are viewed in terms of their leadership qualities. Crucially, the key foundation for effective time management is not relying on memory, but using some form of external memory aid, such as an electronic or paper diary system.

Two key elements need to be engaged with for effective time management. These are producing 'to-do' checklist of jobs or actions, which are then integrated into some form of diary system, whether this is electronic or paper based. If the job tasks have been identified, analysed and assessed in terms of priority, then this provides the foundation for the to-do list, as the examples given in Figure 3.3 illustrate, based on a real managers' to-do-list. This list indicates who is responsible for the action and date of completion, but will need constant up-dating.

To Do List/Action Points

Activity/Action	Who	Notes/sub tasks	Date Completed
Develop new promotional leaflet for course	Delegated PH	Outline content; send to design agency; approve draft, legal scrutiny; then pick-up and distribute	
Confirm staff for holiday cover	Delegated PH	Produce holiday rota; organize additional staff for events; and approve leave	
Review KPI for quarterly performance and produce short interim report	Me	Focus on ratio analysis of efficiency; demand usage and staff costs; explore local statistical reports on crime and deprivation; give short report and actions to any issues to senior management	
Prepare and update induction pack for new staff	Me	Confirm new health and safety policy and update; check compliance	
Organise community festival	All staff	Preliminary contact with all community groups; draft contact letter; check with authorities and policy on any restrictions; check proposed date with other events; produce preliminary risk assessment; designate responsibilities of event organization to staff etc.	
Outline press release for forthcoming sport event for summer	Me	Draft event; send to news agencies, social media platforms, etc.	
Recruitment of new sport assistant.	Me and HR	Update person and job specification; check advert and date; book shortlisting and interview dates when interview panel are available	
Review impact new government policies on data protection	Me and Legal	Audit work practices to check compliance; identify areas where compliance is failed; review security of IT machines and practices; meet with IT and legal team.	

Figure 3.3 Example of an Overall To-Do lists.

Rumelt (2017) observes that some may see the advice about 'making a list' of jobs to do as too simple or of any real use to the experienced business manager. Rumelt, however, stresses how essential simple 'to-do' lists are for effective management, saying:

> Making a list is a basic tool for overcoming our own cognitive limitations. The list itself counters forgetfulness. The act of making a list forces us to reflect on the relative urgency and importance of issues. And making a list of 'things to do *now*' rather than 'things to worry about" forcing us to resolve concerns and turn them into actions.
>
> (Rumelt, 2017, p. 260)

This list of jobs to do is still only part of the way for effective time management. Looking at the previous To-Do/Action point list in Figure 3.3, it should be appreciated that it is impossible to do all of these jobs in a day and will need many hours of attention, spread out over many days, weeks or even months. The manager or SDO therefore has to go further in terms of generating daily to-do lists, drawn from the main checklist of jobs, which are then integrated into a diary system.

In Figure 3.4, some of the complex tasks, listed in Figure 3.3, are broken down into quite specific to-do actions, on the top-right hand of the page. This sample diary page also has examples of delegated work and some reminding trip wires to chase up work and seek answers. On the actual time-line page, examples of B priority-type work have been planned for or scheduled (e.g. the annual report), with a staff meeting in the afternoon. The times in-between are the opportunities when the jobs listed and people to contact can be done, but, of course, this is dependent on whether any new crisis events are generated, as illustrated in Box 3.3, such as needing cover for a member of staff who might be ill. These gaps in the working day can also be considered as the crisis buffers, where the manager can respond to new jobs or problems as they arise in a day. With the staff meeting shown on the page, it will inevitably generate a number of jobs, such as making a note of any staff questions and ensuring that a response is given, even if it is not the answer they want to hear (note that it can be a real source of frustration where people promise to find something out, but fail to respond to the person asking the question).

One might be tempted to think that because so much work can be generated on a day, there is no point of planning on a daily, weekly or monthly basis. The general rule is, however, that it is better to try and plan some (not all) of your time, focusing on some of the key priority areas, as that helps ensure greater control. What is being done here in terms of producing a checklist of jobs and integrating them in some form of diary or calendar system is also a key foundation for project management, discussed in Chapter 6. In order to get a better insight into why these systems work, some of the underpinning theories are explored in Box 3.4.

Job tasks, scheduling and time management 71

Time	Activity	Daily To Do List
5.00		Respond to customer coaching complaint, as they are not satisfied with compensation offer
6.00		Organize cover for sick member of staff
7.00		Financial analysis of annual report
8.00		Update agenda items for staff safety meeting
9.00		
10.00	Work on annual report – finance section (deadline 2 weeks)	
11.00		
12.00		
1.00		
2.00	Staff meeting – new health and safety policy	
3.00		**Contact**
4.00		Has kit supplier sent promised quote?
5.00		Check with assistant manager about preliminary first draft of leaflet to send to advertising agency
6.00		Contact assistant manager to find out about broken window
7.00		
8.00		
9.00		
10.00		
11.00		**Personal**
12.00		Make appointment for dentist

Figure 3.4 Example of a Daily Plan and To-Do List.

Box 3.4 How the mind works (Levitin, 2014)

Levitin offers some useful insights into how the mind works and tips on remembering and completing job tasks. Early in the book he gives some revealing insights into how our brains work, which evolved in different environments to the ones people find themselves in today. He explains how, for example, the brain developed a rehearsal loop mechanism, which was an effective way of remembering things, such as good places to find food, whereby in humans more primitive existence, this would be constantly concern. This mechanism, however, in a modern working environment, where there are numerous jobs which need to be kept track off, can mean people can end up constantly fretting about 'to-do' items, which get tossed around in a persons mind creating stress, insomnia and potential health problems.

Another primitive mechanism which helped humans survive is the novelty bias and startle index. This is where our attention is caught, for example, by sudden movements, such as a predator in the long grass. What then occurs is that the brain delivers a dopamine hit, which can help with the response, such as running away (i.e. fight or flight). But it is also a part of the brain that is easily hijacked in the modern world, such as our attention being caught by an email or phone alert, or helping to explain certain addictive behaviour, such as gambling. He argues that those 'pings' on the phone, for example, tap into a primitive instinct, and we are being rewarded for being distracted. The result is 'infomania' (Levitin, 2014, p. 68) whereby it can become difficult to stay focused on a single task, which can help explain why phones and computers can consume so much of our time, compounded by the fact that so many businesses are actually geared to try and capture our attention (see the earlier point about working days coming down to having productive minutes).

In Levitin book, he offers numerous ways to deal with this overload of information to try and work more effectively, and reduces stress. Here are two key suggestions relevant to operations management:

- **External memory aide and to-do list**: Because there are so many jobs to keep track off, it is too unreliable to use just memory, whereby the rehearsal loop mechanism can end up leading to stress as we churn over, in our mind, the jobs to be done. What is therefore needed is to use some trusted system to capture all the to-do tasks which is 'outside the mind' (Levitin, 2014, p. 69), such as some form of diary system or notebook. He says, 'writing things down conserves mental energy' and 'If it's on you mind, then your mind is not clear', as you need to try and find time to engage with 'to-do' work on some consistent basis.
- **Adopting a culture of *satisficing***: *Satisficing* was a term coined by Herbert Simon, a key writer on organisational theory, which can help deal with the problems of *'decision overload'*. In Simon's various works he observed the numerous limitations on decision-making, where rationality always has its bounds, because managers will never have enough time, or all the information they need, to make a perfectly balanced,

rational decision, so compromises always need to be made. Levitin (2014) reiterates these points about the need to compromise, whereby we may not be able to get the 'best' option, but simply find the one that is 'good enough' – what is called 'satisficing'. Satisficing, Levitin, argues 'is one of the foundations of productive human behaviour; it prevails when we don't waste time on deciding to find improvements that are not going to make a significant difference in our happiness or satisfaction' (Levitin, 2014, p. 4).

Discussion

How many of these issues and problems do you recognise in your working environments?

There are a number of caveats to this prioritisation system. Remember, job tasks exist as part of a dynamic operations system, whereby the longer they are not dealt with, the more likely they can change in terms of priority. Whilst type A priority jobs need to be done first, for type B type tasks, it is crucial that time is found for them at some point, to stop them become crisis scenarios, as illustrated in Box 3.3.

There is a superficial simplicity to some of these practices, but their importance should not be under-estimated as they are critical in being an effective manager, reducing stress and creating confidence in others of your leadership capabilities. Here is a summary of some of the key points which have been discussed, in terms of good operations practice and time management:

- **Produce a 'to-do' lists with deadlines and priorities**: This is drawn from the analysis of jobs or problems, as they arrive and are analysed and the WBS found, with key deadlines or milestones identified, which are prioritised.
- **Produce daily 'to-do' list**: This is vital, as it gives further refinement and detail to the longer to-do list (see Figure 3.3) and is a key ingredient in operationalising plans (see Figure 3.4 for an example). It is important to try and be realistic with a daily to-do list in terms of what can be achieved in a day.
- **Plan your time in a diary to work on complex tasks**: Some work, such as writing reports, can take many hours, requiring an analysis and assessment of data, such as doing an annual performance evaluation report. It is unlikely that this can be done in a day, so it is broken down over a period of weeks, where time is allotted in the diary for it.
- **Plan for a crisis**: Planning is vital, but it is important that not all time is booked out, as there always needs some time to react to crisis-type events.
- **A blank diary page DOES NOT mean you are free**: A common mistake many managers or SDOs make is that they may only show committed time in their diaries for meetings. This can mean that when, for example, they might be asked if they were 'free' on a particular day, they may say yes, when in fact they may have a large amount of more complex work which needs to be completed, as illustrated in Figure 3.4 and why planning by blocking out time is so important.

- **Transfer incomplete tasks to another day's to-do list**: Clearly, the nature of work, whereby new job tasks will be arriving on the day, means that tasks will not always be completed. It is vital, however, that they are not forgotten and transferred to another day.
- **Try and action work once**: This can be tricky, but wherever possible, once a message or task has been engaged with, try and deal with it once, rather than keep coming back to it, unless it is a large, complex task.
- **Place trip wire reminders in diaries**: This can play a critical role in reducing stress as it means work is committed to your diary, not relying on your memory. It is particularly useful for keeping track of promises to respond to questions when you find the information out, or even making a note of other people's promises, to act as a prompt to see if they responded to you (see Figure 3.3 for an example).
- **Use one system to record information**: It is encouraged to try and avoid having lots of reminding notes, or post-it tabs, dotted everywhere, as this can clutter up your mind and lead to confusion or missed work. Try and get into a habit of using one system, such as an electronic calendars or a diary, or even a simple note book. The more you use the single system, the more confident you will become in the system, and it acts as a reliable aide memoire.
- **Don't let urgent, less important jobs push out the important jobs** (Noon, 1989): This is about booking out time during the week to try and work on some of the more complex work, which takes time and which is important but not yet urgent.
- **Work to a clear desk policy and have times away from electronic distractions**: The modern working environment generates numerous distractions, so one way of dealing with this is to work at a clear desk and have times free from electronic distractions which can lead to attention switching, distractions and lost productivity. It can mean that replies to messages can be 'bunched' after more complex work has been dealt with.

3.5 MONITORING, REVIEWING AND ADJUSTMENT

Slack et al. (2016, p. 325) make the crucial point that having a plan in place is not a guarantee that the planned actions will actually happen 'as a plan is formalisation of what is intended in the future'. They state that it is vital to control the plan, in terms of implementation and adjustment, stating that control is '…the process of coping with changes in variables'. It means plans can be redrawn in the short term. It may also mean an 'intervention' will be made in the operation to bring it 'back on track'. Slack et al. (2016, p. 562) also comment that re-planning is not a sign of failure, as long this process reviews on why it failed and the impact on KPIs, discussed in Chapter 2. Time management and performance evaluation need to go hand-in-hand.

One aspect of monitoring which has not been fully discussed relates to delegation. A common definition of management is that it is about getting work done through others. The inference of this is that managers must delegate work. There is not the full scope to discuss the skill, art even, of delegation, which is intimately related to theories on motivation and leadership, as it could easily fill a book in their own right – so just the key points are considered here. Crucially, one can only delegate work, NOT the responsibility. If the person you gave the work to fails, then the manager can be held accountable, because it may well be a failing on your part, by failing to identify the right person, not supporting them or given them the training and resources they needed.

When allocating work to others, it is important to strike the right balance between genuinely empowering people to succeed and develop, rather than simply dumping work on them which a manager does not want to do. Both can have profound impacts on staff motivation and trust. Indeed, writers such as Kanter (1989, cited in Torkildsen, 2005, p. 380) stress how true empowerment is more than delegation, arguing that in an increasingly dynamic and competitive business environment, organisations need to be more flexible and adaptable to change, which requires workforces to have more responsibility and powers to lead innovation.

3.6 CONCLUSION

Getting jobs completed on time, to the required level of quality, creates trust and confidence in the managers and SDOs' management and leadership qualities, whilst also reducing stress. Jobs will be generated from a variety of sources, which vary in complexity and pose different challenges in terms of resources needed. It begins by ensuring all the jobs generated are identified and prioritised in some way, always showing courtesy to others, even if this is to tell them you cannot help them with their task.

In terms of the practicalities and operationalising plans, two basic elements are needed which act as a foundation for good time management: producing dynamic, ever-changing to-do tasks lists, complemented with some form of external memory aid, such as using diary systems or notebooks. Producing to-do lists and using diary systems help ensure work gets done, which in turn can reduce stress as it puts the manager and SDO in more control of their time. People sometimes make the mistake of using a diary to just record committed activities, such as a meeting, where a blank diary page can be interpreted as 'clear' – in fact, this is the time when the more challenging work needs to be organised. These basic principles are returned to in Chapter 6, where a variety of additional tools and concepts are examined in relation to project management.

References

Blinebury, F. (2018). NBA to open NBA academies in three cities in China, NBA website, accessed 28 May 2019, available at: https://www.nba.com/article/2016/10/12/nba-open-nba-academies-urumqi-jinan-and-hangzhou-china

Buzan, T. (2010). *Mind Maps for Business*. Harlow: Pearson.

De Bono, E. (1985). *Six Thinking Hats: An Essential Approach to Business Management*. London: Brown & Company.

FIFA (2019). Regulations on the status and transfer of players, policy document, accessed 28 May 2019, available at: https://resources.fifa.com/image/upload/regulations-on-the-status-and-transfer-of-players-2018-2925437.pdf?cloudid=c83ynehmkp62h5vgwg9g

González, V.M., Mark, G. (2005). Managing currents of work: Multi-tasking among multiple collaborations, In Gellersen H., Schmidt K., Beaudouin-Lafon M., and Mackay W. (eds.), *ECSCW 2005*. Dordrecht: Springer, pp. 143–162.

Levitin, D. (2014). *The Organized Mind*. London: Penguin.

Mark, G., and González, V.M. (2004). "Constant, constant, multi-tasking craziness's": Managing multiple working spheres. *Conference Proceedings of the SIGCHI Conference on Human Factors in Computing Systems*, pp. 113–120.

McNicol, A. (2018). How the NBA became China's most popular sports league, with a boost from tech giants such as Weibo and Tencent. *South China Morning post*, accessed on 28 May 2019, available at: https://www.scmp.com/sport/china/article/2112972/how-nba-became-chinas-most-popular-sports-league-boost-tech-giants-such

Nichols, J.M. (2001). *Project Management for Business and Technology*. New Jersey: Prentice Hall.

Noon, J. (1989). *'A' Time*. London: Van Nostrand Reimhold.

Rumelt, R. (2017). *Good Strategy, Bad Strategy*. London: Profile Books.

Sogut, E., and Pentol-Levy, J. (2019). *How to Become a Sport Agent*. Kibworth: Matador.

Slack, N., Brandon-Jones, A., and Johnston, R. (2016). *Operations Management*. 8th ed. London: Pearson.

Syed M. (2016). *Black Box Thinking*. London: John Murray.

Tenner, E. (2003). *Our Own Devices*. London: Knopf.

VanGrundy, A.B. (1998). *Techniques of Structured Problem Solving*. New York: Van Nostrand.

4
CREATING SPORT PROGRAMMES TO MEET NEEDS AND WANTS

> **Challenges for managers**
>
> - How does a manager or sport development officer (SDO) begin to create a new sport programme or improve existing ones to maintain demand?
> - What is the difference between designing services which meet a *want* or a *need*?
> - How are programmes costed and designed?

4.1 INTRODUCTION

Designing a sport service or programme is at very heart of most sport operations and should be considered as inseparable from the business function of marketing. It refers to the services which a sport manager or SDO offers to people to play, watch or support. In this chapter we primarily focus on the *creating* part of the operational process, for designing programmes which meet people's needs and wants – terms which should not be used inter-changeably – which can be done for profit, or to achieve some broader social-orientated objective and outcome.

This chapter begins by outlining a number of practical marketing concepts to explain how a sport programme is researched, developed and priced. The chapter then develops a programming process model, illustrated with a variety of applied case studies.

4.2 THE IMPORTANCE OF MARKETING THEORY TO SERVICE DESIGN

Torkildsen (2005) states bluntly that marketing and programming go hand-in-hand. He describes it as the 'what and why' of leisure and sport, arguing that:

> Programming is important. It is highly underrated factor in leisure management, yet the programme is the single most important product of a leisure and recreation organization. Everything that a service or department is concerned with – facilities, supplies, personnel, budgets, marketing, public relations, activities, timetabling and administration – is solely to ensure opportunities exist for people to enjoy or experience leisure in ways satisfying to them.
>
> (Torkildsen, 2005, p. 447)

Whilst the scope of this book goes beyond Torkildsen's facility management focus, the point about the importance of designing sport programmes for people to consume still holds. And if this proposition is accepted, then it in affect means accepting the central importance of the marketing business function in sport operations. Whilst it is beyond the scope of this book to fully explore all the key marketing theories which are relevant to sport operations and SDO work, it is possible to identify some core concepts which are invaluable for sport operations, which the sport manager and SDO should be familiar with.

Marketing has various definitions. The problem with some is that they simply focus on making a profit from want satisfaction. In a sport context, as was explained in Chapters 1 and 2, one of the unique features about many sport services is that they are often provided on a non-profit basis, designed to achieve both outputs and many unique outcomes, which need to utilise marketing theories and practices just as much as profit-orientated services. Therefore, the preferred definition of marketing is:

> Sport marketing is a matching process – the matching of sport products and services to the demands of sport consumers and customers. It helps to bring supply and demand into balance. Sport consumers (i.e. those who use sport services) and customers (i.e. those who buy them) require products and services to satisfy the needs and wants they have in life.
>
> (Blakey, 2011, p. 2)

It is important to explain the difference between a *need* and a *want*. Saipe (1999, p. 16) frames it quite simply by saying 'needs are essential, wants are desires'. Maslow's (1943) ubiquitous hierarchy of needs gives a simple insight into these needs, framed around a progression through five broad needs: physiological needs, such as food, water and rest; safety needs, such as security and shelter; belonging and love needs, such as having friends and family; esteem needs, such as prestige and status; and self-actualisation, which can be a little hard to pin down, but relates to people reaching a sense of self-fulfilment and happiness. Maslow's theory is a little simplistic and deterministic in the sense that humans are not so mechanically driven that one need has to be met before progression to the next level. Despite these limitations, it gives a simple starting point to understand needs. Torkildsen (2005) helps frame where sport and leisure services fit into the discussion on needs, arguing that we have human needs, which sport services can help satisfy, such as meeting belonging needs, because of the opportunities sport offers for creating social interaction.

Sport, then, has the potential to meet people's human needs, but how is this different from a want? A want is something people desire. It is rooted in a need, such as the need for food and water, which when felt, creates a sense of arousal, which would be described as being hungry or thirsty, and so a desire or *want* is created. The problem is that at times, satisfying a *want* can be detrimental to a person's *needs*. A simple example is that people need to eat, but satisfying hunger *wants* with 'junk' food can lead to obesity and health problems. Another example can relate to gambling, which can meet a need for stimulation, giving rewarding

Creating sport programmes to meet needs and wants 79

dopamine hits, but unfortunately can also become addictive, which in turn can damage their social relationships and health.

What these examples also help illustrate is that there can be a moral and ethical dimension to programming, where consideration should not always be given to simple want satisfaction, even though this can be very profitable. Into this mix of the ethical considerations, is that sport and active recreation should not be considered as *discretionary item* or a luxury, to be consumed when other basic needs have been met, which should be considered in relative terms of deprivation, not absolute (i.e. comparing recreational opportunities with others in the society, not between the richest and poorest countries).

In this chapter, just two basic marketing concepts will be periodically referred to in the applied process of designing, costing and delivering services. These are:

- **Product life cycle (PLC)**: This refers to the idea that products and services, when introduced to the market will go through a cycle of demand growth, demand maturity, then demand decline, unless the service is changed or rejuvenated. The PLC is important because it shows why operations management should always be considered as a dynamic process, where failure to renew, improve and regenerate facilities and services can lead to decline. See Box 4.1 for how this can be applied in practice.
- **Marketing mix**: There are a number of variations, but it is sufficient to briefly consider the basic 4 Ps, in relation to: the product (for simplicity here, we include the services, even though they have different attributes); the price of the service; its place and promotion.

Box 4.1 The product lifecycle (PLC) of keep fit services

According to the IHRSA (2019) report there was estimated to be over 210,000 health clubs around the world, worth $94 billion, with the USA the largest market, followed by Germany, then the UK. The health and fitness market sector is also one which reveals many paradoxical trends. For example, in many developed countries, there is the problem of obesity, yet at the same time, there has been a significant growth in gym membership and participation rates in keep fit-type classes. IbisWorld (2019) in their review of the gym, health and fitness industry in the US noted how gym membership has grown by 2.9% annually, between 2013 and 2017, which was driven by a mix of external factors, such as campaigns to fight obesity, trends of people trying to improve their health, rising consumer incomes and a more competitive supply sector.

An important part of the services in many of these fitness centres offer is the various keep fit/aerobic-type classes. Doing non-competitive physical

(continued)

Box 4.1 (continued)

activities to improve fitness, has a long history, rooted in military and educational training (i.e. school P.E classes). In the 1980s however, these activities broke out from these more traditional confines, with the rapid growth of rhythmical physical activities performed to music, usually marketed as aerobic or keep fit classes. In the early years, these classes were limited in range, which, in terms of the PLC, would be described as the 'growth' stage. By the 1990s, the market had matured or was in some areas going into decline. What needed to be done in order to both maintain demand or create new demand was to develop new classes and services, which could help 'rejuvenate' services. Hence, over the years the variety of aerobic-type fitness classes has grown. Today, if you look at a range of classes offered in a gym or a multi-use sport facility from around the world, it reveals numerous different types of keep fit classes, such as:

- **Keep fit classes** – Simple rhythmic movement classes to music
- **Legs, bums and tums** – An aerobics class designed to target certain parts of the body
- **Zumba** – In many ways this is simple way of rebranding older aerobic courses, but it focuses more on high tempo Latin music, with salsa, flamenco and hip-hop beats, which can even weave in martial art movement beats
- **Aquarobics** – Using swimming pools for rehabilitation of injuries has a long history, as the water can help support the body and aid in gradual movement. They were often initially marketed to older consumers, whose mobility might be reduced, but today they have a much broader appeal
- **Body pump** – This has many aerobic elements, but brings in more resistance exercises, such as using weights to music
- **Dancercise** – Again, this can be something of a rebranding exercise, for what previously may have been called an aerobics class or a keep fit class, as it is exercise to music with more dance elements built in
- **Pilates** – This is more of a low impact exercise class that at times can be more akin to yoga, with its more controlled movement of the body

The variety of keep fit classes seems set to continue to grow, having become a core part of many fitness centres and gyms, core services. The changes shown in the fitness market illustrate the challenges that operations managers and development officers face in terms of how they need to constantly think about creating new services to meet demand, or to rejuvenate older services to try and improve their market appeal. In some instances, the experience of consumers can be improved by changing the classes, such as changing instructors, and the types of music used, or alternatively, a completely new type of class can be introduced, which blends in new technologies and helps to keep fresh and 'rejuvenate' the service.

Questions

If you were the manager of a budget, low cost gym, how would you try and maintain people's interest in your gym?

Creating sport programmes to meet needs and wants 81

4.3 HOW TO CREATE A NEW SPORT PROGRAMME

The process outlined here blends in some of the key elements from the business functions of marketing, finance and HRM. Consideration also needs to be given to applying the management functions (e.g. controlling, leading, communicating, etc.) and the different scientific disciplines (e.g. psychology and understanding human behaviour, economics and the types of demand and the elasticity of demand). In Figure 4.1, a simple flow chart is presented which outlines how a sport service can be created, which needs to draw on different aspects of the

Context

How does the sector operated in shape the organizational strategies and policies?

What is the balance between the social objectives vs commercial profit objectives?

(Section 4.4.1)

Idea and Demand Research

How do we generate ideas for services? How can the following methods be used, such as heuristics, mind mapping, internal and external environmental analysis, trade journals and news scans, competitor analysis, analysis of usage data, secondary databases, primary research, consumer analysis, modelling?

(Section 4.4.2)

Assessment of Resources and Risk

What resources are needed? (Staffing, equipment, insurance, spaces, service design such as time, skill level, target group, etc.. What are the key risks and areas of legal regulation which must be) complied with?

(Section 4.4. and Chapter 9)

Planning and Marketing

Costing & prices (staff, equipment, insurance, energy, administration) and pricing, promotion (posters, social media, press releases, etc.) (Section 4.5. and Chapter 9)

Implementation and monitoring

Booking forms, observations, data analysis, record for medicalments,

Figure 4.1 Programming Checklist Flow Chart.

business and management functions, and theories and concepts from different scientific disciplines. This flow chart can also be used as a checklist of actions (see Chapter 3) to help keep track of all the job tasks that need to be kept track of.

A couple of observations need to be made about this flow diagram. The first is that it focuses on the *who, what, where, when* and *how*, discussed in Chapter 3. Second, at its heart, it adopts market-orientated approach, which means managers and SDOs should always attempt to try and understand the needs and wants of customers and how any sport services meet these needs and wants. It is also a process model which adapts generic operations models designed for product development, such as Slack et al. (2016) five-stage model (stage 1, concept generation; stage 2, concept screening; stage 3, preliminary design; stage 4, evaluation and improvements; and stage 5, prototype and final design). Finally, for ease, it utilises the 4 Ps (Product, Price, Place, Promotion), but more sophisticated marketing templates can be adapted and utilised if needed. The four stages are used to frame the subsequent sub-sections of this chapter.

4.3.1 Stage 1 – rationale and context of service design

Reflecting on the rationale of the organisation and the purpose of its services, whether this is for profit or to achieve broader social objectives, or even a mixture of the two, helps kick-start the concept generation process. The expectation would be for the sport organisation or business to have some sort of strategic plan written – discussed in Chapter 2 – whereby the purpose is encapsulated in a mixture of the vision, mission and value statements, or their variants. These should, in theory, then be given more detail in the aims and SMART objectives (or their variants in terms of the terminology, all discussed in Chapter 2). In Box 4.2 some examples of social enterprises and the types of sport programmes they have created to meet their aims, objectives and hoped for outcomes are shown.

Box 4.2 – The rise of social sport enterprise programming

Over recent years, around the world, there has been a growth in organisations and charities using sport programmes and events to help achieve some broader social objectives. They have a strong focus on sport development and sport *for* development. Broadly speaking, organisations can use sport as a core or ancillary part of their operations as the following examples illustrate:

- **Core operations**: Social enterprises and charities where the central focus of their operations is using sport to achieve broader social outcomes and changes.
  - **Example 1 – Homeless World Cup Football Foundation**: This is a charitable enterprise that attempts to deal with the huge problem of homeless

people, which globally has been estimated as affecting 1.6 billion people (Homeless World Cup Foundation, 2019). The sport of football is used to engage homeless people (the outputs), which can be leveraged to try and build confidence and change behaviours, for them to rebuild their lives (oucomes).
- **Example 2 – Football 4 Peace Korea**: This uses football as a mechanism for peace education, community relations and reconciliation initiatives between North and South Korea, for players, coaches and community leaders. It was instrumental in the combined North and South football team who is playing in a football match as a single team.

- **Ancillary operations**: Organisations or charities, who may use a sport activity or event, to raise money or awareness of their cause.
  - **Example 3 – UNAIDS**: This is a project linked with the United Nations (UN) designed to combat the disease of AIDS around the world. Over the years they have helped support and develop a variety of initiatives, where sport has been used as a mechanism to educate people, such as using basketball or football to educate people about the risk of AIDS.
  - **Example 4 – Care**: This is a broad-based charity setup in 1945, which focuses on combating global poverty (Care, 2019). It is regularly involved in nearly a thousand programmes around the world, some of which are sport related, such as developing leaders and building confidence in young people, by offering boys and girls equal opportunities to play a variety of sports in poor villages.

Question

For a country of your choice, focus on a social issue and consider how sport may be used to deal with the issue or alleviate some of the negative conditions people may be experiencing.

4.3.2 Stage 2 – ideas and demand research

Data and information collected from research is in fact a key underpinning of all areas of operations management. The practical management actions of researching and collecting data are explored in more detail in Chapter 10, such as how to identify market gaps or the barriers to participation. If we assume for now that aspects of the market research, as outlined in Chapter 10, have been engaged with, then this can be used to help inform some of the creative thinking techniques already discussed in Chapter 3, Section 3.4. There is in fact no set time or limit for the use of creative thinking techniques. It can be the first thing that can be done, which then encourages more focused research; alternatively, after doing some research for ideas or examples of services, mind-mapping techniques might be utilised to further explore the ideas. Crucially both demand analysis and the barriers to participation should be explored, with some examples explored in Box 4.3.

Box 4.3 Exploring group needs and barriers for swimming

Swimming pools have the potential to deliver numerous positive social outcomes, for many different groups in the community. They are, however, notoriously difficult to run profitably because of the high maintenance and energy costs; in addition, the humid environments and heavy use of chemicals can quickly degrade fixtures and fittings in buildings. These high operational running costs is one of the reasons why budget gym providers (See Box 4.6) have no real interest in having pools, because of the impact on profits. For the high-end gyms, having a range of pool facilities, whilst costly, is also vital in conveying a sense of quality. Despite these high costs, the benefits from swimming for many groups is one of the reasons why pools are so frequently subsidised by either central or local governments, in order to keep prices low.

There are a variety of markets for swimming pools, with three considered here:

- Pools as part of a more exclusive suite of health and fitness facilities at the high end of the market
- Pools for elite swimmers
- Pools for community users, with low prices charged to allow equality of opportunity for all, but where the prices set are dependent on subsidies

Managers and SDOs are encouraged to research the barriers to participation as that can shape the demand for their services, or what can act as a barrier to participation. To illustrate this process, we will focus on a particular target group of disabled users. Using pools for therapeutic purposes or rehabilitation from injuries is well established, which offers the additional benefits of social interaction and challenge that create a stimulating activity. Whilst price is often an important consideration, it is not the only one, as it is dependent on the elasticity of demand (this is the term economist uses which relates to how responsive demand is to price changes, where if demand changes in response to a small price change, then it is described as elastic).

Using systems theory and the research of French and Hainsworth (2001), it is possible to identify a fuller range of potential barriers to participation, represented in Figure 4.2. What this figure illustrates is participation, which is affected by a complex interaction of many factors, rather than a single factor, such as a simplistic focus just on physical impairments limiting participation.

Here are some other examples to illustrate some of the management issues of programming.

Case Study 1 – Seoul Olympic pool: The Seoul Olympic pool was constructed for the 1988 Olympic Games and saw many swimming WR (world records) broken. At the time it was considered an innovative pool, with its turtle-like design. Many years on, however, it is showing its age. It is a pool whose design means it is particularly prone to condensation, which can play havoc with the actual building and fittings, resulting in problems of rust,

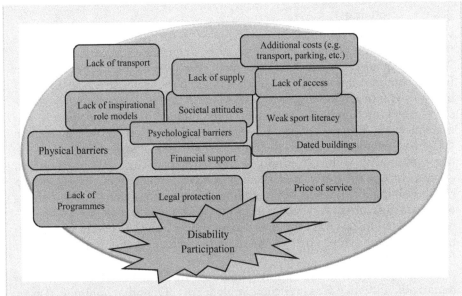

Figure 4.2 System Showing the Barriers to Participation for People with Disability.

peeling paint, concrete distress and mould. What is more, because it was a space designed for thousands of spectators, it means that when it comes to the day-to-day community use, huge amounts of energy will be wasted heating the large cavernous space, where the lack of modern insulating materials only compounds the waste in energy. One of the attempts to deal with this issue was the erection of a huge tent-like structure, almost like one of the old circus big top tents, which reduces the area to heat; unfortunately, in classic boomerang fashion, where one action taken to solve one problem only creates a new set of problems (see Chapter 3), which in this instance was the intensification of the humidity and the damage to fixtures and fittings.

Despite these problems, it is still heavily used by different community users. It is still publicly owned, where the prices for swimming are subsidised, which allows for a wide number of community groups to use the facility, particularly the elderly and retired groups. (The importance of catering to this group has added salience as South Korea has a rapidly ageing population, with many having a poor pension provision.) The daily demand for the pool is impressive, where large part of the pool timetable is for 50-minute lane swimming sessions, which can often have over a 150 people swimming, meaning thousands of people use the pool each day. They also offer a range of other activities, such as swimming clubs, aqua-aerobics and swimming lessons, with a range of different pricing structures, from monthly membership fees to a pay-as-you go fee of around $6.

Case Study 2 – Sri Lanka Women's Swimming Society: After the 2004 Asian Tsunami, one of the striking statistics was that 80% of the casualties

(continued)

Box 4.3 (continued)

were women and children. One of the reasons for this high death rate was that even though many of them lived near water, they still could not swim. As a consequence, Christina Fonfe set up a charity to try and go out into poor, fishing communities in order to teach women basic water survival skills and how to swim (e.g. showing them how to jump in the water, submerge themselves, float for 10 minutes and swim a 100 metres). It is classic sport development work. There were many barriers for this project to overcome, such as: getting people to coach in the remote areas; lack of swimming costumes; and building up women's confidence to participate. In terms of resources, equipment was relatively modest, such as having small mobile pools to help build up initial confidence, before moving the participants to lagoons, rivers or the sea to swim in. A crucial part of the project was to make it sustainable, so it was vital to also train up locals, who could carry on teaching swimming to others, where swimming was not done for recreation, but as a skill to help people survive.

Case Study 3 – The summer of pools in New York City: In 1936 a remarkable initiative was launched in New York. Over that summer, 11 new swimming pools were opened in different parts of the city, which were built from public money, and when they were all operational, could accommodate 49,000 users. They were constructed partly to improve public health, but also as part of a scheme to create employment during the Great Depression. Mayor Moses, a key driving force of the projects in 1936, told the New York Times:

> It is an undeniable fact that adequate opportunities for summer bathing constitute a vital recreational need of the city. It is no exaggeration to say that the health, happiness, efficiency, and orderliness of a large number of the City's residents, especially in the summer months, are tremendously affected by the presence or absence of adequate bathing facilities.
>
> Levine (2018)

These different pools, some of which were outdoor, had many bold innovations and striking designs, and are interesting examples of government intervention, offering sport and recreation services for public good. Despite some highs and lows such as public funding cuts which have threatened their closure, they have continued to offer a variety of water-based activities at low prices or free, which can help achieve a variety of social objectives. They run a subsidised member scheme which costs $150 for an annual membership, and $25 for seniors and young adults, whilst for under 18 it is free. This membership gives free access to year-round swimming for the indoor pools and the opportunity to attend free aqua programmes, such as learn to swim programmes.

The free 'Learn to Swim' for adults and children classes are particularly interesting, as they are deemed almost as a social service because of the many benefits this can offer, such as learning to swim can reduce the risk of drowning and improve health, fitness and wellbeing. There are, however, limited places, where demand exceeds supply, therefore, the allocation of places is done via a lottery. Whilst it raises some questions about equity and fairness, as it can still mean some people will be excluded if they are not lucky enough to get drawn in the lottery, it shows that sport and recreation is seen as a social benefit. It may also come as something of a surprise to some as these free or subsidised low-cost leisure activities take place in the USA is usually associated as a country with its free market and entrepreneurial activities, but it shows the value and the belief in the social benefits of sport and recreation.

Discussion
What are the barriers which would need to be researched to try and encourage low-income groups to learn to swim?

Other considerations for preliminary planning relate to what type of activities can give the best return on the utilisation of space, as the following example illustrates:

- A sport hall has four badminton courts hired at a cost of £9 per court per hour, which can have up to 16 people using the facility (i.e. making the presumption that people play doubles, but which could also be more if it was a badminton club), so at 100% utilisation it could generate £36 per hour.
- The same sport hall could however also be utilised for keep fit classes, where an instructor could lead a session for up to 40 people, who, if they paid $5 for the session, at a 100% utilisation, could generate £200 per hour.

It is a simple example, but illustrates how the same space, depending on how it is used, can generate different amounts of revenue and usage numbers. So, should this mean that time should not be made for a badminton club? Of course not. Badminton can help deliver on different outputs and outcomes. For the operations manager and SDO it is a constant consideration about the various benefits, different services can bring, where a balance needs to be given between generating revenue and achieving social objectives.

4.3.3 Stage 3 – assessment of resources and risks

What can decide whether to progress with developing a new service depends on the availability of resources, the risks involved and how realistic it is to deliver on the proposed time scales. In terms of resources and the assessment of the feasibility, the following checklist areas should be considered:

- **Equipment needed**: Consideration needs to be given to the capital investment required to purchase any new equipment. For some services, such as those which an SDO provides, the costs may be relatively modest, based around sports equipment and clothing, such as bats, balls, bibs and any

protective gear. In others instances, the investment may be considerable, such as for adventure sports, as illustrated in Box 4.4 or in Box 4.5.
- **Space needed**: This can be another key P in the four marketing Ps, in relation to the place or location of the service. For many sport facilities, they are designed to be multi-use in the variety of sports that they can run, such as a sport hall being able to be used for games of football, basketball or keep fit classes. Similarly, SDOs can often be very pragmatic, whereby they go out and seek a variety of spaces, such as playing fields, or community spaces, where they can run their services. In this instance, the idea of place is a moveable one, where the SDO reaches out into communities to find out what is needed and the recreational spaces available for accommodating sport services.
- **Staff needed**: Considerations need to be given to the number of staff, their qualifications and whether new staff are employed or volunteers used.
- **Training and checks needed**: Before certain courses or services can take place, consideration may need to be given to training staff, such as getting a relevant coaching qualification or first aid. Furthermore, if the services involve children then any relevant checks must also be done, although it should be noted that the legal obligation to do this varies in countries around the world.
- **Regulatory compliance**: For certain services, it can be essential that any guidelines of good practice are consulted, whereby if standards cannot be complied with, the service may not be able to go ahead. Types of insurance cover can relate to indemnity insurance, third- party liability cover and licenses, such as in the UK, obtaining license for Public Entertainment, Performing Rights or Phonographic performance.

4.3.4 Stage 4 – planning, pricing and promotional marketing

So, if the idea, demand and resources needed are all identified and are deemed as feasible, this can allow for engagement with other marketing activities, relating to the pricing, branding and communications strategies. Again, there is not the scope to go into all the marketing theories and principles which need to be understood and applied here, so just a few key concepts are looked at in relation to the operational elements that can be involved with setting a price for a service.

Pricing is a crucial marketing decision, which must be underpinned by good financial management. The size of the organisation and enterprise can influence the extent that an operations manager or SDO will get involved with setting a price for a service (if one is set all). Whether the operations manager or SDO set the price, it is still vital that they understand some of the process for price setting. Price should also be considered in relation to how it helps position the service in the market place (see also Box 4.5).

Price can send an important signal about the quality of service. For social-orientated, non-profit sport services, price may be set to just break-even,

Expenditure and Income Items	Costs/ Income
1. Staff Needed and Costs ......£ ...... rate per hr x ....hrs x ....week(s)/day(s) ......£ ...... rate per hr x ....hrs x ....week(s)/day(s) Etc. (Guidance Note: a simple way is to calculate the cost per session then decide how you want to multiply it to work out total costs)	
2. Equipment Needed and Costs .... (Guidance Note: Need to depreciate costs by calculating the total equipment costs divided by the approximate number of years used, before it needs replacement)	
3. Promotion/advertising needed and costs .... (Guidance Note: calculate costs of materials, design, adverts, etc. then depreciate over the length of time the programme runs for)	
4. Facility charge/lost income (if appropriate) .... (Guidance Note: Relates to considering the lost income from different users)	
Total expenditure	
Less Potential Income	
Maximum number of participants .... (Guidance Note: consider maximum number that can be accommodated safely or in line with regulatory standards)	
Minimum number to achieve break even at 80% take-up (Guidance Note: consider price based on 80% of the maximum number which gives a 'buffer' or safety gap)	
Cost per head per course/session/Tax (e.g. VAT) if necessary	

Estimated income
    Full price £ ....x (number) ....
    Concession £ ....x (number) ....
                                       Estimated total income	

Surplus/deficit	

Figure 4.3 Pricing Calculation Form.

which means covering the operational costs of running the service. For commercial businesses, the price set needs to cover the input costs and has a mark-up for profit. Of course, sometimes commercial businesses may set a price of a service which means it is unable to make a profit at the price set (this is called a lost leader); alternatively, a non-profit organisation may set a price to make a profit, which helps to cross-subsidise other services for certain target groups. What this shows is that pricing is a strategic decision, which can be used to achieve different objectives. Some examples of pricing strategies can be:

- Break-even pricing (i.e. covering all the input costs)
- Matching the price of competitors
- Lost leader pricing
- Subsidising the price
- Marginal cost pricing
- Cost plus pricing (e.g. adding an additional percentage amount for profit, once all the basic costs are covered)

In Figure 4.3 a Pricing Calculation form is presented, which broadly follows a rate of return pricing strategy, where a satisfactory level of return is expected in terms of the level of investment put into the service. An applied example of costing and pricing is given in Box 4.4.

Box 4.4 – Pricing strategies

The following cases give two different examples of pricing strategies, with the first having a clear operational focus and the second being approached more from a strategic level.

Case Study 1 – Pricing a new children's water sport service: A small commercial outdoor activity centre, based on urban reservoir in a large city, is looking to expand its summer activities for children during the school holidays. So far, it has not run any windsurfing classes for children, so it has decided to purchase some windsurfing boards to expand the range of activities. They use the basic checklist process represented in Figure 4.1, together with the more detailed Pricing Calculation Form in Figure 4.4.

a. Preliminary ideas and research conducted

Some preliminary research was done which included: looking at the catchment of school children in the local area; analysing market trends of water sports; and having some informal discussions with some school teachers who said they would be interested in such a service. Based on this analysis, the business has decided to expand its provision of services, such as offering:

> Three two-hour windsurfing lessons each week (Saturday, Tuesday and Thursday), running for four weeks.

Expenditure and Income Items	Costs/ Income
Staffing costs: 1 coach $15 per hour x 3 hours x 3 days x 4 weeks 1 Safety instructor in boat $10 x 3 hours x 3 days x 4 weeks Note: although the sessions only last for two hours, the extra hour is paid for to include staff setting up and down the sessions. Also the safety instructor has a lower pay rate.	£540 £360
Equipment costs (depreciated) 10 boards x £500 = £5,000 ÷ 36 (3 days x 4 weeks x 3 years) = £139 (average cost of equipment to cover costs) Note: the cost of the beginner's wind-surfing boards is approximately £500 and will last around 3 years, depending on use and maintenance. It is also possible to depreciate the costs further by taking into account how they could be used in other sessions, such as hire, adult sessions etc., but for now we will just consider the holiday activities in the initial calculation)	£139
Marketing costs: £250 Note: this money could again be spread amongst other costs, such as if it is used as part of a general leaflet for all the centre activities.	£250
Total Operational Costs	£1289
Less potential income	
Maximum number of participants **8 Children per session x 3 sessions x 4 weeks = 96 children** Note: this relates to a recommended safety standard. Note also that 10 boards have been bought, which creates some spare capacity, in case 1 board is damaged	
Minimum number to achieve break even at 80% take-up **6 children x 3 sessions x 4 weeks = 72 children** Note: this has been rounded slightly. Note that if the 80% is exceeded then it can mean more profit, but by calculating for 80% of the usage, it builds in some contingency or buffer.	72 people
Price per head to break even (cover all operating costs) =	
Price per head to break even (cover all operating costs) at 80% : $1289 ÷ 72 = £18 price per head	£18

Figure 4.4 Application of the Pricing Calculation Form.

(continued)

Box 4.4 (continued)

This obviously can be increased if demand is exceeded (e.g. a waiting list builds up), along with thinking about how the different classes will cater for different abilities.

The courses are ultimately designed to make a profit, but, just as crucially, to create a demand base for hiring their equipment on a pay-as-you go basis, where customers who have learnt to windsurf come back in their own time.

b. Assessment of resources and costing

For some of the costs, these are easy to identify, as they are the marginal costs accompanied with the activity such as staffing. For other costs, they can be more difficult to attribute to a particular session (e.g. the centre will have to pay for insurance which could cost the centre thousands each year, but where the costs recovery would be spread out through all the services offered).

For simplicity sake, what will be done here is to just represent some of the tangible marginal costs (i.e. inputs) which can easily be identified based on the pricing costing form (Figure 4.4), which is presented in Figure 4.5.

So, based on this simple preliminary calculation, the charge that would need to be charged to break-even and cover the operating or marginal costs is $18 for a two-hour class.

But this is not the end of the pricing process. More considerations need to be factored in, such as the mark up price to help generate a profit, which in this instance is set at 60% (remember there are many other costs, such as management costs, other equipment costs (e.g. wet suits), building maintenance and cleaning, which have not been factored into the costing price, hence, what may seem a high mark-up price, but which could in fact be even higher).

This brings a potential rounded up price to £29 per session.

This price is still only a provisional one as other factors need to be considered to help set the final price charged. This is where it becomes strategic, such as considering what the competition might charge for a similar children's holiday course might be around £45 dollars. This creates some more options of whether to match the price in terms of maximising income or have a lower price to try and gain more market share.

This simple example shows why pricing is a key marketing decision and should not just come down to the accountant deciding what price is charged.

Case Study 2 – Cricket World Cup pricing strategies: The pricing strategy use for the 2019 Cricket World Cup, held in England, was designed to achieve a variety of objectives. For a large-scale event, such as the Cricket World Cup, it can be near impossible to recoup the capital outlay of the events just from ticket sales of the live events, but this does not mean they are unimportant. For certain games, such as the England vs. Australia, India vs. Pakistan or England vs. India at Edgbaston in the City of Birmingham, demand far outstripped supply. In theory, the demand would be relatively inelastic (i.e. unresponsive to price changes) so it could have been an opportunity to maximise revenue by charging very high prices; but other strategic objectives needed to be considered, such as appealing to younger people and families, as they would be the supporters of the future. Hence, they offer a range of cheaper, discounted seats for people, even though they could have charged higher prices (but in comparison with other games, this is likely to be a smaller proportion). Here are some examples of the different prices charged:

> The platinum adult tickets cost £175, with other prices going down to £125, £95, £55 and £44 for restricted view seats. Crucially, however, the ticket prices for children went from £20 down to £6, with a number of alcohol-free family zones, and tickets for adult wheel chair users being £55.

Discussion

To what extent should the prime goal be to maximise revenue from tickets, or try and encourage lower-income groups to attend the events?

4.3.5 Stage 5 – monitoring and evaluation

The monitoring and evaluation of a service has been extensively discussed in Chapter 2, and themes will be returned to in Chapters 5 and 10, so it is not discussed in any length here. All that needs to be reiterated is how vital it is to constantly reflect and evaluate services delivered, to help ensure that the quality and safety of the service is maintained, whilst always looking for ways to try and improve the quality of the service. The irony is that from the moment the service is designed and delivered to the market, it begins its ageing process on the PLC, going through a process of growth, maturity and, unless something is done to prevent it, go into decline, as illustrated in Box 4.5.

Box 4.5 Comparing health and fitness services and market placement

It is important for managers and SDOs to understand the concept of market placement, whereby different services can be priced and promoted to different market segments, even though at the core, they offering a similar service. Here are examples of four providers of health and fitness services and where they fit in terms of the market, represented in Figure 4.5.

(continued)

Box 4.4 (continued)

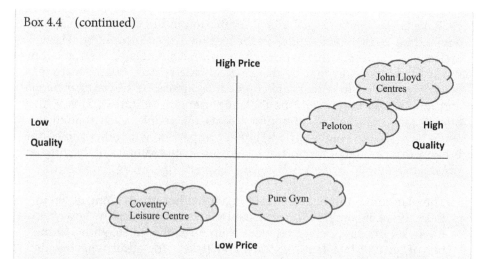

Figure 4.5 Service Market Position Map of Competing Facilities.

Case Study 1 – The David Lloyd health and fitness leisure centres: The Lloyd centres primarily operate in the UK, but have expanded into Europe. It is a commercial business and is placed at the 'high-end' of the fitness market. This is based on the membership fees charged and the range and quality of the facilities and services offered, which can include indoor and outdoor swimming pools, tennis courts, squash, gym and spa facilities. To use the gym, people must be a member, but as part of their marketing strategy, they rarely openly advertise the membership rates. Part of their sales techniques is to entice people to visit, as it can be more likely to get people to sign up. As part of this membership scheme, they require three months' notice period to end the membership – a common market practice by fitness suppliers, but one which is increasingly being challenged by competitors, such as PureGym's cheaper, more flexible approach.

Looking at their range of keep fit classes, it is obvious how they constantly seek to rejuvenate their services. In addition to a range of familiar services, such as Pilates, yoga and Zumba classes, they have introduced new technologies, such as the indoor cycling spinning classes that are done to music, or the RPM Virtual Reality workout environments. Other interesting variation is the Blaze fitness class, which is described as a 'boutique-style' high-intensity workout, using treadmills, weights, martial arts bags, music and heart monitors, so that participant fitness can be monitored during the classes to check on improvements over time.

What this variety in services shows is the dynamic nature of programming, where even to just maintain demand, there is a constant need to improve the quality of service experience offered (e.g. integrating more technology to add to the novelty of the experience) if people are to return.

Case Study Example 2 – PureGym: In more recent years, there has been a flourishing of budget gyms, such as PureGym which is placed at the low price, medium quality end on the Market Position Map (Figure 4.5). They have been innovative in their pricing and membership strategies, by offering cheap membership that is easy to cancel, which is particularly important for the locations which have large student populations. Many also have longer opening times, with some open for 24 hours.

They are able to charge lower prices, because they know how to reduce operational costs, such as: not having expensive swimming pools; not having a staffed reception area (customers are simply given a code to enter the gym) and having instructors who have only part of their salary paid by PureGym, but who can supplement their income from the additional fitness classes they run and promote.

These changes went against the traditional model of fitness centre operations and has meant the PureGym brand, in a very short period of time, has become one of the largest UK providers and continues to expand into Europe.

Case Study Example 3 – Coventry leisure centre: In the City of Coventry an ageing leisure centre had to be closed, after many successful years of operations. It is placed on the low price, lower quality end of the map in Figure 4.5. The leisure centre was built in 1966, on the foundations of an old public baths, which was destroyed by war time bombing, with the new facility having a 50-metre pool, diving pool and many other sport facilities.

When it was built, it had numerous innovations and was hugely popular, but eventually the age and deterioration of the building, along with changing market conditions, meant that it became increasingly un-economic to run. For example, it initially enjoyed a high proportion of the city's fitness market because of a lack of competition. Over time, more private gyms opened up, which initially did not impact too much on the demand for its fitness services. The opening up of the first budget, PureGym, actually helped the old leisure centre, as it encouraged them to improve the quality of their services and so the demand went up. The opening of a second PureGym however was more decisive, particularly in diverting the key student market segment. Whilst both organisations could compete on price for certain markets, what the leisure centre could not match PureGym was in the perceived quality, as the newer purpose-built budget gyms felt fresher, had greater flexibility with opening times and has a more attractive design aesthetic. With declining income, yet rising maintenance costs (see back to Box 4.2 for some of the challenges of managing swimming pools), it meant it was more economic for the council to close this leisure centre and build a new, smaller and more efficient leisure centre, which would appeal to the local community.

Case Study Example 4 – Peloton rise: Peloton is a commercial company which was launched in 2012 and describes itself as an 'indoor cycling studio in your home'. What is different about the service is that customers use a special indoor bike, then book onto various interactive online cycling fitness

(continued)

Box 4.4 (continued)

spinning classes, where you can link up with other people around the world. It claims that more than one million people use the online streaming classes, where there are various service packages, ranging from buying the bike, then paying for classes on a pay-as-you go basis or hiring the bike on a monthly subscription basis. Classes can be done through live, or use archived classes, which allow for a structured development.

This service offers an interesting development, which has been very popular in the USA and has been expanding around the world. It offers the type of class which people would have had to go to a fitness club for, but in the convenience of the home. It is likely to tap into some new latent demand (i.e. people want to try the service but haven't had the opportunity to do it yet) and has the potential to divert demand from fitness centres.

Discussion

Select a country of your choice and analyse the potential market growth in terms of fitness and health centres and keep fit classes.

4.4 CONCLUSION

This chapter primarily focused on the practical steps of designing a sport programme, which blended in theories, concepts and practices from the broader business functional areas of marketing (a key area), finance and HR. It is also a chapter where it is essential to appreciate how the themes discussed in other chapters need to be drawn on. For example, the initial rationale for the types of services and how they can be evaluated was discussed in Chapter 2. The practicalities of delivering on all the tasks which needed to be completed in order to bring a service to market were explained in Chapter 3. The critical role of research and demand analysis which acts as a key foundation for developing a sport programme is explored in more detail in Chapter 10. The key point which managers and SDOs should take away is that the design of services takes place within a dynamic and complex operational environment, when no sooner is a service designed and offered, then it already begins an ageing process in terms of the PLC, where unless it is refreshed or rejuvenated, demand for the service will inevitably go into decline.

References

Blackey, P. (2011) *Sport Marketing*. Exeter: Learning Matters.

Care (2019). Our work, accessed 1 June 2019, available at: https://www.care.org/about

French, D., and Hainsworth, J. (2001). There aren't any buses and swimming pool is always cold!: Obstacles and opportunities in the provision of sport for disabled people. *Managing Leisure*, 6, 35–49.

Homeless World Cup Foundation (2019). accessed on 2 April, 2019, available at: https://homelessworldcup.org/cardiff-2019/

IbisWorld (2019). Gym, health and fitness clubs industry in the US, accessed 24 March 2019, available at: https://www.ibisworld.com/industry-trends/market-research-reports/arts-entertainment-recreation/gym-health-fitness-clubs.html

IHRSA (2019). Global report, accessed 1 July 2019, available at: https://www.ihrsa.org/publications/the-2019-ihrsa-global-report/

Levine, L. (2018). The 1936 'Summer of Pools': When Robert Moses and the WPA cooled off NYC, 6sqft, accessed on 20 September 2019, available at: https://www.6sqft.com/the-1936-summer-of-pools-when-robert-moses-and-the-wpa-cooled-off-nyc/

Maslow, A.H. (1943). A theory of human motivation. *Psychological Review*, 50(4), 370–396.

Saipe, R. (1999). *Working in Sport and Recreation: A Practical Approach*. Cheltenham: Nelson Thomas Ltd.

Slack, N., Brandon-Jones, A., and Johnston, R. (2016). *Operations Management*, 8th ed. London: Pearson.

Torkildsen, G. (2005). *Sport and Leisure Management*, 5th ed. London: Taylor and Francis.

5 CUSTOMER CARE, QUALITY SYSTEMS AND REGULATORY COMPLIANCE

> **Challenges for managers**
>
> - How does a manager or sport development officer (SDO) ensure consistency in the services delivered, which meet with customers' expectations?
> - What factors need to be managed with the customer encounter and their journey in consuming in a sport service?
> - What factors act as an influence or barrier to their participation?

5.1 INTRODUCTION

How do managers and SDOs ensure that customers get the best quality service first time, every time? It is a vital question to ask which should concern all sport managers and SDOs. By asking this question and looking for the answer, it will help develop a working culture which always strives to maintain and improve the quality of service consumers and customers experience, laying down a key foundation for retaining existing customers and attracting new ones. A critical part of this notion of quality relates to the customers' expectations of the type of service they believe they should receive, for the price they have paid. Even services that are free still need to consider aspects of quality, as they require the delivery of services that meet the needs, wants and expectations of their users and try to achieve a variety of outcomes.

In this chapter, the importance of customer care and the value of retaining customers is explored using quality management practices and theories. Consideration is given to the customer journey and what factors create customer satisfaction or dissatisfaction, which is framed using systems theory and the principle of marginal gains, or the small wins approach (see back to Box 1.4, in Chapter 1).

5.2 THE IMPORTANCE OF CUSTOMER CARE

At its simplest level, a customer is anyone who consumes a service provided by the sport organisation. Many definitions of a customer would also include the notion of a purchase or financial transaction, but in the sport context, because some sport services may be provided free of charge, these definitions are less satisfactory. Some writers, such as Blakey (2011, p. 2), make the distinction between

Customer care, quality systems 99

paying customers and consumers who use the service, but in this chapter, for convenience, we will use the word customer to include both, whether they pay for the service or not. This means that the supplier has a *responsibility* to ensure that the service meets the customers' *expectations*, gives *satisfaction* and is kept *safe*.

Taking care of customers begins by designing services that meet their needs and wants, then continues by meeting or exceeding their expectations for the service they are consuming, which creates – as Carlzon (1987) describes it – the 'moment of truth'. This is point where people decide if they have had a good or bad service, which has been shaped by many different elements of the customers' journey, ranging from booking a service to how they are treated by staff. Using this approach means the manager and SDO is trying to adopt a market-orientated working culture (discussed in Chapter 4), which can create a reciprocal causation process, represented in Figure 5.1 (e.g. staff look after customers – customers are happy and give positive feedback – staff feel their effort is recognised, so want to do a better job for the next set of customers – customers gain a positive experience and so on).

Failure to look after customers can be costly. Lost customers reduce revenues, and it is often regarded that it can be far more expensive to create new customers, rather than retain existing ones (Kumar et al., 2011). Leboeuf (2000, p. 3)

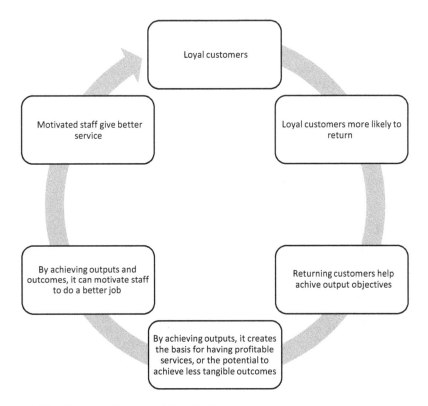

Figure 5.1 The Virtuous Customer Care Cycle.

argues how important it is to make many small improvements to the customer journey and experiencing, saying:

> Stop for a moment and consider how valuable customers are. They alone make it possible for you to earn your livelihood in a way that you do. Treat them well and satisfied customers will be your best source of advertising and marketing. Give them good value and they will continue to reward you with their dollars for years and years. All the slick financial and marketing techniques in the world are no substitute for an army of satisfied customers …every company's greatest assets are its customers, because without customers there is no company. It's that simple.
>
> (Leboeuf, 2000, p. 3)

Leboeuf echoes one of the key writers on business management, Peter Drucker and his often used, but simple, statement of:

> There is only one valid definition of business purpose: to create customers.
>
> (Drucker, 1973, p. 61)

An old, often-cited truism used in customer care literature and training is that a customer who has received a bad experience is more likely to tell ten others (LeBoeuf, 2000, p. 84), whilst those who receive a positive experience will tell half that number. What research was used to underpin this is far from clear, but if one worries less about the actual figure and more about the general principle that people are more likely to tell others of a negative experience, which can potentially deter others, then one has an important principle to help guide service operations. Today, with social media, that nine or ten could now be thousands, as people post up their experience off services on platforms, such as Instagram, Twitter, Facebook, trip-advisor or a whole host of other social media sites. Getting it right first time, every time has perhaps never been more important. A variety of examples of customer complaints from around the world are given in Box 5.1.

Box 5.1 Examples of online customer complaints when reviewing sport services

Social media has transformed how customers convey their experience of a service, which has the potential to be read by thousands in a very short space of time, so the importance of getting a sport service right first time, every time, is vital. Here are some real examples of customer comments about a variety of sport services from different countries, posted on a well-established review website, but which contain information which a manager or SDO can evaluate to help refine and improve future service delivery:

- *'Nowhere to park, no mobility aids, poor signage in and out of the park …awful experience'.*

- Food appalling ... show brief and boring, food tasteless, staff looked unhappy, absolute rip off! Never again.
- 'Bag searches were – well let's just say the staff could do with some more training!! The venue itself was a bit tatty and could do with a bit of TLC!! Leaving the venue, it's a wonder we didn't break a bone because the floor could do with some anti-slip treatment!!
- 'The games had been postponed and.... It was hardly raining!! I've seen games played in worst weather!! Why bother opening up the ballpark and letting fans in if you're not going to at least try to get the games in?'
- 'Poolside is always dirty and smells, the staff always look so unfriendly and grumpy...this place needed to go as it was so unhygienic and unsafe'.
- 'Awful staff member behaviour, while the cleaning of the locker room in the evening, before closing hours, with buckets and puddles of filthy water full of hair knots and such ending up under my feet while I was still changing with no warning or request to move in an area that had been cleaned already. No reaction from the headphone wearing ...(person) making the mess (cleaning the floors)...Won't be going back, DO NOT RECOMMEND!'
- 'As the staff are unpaid, they use their time in the gym trying to constantly sell their one to one personal training, which is extortionate. To cut corners the gym is cleaned at night from 22:00 to 05:00 BUT no further cleaning during the day (or so it would appear) showers are filthy smelly and disgusting...'
- 'Why can't they manage their car park properly, this happens frequently. Can't get through on the phone to flag it'.
- No human touch. Impersonal, automatic email responses. You are not a valued individual – you are just a walking moneybag.

These simple examples are drawn from the USA, UK, China and Korea. In a few lines, they illustrate some simple, universal truths which can irritate customers, ranging from the frustrations of delays, cancellations, rude staff, dirty, unhygienic spaces and a feeling that you are not valued as a customer.

These comments should also be viewed by managers and SDOs as opportunities to review and improve performance, as they can represent the feedback loop to develop a marginal gain or improvement to service quality. Yes, these comments could be wrong, based on false assumptions, could prove irritating and ignore all the hard work done by staff, or even could be made by malevolent competitors, but they have been made and so must be dealt with. You are encouraged to look at a variety of review sites and scan for bad reviews, and if a response has been given, because even at that stage, it still represents an opportunity to try and save the customer, or prove to others you have dealt with the issue, which helps retain trust and confidence in the provider.

Discussion questions

For each of the issues raised above, outline how you would respond to each of them.

In many quality management theories, they develop the concept of the internal customer, which means treating all staff – whether they operate above, below or parallel in the organisation hierarchy – as customers. This principle of treating all staff as customers can, in theory, bring the benefits of better teamwork, efficiency and job task completion, which will all combine to create better external customer satisfaction. In effect, it is using the principle of marginal gains or small wins approach. Not all agree with this approach and tensions can be created in terms of prioritising work, discussed in Chapter 2, where another employee's urgent/important task may not be yours, so ultimately it will be a judgement call, but it is a useful reminder for the manager or SDO that they operate in an interactive system, where decisions and actions (or sometimes inaction) can reverberate through the organisation.

5.3 IS THE CUSTOMER ALWAYS RIGHT?

Considering all these points, it is perhaps not surprising that so many books on marketing or customer care will cite the common mantra that the 'customer is always right'. It is not a bad mantra for managers and SDOs to have, but its limitations in the sport sector should be recognised. It goes back to Blakey's (2011) comment on the distinction between paying customers and consumers, together with the difference between need and want satisfaction, discussed in Chapter 4, Section 4.2. For example, sport can provide many useful analogies on how engaging with an activity is not always pleasurable at the time, but worth it in the end, such as a tough workout session, doing a challenging adventure sport activity, or watching your team going through the rhythm of winning and losing a game (See Box 5.2 for more examples). The principle of the 'customer is always right' may also not be appropriate when dealing with issues of risk. At times, people participating in sport may not be fully aware of the risks involved (e.g. using a piece of gym equipment incorrectly, or wanting an event to go ahead in poor weather conditions), so the manager and SDO have both a moral and legal responsibility to not let the customer do what they want, even if they have paid a lot of money for the service. It is perhaps therefore better for managers and SDOs to try and add a proviso to classic mantra:

The customer is (nearly) always right!

Box 5.2 Testing the loyalty of sport fans and the future of the stadium experience

Around the world, football fans have had a long history of receiving poor customer care from their clubs, where the most extreme manifestation of this poor care has resulted in severe injuries and deaths. There are many examples of stadium disasters from around the world, where people have died or been injured because of operational failures and poor working cultures.

The conditions for the disasters were often there lying dormant for years, just needing a triggering event to initiate the disaster, as the following examples illustrate: 1964, 328 people died in Lima, Peru, in the Estadio National stadium; 1971, 66 died at the Ibrox stadium, UK; 1982, 66 died in the Luzhniki stadium, Moscow, USSR; 1985, 39 died in the Heysel stadium, Belgium; 1987, 56 died in the Bradford City stadium fire, UK; 1989, 96 died in the Hillsborough stadium, UK; 2001, 127 died at the Accra sport stadium, Ghana; 2012, 74 people died at the Port Said stadium, Egypt. Many other incidents could be cited. It is quite shocking that over the past century thousands have been injured or killed, around the world, in a recreation activity which is supposed to give enjoyment and fun, and offer opportunities social interaction from the shared experience.

What can make these deaths more startling is that in many of the instances, one of the contributory factors were poor, complacent working cultures that consistently failed to learn from the past mistakes and treat fans with disdain. Despite these years of neglect, poor customer care and tragedy, football fans, amazingly, still returned to games. This suggests that the sport fan is more resilient (but not immune) to poor customer care.

Thankfully, in many countries around the world, customer care and the treatment of fans have been changing, sometimes quite radically, for the better. There are now a many regulations and guidelines on how to stage safe sport events, which act as quality standards that must be complied with and operationalised (e.g. FIFA's (2015) stadium safety regulations).

The new stadium built for the English Premiership football club Tottenham Hotspur illustrates many of these changes. The stadium, opened in 2019, on the site they have occupied for over a 100 years has been described by some as a game changer and laid a standard for future stadiums built in the 21st century. It costs over £1 billion and has a seating capacity of 62,000.

Moore (2019), reviewing the stadium, commented that whilst there is no doubt that it is designed to maximise revenue at every opportunity, he still acknowledges the many ways the club tried to create a positive experience from the many points of the service encounter such as: using design to create warm and attractive spaces to walk through; having a more varied food offering, with plenty of service points (reputed to have the longest bar in Europe); new technology to speed up the service process; having fewer corporate hospitality boxes in comparison with other stadiums, but with more boxes which can be booked by groups, such as friends and family for special occasions; and having a large retail spaces, but not an over-whelming amount, so, Moore observes, it 'still feels like a stadium, rather than a shopping mall'. Security and safety are also embedded in the operations systems, such as airport-type scanning machines and sniffer dogs. As part of the design, they have also worked on integrating their heritage, with memorabilia, pictures and a gallery space to showcase local arts and music, which are important elements in developing connected and committed fans.

(continued)

Box 5.3 (continued)

At the of core of the experience is the football game, where the design of the stadium is contrived to try and add to the emotional intensity of the game, such as the consideration given to the soundscape and how close fans can feel to the pitch and action. These experiential elements are particularly evident in the 17,500 single-tier stand, which Moore (2019) described as creating an 'imposing wall of humanity' from the chanting fans, who can play such a pivotal role in generating the atmosphere.

What is also of interest from an operations point of view is how Tottenham has created flexibility in how the stadium can be used for other services and events, such as being able to have the grass pitch slide away, to reveal an artificial pitch beneath it, which can allow American Football and concerts to take place. There is also the stadium, museum and a sky walk tours (people scale the stadium and walk on the 40-metre high walkway).

All these developments help the club, in their words, to encourage fans 'to arrive earlier, stay longer': a principle which is vital for modern stadiums that are open for both sport and non-sport activities need to consider how they can generate revenue every day and every minute.

Discussion

Try and identify and map out some of the biggest frustration's sport fans who may experience at large-scale sport events.

5.4 QUALITY SYSTEMS AND CUSTOMER CARE

Using quality management theories and systems can be a key bedrock with which to ensure good quality customer care, together with compliance with legal regulations. Indeed, elements of using quality management theory have already been used in this book, such as the importance of understanding service operations as part of an interactive system (Chapter 1), having measurable objectives (Chapter 2) or the principle of marginal gains. Here, it can be helpful to elaborate more on quality systems theory and practices as they are so important in shaping customer care working cultures and philosophies.

The word 'quality' can sometimes be misunderstood, having a simplistic link to something which may be considered as expensive, high calibre, excellent or seen as superior in some way. These elements are important, but they do not fully represent the concept of quality as it is used in the context of business quality management theory. In business, quality refers to how effectively a service or product meets customers' expectations, needs and wants to deliver satisfaction. It is often encapsulated by the phrases 'fitness for purpose' and 'quality is remembered long after the price is forgotten'. Mitra offers a useful, synthesised definition of quality:

> The quality of a product or service is the fitness of that product or service for meeting or exceeding its intended use as required by the customer.
>
> (Mitra, 2008, p. 7)

The various works of Deming, Crosby and Jura are key writers in developing quality management theories and quality assurance systems, which have been of critical importance to the whole subject area of operations management. There is not the scope here to discuss all their works, so what is done here is to identify a few important points of quality management relevant to operations management used in this book:

- Quality is not a one-off practice, but a continuous, never-ending process or approach to operations (Deming, 1986; Mitra, 2008, p. 56), which is part of the foundation for TQM (Total quality management).
- TQM is encapsulated by the expression of 'getting it right first time, every time' and is designed to seek continuous improvement (e.g. from Deming's (1986) 14 points of quality).
- The theory of marginal gains and small wins approach can be understood as quality management theories, as they emphasise the importance of understanding operations as part of an interactive system, where small improvements can add up to big wins.
- In quality systems, such as the Kaizen business philosophy (which literally means *change* to become *good*) developed by Imai (1986), he stresses the importance of having data to monitor the operations, which can help identify problem areas.

Quality assurance systems are the ways quality management theory can be put into practice. In essence, a quality assurance system gives more specific guidelines and benchmarks to adhere to and comply with. Quality assurance systems for services work by focusing on scrutinising inputs and processes, to try and assure the quality of output. For example, a quality assurance system may stipulate the training and qualifications of staff, as this can help assure (but by no means guarantee) the quality of the service provided and its safety. There are a wide variety of quality assurance systems that can be utilised by businesses, whereby compliance to their standards can mean the award of a quality standard or certificate, which can then be leveraged for marketing purposes (e.g. stating that the service or organisation has been awarded a quality benchmark, which can create more trust in the service for customers). There are various quality systems which can be used in sport, such as QUEST, a UK-based quality assurance, which in turn is based on the European Foundation for Quality Management (EFQM) Excellence Model.

Quality management is underpinned by the theory of the triple constraints, which relates to managers and SDOs having to decide if a service is either delivered quickly, delivered cheaply or delivered to a high quality (including safety). Of these three, the manager or SDO *must choose just two*, as you can never have all three. There are a number of variations of the triple constraints. For example, Slack et al. (2016) add the dimensions of dependability (the extent the service can be relied on) and flexibility (the extent the services can innovate and be adapted). The SERQUAL model (Parasuraman et al., 1988) is another variation designed to measure service quality based on five dimensions of tangibles, reliability, responsiveness, assurance and empathy. Mitra (2008, p. 51) gives other variation of the key areas of quality, relating to:

- **Efficiency** (concerns the time required to prepare and deliver the service)
- **Effectiveness** (deals with meeting the desirable service attributes that are expected by the customer)
- **Quality of service** (this relates to have faith and belief that the service purchased is safe and a positive experience is enhanced by polite and welcoming staff)
- **Value for money** (what the actual price charged – if at all – for a service is less important, then the expectations of what people expect for the money they have paid)
- **Speed** (this is a basics of operations management, which is about avoiding customers waiting around and ensuring that the sport service starts at its specified time)

The final point to consider is embedding legal regulations and best practices guidelines into quality operational procedures (e.g. stadium safety regulations). Legal regulations can form a key benchmark for quality standards which must be complied with. Whilst some may feel it adds to the bureaucracy of sport operations, being time-consuming and costly, it is a view which should be contested. Managers and SDOs should reflect on the quote: 'If you think safety is expensive, try an accident!' (Kimberly-Clark Worldwide, 2009). This is because the costs of mistakes from poor or inadequate operations practices can be huge, which can lead to compensation claims; operational disruptions; lost income; customer frustration; reputational and brand damage and loss of trust; and it can mean the guilt of knowing that you could have done more, which can even lead to a prison sentence.

5.4 THE CUSTOMER SERVICE ENCOUNTER AND JOURNEY

Using quality management theory provides an important foundation for approaching customer care. As in other chapters, we will use systems theory to explore the dynamic interplay of forces and touchpoints customers have with the service provider, in which each point of contact can represent a moment where the customer experience can be enhanced or eroded. One further consideration is also to reflect back to Chapter 1 and the different leveraging mechanisms that can be used to nudge people's behaviour. These concepts are integrated in the customer journey and service encounter, represented in Figure 5.2.

The encounter begins with the potential customer becoming aware of a need or a want, which a sport service may help to satisfy, such as wanting to stay fit or relax. Whatever the motivation, this can initiate a drive to seek out a sport service, which can start the customer going on a journey through a complex, interactive system (represented by all the smaller circles in the diagram), where each element has the potential to have profound effects on the customer experience and their satisfaction. In turn, this customer experience, for good or bad, is also one that can be communicated to others, which can impact on future demand. This is why Buswell (2004, p. 4) argues this service encounter cannot be

Customer care, quality systems 107

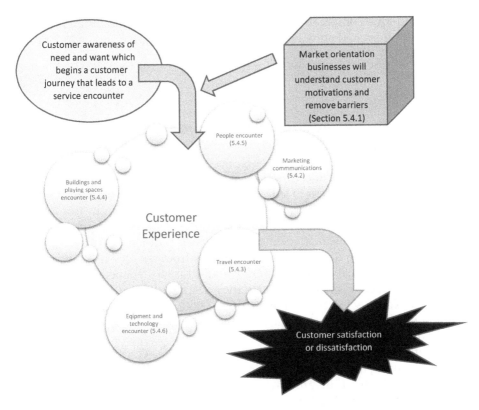

Figure 5.2 Overview of the Service Encounter.

left to chance. These different touchpoints, represented in Figure 5.1, are given more detailed discussion in the subsequent sub-sections in this chapter.

5.4.1 Points of encounter – awareness of customer needs and removing barriers

The importance of understanding the motivations for different customers was explained in Chapter 4, with consideration given to how these can be researched (continued in Chapter 10). It is a subject area with a good body of literature, which managers and SDOs are encouraged to explore in order to help give more depth to the analysis of target groups and the system of potential barriers to participation. In Wilson and Piekarz (2015) they give an overview of the many potential barriers which can prevent sport participation, drawn from a variety of literature. In that discussion, they highlight how different factors can interplay to shape motivation and potential demand, such as motivational needs for belonging, stimulation and excitement; economic barriers to participation, such as price of the service; social barriers, such as peer or cultural pressures; physiological barriers, such as poor physical mobility, and health; supply factors, such as ability to actually attend the service and a lack awareness of services. The list of factors that shape demand really is a long one, where different segments have their own unique combinations. An illustration of how these different factors can come into play and entwine is given in Box 5.3 (see also Chapter 10 for more examples).

Box 5.3 The service encounter, women and removing barriers

In many countries, significant strides have been made with women gaining more equality of access to sport. It is, however, an area where parity has not been achieved between girls and boys, men and women, in relation to sport participation rates, financial returns for elite players, or representation in senior coaching and management governance positions. Whilst this balance of participation and representation varies from country to country, the broader issue of equality of opportunity and access for women is one which has entered the mainstream discourse for governing bodies of sport around the world. Not only is it important on grounds of social justice and ethics, but sport bodies have also realised it makes good business sense, as it can represent key areas of market growth, when the more traditional male markets have matured or gone into decline (see Box 4.1, Chapter 4 on the PLC concept).

To focus on the issue of increasing women's participation in sport, there is now a rich body of literature which can help illustrate the complex interaction of factors that shape women's opportunities for active recreation and sport participation. Here is a simple overview of some of the barriers in the system which can shape potential demand for sport by women, represented in Figure 5.3.

Clearly, managers or SDOs have varying degrees of control over these issues and points of contact (e.g. the challenge of dealing with broader and deeply held social attitudes towards women, which needs to be combatted from a variety of sources). Furthermore, managers and SDOs should also appreciate that care needs to be taken about 'women' represented as a single, homogenous group; here the theory of intersectionality can give a deeper, philosophical way of analysing the issues. AWID (2004) discusses the feminist theory of intersectionality, which relates to the idea of women having different sets of identities which can impact on access and participating in sport. It is a relativist theory, which means that individual factors and context always have to be considered, such as how two women, coming from the same town, can have different opportunities because of other relative factors, such as ethnicity, income and religion.

Reflecting back to Figure 5.2 the operations manager or SDO can take a variety of management actions to try and remove these barriers and nudge behaviours. These can relate to have women-only targeted sessions, providing creche facilities or launching media campaigns to try and build the confidence to participate in sports, to name but a few (refer back to Chapter 1,

Customer care, quality systems

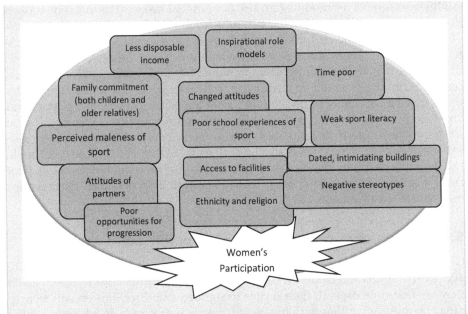

Figure 5.3 Sample Barriers to Women's Participation in Sport.

Figure 1.3). It is recommended you explore the programming checklist model and the discussion of nudge theory, given in Chapter 4.

Discussion

Select a specific sport or sport service which is under-represented by women and identify the key barriers that may prevent girls and women from participating in a sport, together with how they could be overcome.

5.4.2 Points of encounter – marketing and communication

If there is a potential market (latent demand) for a service, which has been identified from research (see Chapters 4 and 10), then the next critical task to consider is how can customers be made aware of the services available to them. This is starting point for the customer journey in terms of helping them find out what sport services are offered, when they are on and what is the cost. A little obvious perhaps, but effective marketing communication (e.g. websites, posters, adverts, leaflets, taster sessions, press-releases, etc.) is a critical foundation for operations management. Here are some examples of things which can go wrong in this encounter area.

- Webpages not being updated
- Incorrect information or spelling mistakes
- Not enough detail on the promotional materials to help make the service more tangible in terms of the potential experience
- Leaflets and posters not put up in enough time to promote activities
- Wrong advertising medium used to target a particular group

All these examples represent again key operational tasks which must be broken down and turned into a task job list, which must be managed and kept track of. The mobile phone and the internet have created a crucial nexus for people to connect with others and the world, which has had a variety of upsides and downsides. It is, however, important to remember that using mobiles and social media technologies is not appropriate for all user groups. For example, older users may be less likely to use certain technologies, such as mobile phones and various social media platforms, so different, more traditional communication strategies may need to be used, such as posters, leaflets and focus group conversations in key locations. This is also important for SDOs who may be working in more remote destinations, such as delivering a sport campaign in a remote, poor rural locations, where using local word of mouth networks and partnerships may be the key to success.

5.4.3 Points of encounter – travel directions and queues

Giving clear directions and having good signage are of critical importance to avoid frustrations and delays. It begins by giving clear directions to the venue, if they are first-time users. It then relates to signage and directions on site, to help direct people not familiar with the venue or arrival protocols. In addition, giving clear directions and having good signage are communicating to customers what is and is not allowed, such as restrictions on clothing, food, drink, bags, umbrellas and flags. Here are some examples of common frustrations in terms of the travel encounter:

- Poor signage to venues or events, or in venues, meaning people are easily lost
- Inadequate parking or too costly
- Contradictory information about location of services
- Not being clearly informed on what can be brought into venues
- Queues and delays for refreshments, using toilet facilities, leaving the venue or event

In relation to the more specific operational practices for dealing with the flows of people and queues, this can almost be a whole science in itself in terms of the psychology that underpins behaviour, or the mathematical calculations needed to work out the carrying capacities of areas. To illustrate these points, some practical examples are explored in Box 5.5.

Box 5.4 Carrying capacity, queue management and the impact of social distance measures

In order to manage queues for sport services and events, you need to understand the principles of carrying capacity. Carrying capacity relates to how many people a physical space can accommodate safely, or before the experience, or even the environment, becomes degraded in some way. Sometimes these limits may be set by legal regulations, such as fire and safety, which specify the safe numbers of people who can be accommodated in a room. At other times, it relates to the type of experiences offered, such as for a sport event, where having a full stadium can be vital in terms of generating an atmosphere; alternately, for a fitness class, it can be more comfortable if people working out have plenty of space, but not so quiet that no atmosphere is generated.

The importance of understanding carrying capacity has also gained further importance because of the impact of the 2019/20 COVID-19 pandemic and the need to regulate crowds and the distance between people, if some sport services are to take place.

As services are designed and events staged, it is important that the flows of people and how they are managed are carefully explored, as it can play a pivotal role in the customer experience (Wakefield et al., 1996a, 1996b). In order to do this, it is vital that the following concepts related to carrying capacity are used and understood by operations managers:

Design Day Capacity: This relates to the average number of visitors who are usually expected to turn up to consume the service.

Peak Day: This relates to the maximum number of people recorded, which can be similar to the design day, but it can exceed it (i.e. this can manifest itself by the length of the queues of people waiting to get into a facility, or their turn for the activity), which also raises issues over safety and the customer experience (e.g. In Box 5.1, for the new Tottenham stadium the peak day has matched its capacity of 62,000 people).

Peak arrivals: This relates to the time of the day when most people are likely to arrive, to purchase a ticket or waiting to enter a stadium for a sport event, such as the hour before a sport event begins.

Design arrivals: This relates to how many people can be accommodated in a specified time, such as how many gates or serving points are open, to deal with queues.

Average service time: Through observations, it can be calculated how long, on average, it takes to serve someone, or to enter a location, or to even do a security bag search.

Throughput: This allows someone to calculate how many people can be processed or served, which uses the service time and peak arrival data.

Social distancing: A new consideration that operations managers may have to factor in at times is any government guidelines on social distancing (i.e. the required distance people need to maintain between each other, which can vary between one and two metres) which may be brought in to deal with the risks of disease transmission.

With these concepts, operation managers and SDOs can consider how to manage the flows of people to try and reduce the frustrations caused by delays.

(continued)

Box 5.4 (continued)

Consider, for example, how a large, multi-use leisure facility can manage its visitors if it has the following information:

Annual visitors – 350,000
Peak Day – 4,400
Design Day – 3,800
Peak arrivals – 2,100 (56% are likely to come in first three hours)
Design arrivals – 1,900
Average service time – 30 seconds (people to purchase tickets)

Whether any queues build up depends on the number of service points. The operations manager can consider how many people to utilise in these early peak hours of the day, which can occur at certain times of the year. For example, this is how many people could be processed by the ticket offices:

Two people serving in a ticket kiosks in one hour can serve/process: 240 (60 minutes × 60 seconds ÷ 30-second average service time × 2 people serving), means there will be long queues, if 1,900 (the design hour) people turn up.

Four people serving in the ticket kiosks in one hour it can serve/process: 480 people.

Ten people serving in the ticket kiosks in one hour it can serve/process: 1,200 people.

Beyond this, it is impossible to have any more tills open, as there is not the space, so delay on some days, at some points, seems inevitable.

When queues are inevitable, other things can be done to help improve the experience and make sure that people are kept safe. For example, considerations can be given to different waiting line configurations. In theme parks, for example, rather than have a long snaking line of people queuing for a ride, they can be made to zig-zag, by using a system of cordons, which can be adjusted depending on demand (something which can also be seen at airports at busy time so of the day, such as going through passport checks). Other simple techniques to reduce queues can relate to: customers printing their tickets at home; providing entertainments to encourage people to come to the stadium earlier; and placing restrictions on the types of bags allowed into the stadium (e.g. at the new Tottenham stadium fans are encouraged or nudged to use the club branded clear plastic draw string bags, sold online or in the stadium shop, which is also a useful source of additional revenue), which speeds up the security bag checks. The good manager should also keep an eye on queues, where considerations can be given to offering other forms of entertainment or refreshment, particularly if people are queuing in the sun.

The final point to consider is what compromises might need to be made to speed up security checks but not undermine safety in terms of the numbers who check and how thoroughly they check (i.e. the triple constraints principle again). At times, there may be a temptation to compromise on security checks to speed up the process of people getting through the system, but caution is urged here to take care not to compromise on quality checks relating to safety. In France, in 2015, a more serious terrorist attack on Stade de France was prevented because of the vigilance of the security guard spotting the bomb on the person trying to get into the stadium, forcing the terrorist to flee, prematurely detonating his bomb, which sadly killed one person. In the UK, on the other hand, the Manchester arena terrorist attack killed 23 people and wounded another 139, after a suicide bomber detonated a bomb at the end of the concert, when security checks had stopped.

If one factored in a requirement of a one- or two-metre social distancing measures to be applied to queues, as part of a government requirement to deal with disease transmission, then it would not be possible to have the classic zig-zag queue, but instead require linear lines. To give a sense of the challenge, if, for example, a two-metre distant rule, it would just take 500 people to create a linear queue of 1 kilometre! These measures can also mean that the capacity of some sport services and events can be radically reduced, which in turn can have profound implications on revenues, atmospheres and the customer experience.

Discussion
Adapting the theory of the triple constraint, what should take priority in terms of speed of service (e.g. doing quicker bag checks), safety or customer care?

5.4.4 Points of encounter – physical spaces and playing environments

Design influences behaviour and the customer experience. Buildings or playing spaces are obvious and important points of contact which can play a critical role in shaping the customer experience, for good and bad. When looking at reviews of sport service experience elements relating to the design and the flow of people through areas, there are a number of complaints, some of which the manager or SDO can have some control over, as the following list illustrates:

- Dirty, untidy spaces, such as changing rooms or toilets
- Lack of atmosphere, which can reflect the poor design
- Poor quality refreshments
- Uncomfortable environments, such as being too hot or cold

The list could go on, as there are so many points of tension when people interact and move through buildings and playing areas. Some of these things can be quite tangible, such as poor design, which means queues may build up, or buildings in need of repair or decoration. Other elements can be less obvious, but still relate to the design of the space, and relate to what is called the servicescape (Bitner, 1992), or more specifically the sportscape (Wakefield et al., 1996a). In essence, the servicescape is rooted in the customer encounter but helps give another dimension to evaluate what shapes the customer experience. According to Bitner (1992), the servicescape is considered in relation to:

- **Ambient conditions** (e.g. weather conditions, air quality, noise, odours, etc.)
- **Spatial layout and functionality** (i.e. the way equipment and furnishings are arranged)
- **Signs, symbols and artefacts** (i.e. signage and décor used to communicate and enhance a certain image of mood, or to direct customers to desired destination)

Here are some other areas, which an operations manager may be able to have some control or influence over, based around Wakefield et al. (1996b) broad categories, which adapt Bitner's servicescape area, all of which the operations manager can control, summarised in Table 5.1.

It is important to consider the time element in physical spaces. Simply put, the longer the time spent in an area, the more important certain elements of design and support facilities are. If, for example, someone just wanted to buy a few items from a shop, then the design may be less important, where the key criteria for satisfaction is having the item, which they can quickly buy at the expected price. For many sport services however, the duration of time spent there can be much longer, meaning considering the servicescape becomes vital, such as how comfortable the space is, or whether it has supporting services, such as toilets and refreshments. In essence, the more comfortable and happy people are made to feel in a space, the more likely they are to stay for longer, which can create more opportunities for secondary spend and revenue generation, or even opportunities for more social interaction and developing a sense of community (i.e. outcome-related objectives).

Table 5.1 Servicescape Dimensions

Servicescape Dimension	Examples of Operational Controls
Layout accessibility	Layout of furnishings and equipment for users; considerations of ease of entry and exit to spaces; areas for refreshments and clear directions; reception area location
Facility aesthetics	Design and décor within the building, such as colour schemes and decorations; design on approach to area, such as landscaping and signage; facades and floor coverings; open reception area (if used – see Chapter 3)
Seating comfort	Places to relax and enjoy activities if a spectator-based service; places for refreshment and conversations; style of furniture
Electronic equipment	This can relate to the lighting and soundscape, such as: how music and lighting can be used to enhance the workout experience, or using technology which gives information, such as large screens showing scores, advertisements and even game highlights
Cleanliness and maintenance	Ensuring facilities are kept clean on a regular basis; having cleaning rotas; making repairs to buildings and machines; developing maintenance schedules. This can relate to pre-events and post-event tidy ups. It is sometimes regarded as one of the simplest indicators of quality

Source: Adapting Wakefield and Blodgett (1996a and 1996b) service scape dimensions.

Realistically, the manager or SDO has little control of the main structure of the building or playing space, but there are still opportunities to shape and manage the conditions. There will be some areas of control in relation to the design of furniture, decor and signage, which can be of critical importance in conveying the relevant atmosphere for the target group, such as creating calm environments in fitness and spa areas, or colourful spaces for children. The attempt is to try and develop a provocative experience, which may be designed to inspire, build up a sense of anticipation or create feelings of calm and relaxation.

The one area of the operations which should *never* be forgotten or underestimated in terms of physical spaces is cleaning and maintenance. It is not always the most glamorous or interesting areas of operations management, but the importance in terms of the quality of experience and safety should never be forgotten. If you reflect back to some of the common complaints given earlier, or the salutary case study of the Bradford Fire, given in Chapter 1, then the importance should be clear. In Box 5.6 an example of adopting quality assurance system for operational cleaning and maintenance is given.

Box 5.5 The importance of cleaning and maintenance schedules for facilities and equipment

Ensuring sport facilities and equipment are well maintained and clean is a vital in terms of quality of service and safety. Not only does it give a simple indication of quality, but it also has a vital relationship to health and safety and avoiding operational delays, by preventing systems and equipment failures. And if these were not enough, the impact of the 2019/20 global pandemic has only elevated the importance of cleaning, as it can make the difference of whether sport services can operate, whereby the term 'deep cleaning' has entered the lexicon of operations managers. What is more, cleaning was often seen as something of a hidden activity, but in the post-COVID world, having visible public demonstration of cleaning areas, to give users more confidence can be seen as a virtue, such as being seen to wipe down equipment after use.

Using the principles of TQM and quality assurance approaches can be a crucial method to ensure proper cleaning and maintenance schedules are developed. Here is a simple extract of a maintenance schedule for a sport facility represented in Table 5.2.

It should be appreciated that this extract of a maintenance schedule gives a simple plan for how different parts of the facility need to be maintained on a daily, weekly, monthly and annual basis. Some of this work can be done by non-expert staff, whilst others require technical expertise and an outside contractor brought in. In relation to the longer time scales for bigger maintenance projects, such as for the pool being relined, there are some

(continued)

Box 5.5 (continued)

Table 5.2 Example of Maintenance Schedule

Area Situated	Item for Maintenance	Type of Service	How Often	By \ Who	Interim Maintenance	Estimated Cost
Reception/ foyer	Decoration Vending machines	Painting of walls/ redecorate Service as req' Yearly overhaul Carpet	Two years Twelve months Cleaned monthly	DLO Centre	OIL moving parts Hoovered daily	
Pool	Relined Ventilation extracts Pool cover	New 'skin' for pool lining	Five to seven years Cleaned	DLO		£15,000
Wet changing room	Lockers Hair dryer Walls Benches	Oiled Annual overall and electrical check Decoration Metal fatigue	Two months One year Two years One year	Centre DLO DLO DLO		£10

additional budgeting issues which need to be considered. For example, it can be deemed as good practice where each year, as part of the operations budget, that money is set a-side or saved for the larger maintenance or equipment replacement elements, so that when it comes to doing the work or replacing the equipment, it does not place a strain on the annual operations budget.

For an SDO, looking at this facility-orientated maintenance schedule, they may think it has little to do with them, but this would be wrong. Simple maintenance schedules are just as relevant in terms of any equipment used and how it is looked after, which can range from the sports equipment to mini buses.

Discussion

How would you ensure and check that facilities are being cleaned properly and on a regular basis?

5.4.5 Points of encounter – human contact

At the heart of many quality management systems and theories is ensuring staff are committed and understand the quality goals and objectives of the organisation and service. The importance of the 'human factor' is a critical ingredient in ensuring customer care, but is also one which is prone to variability, which in turn impacts on the quality of the customer experience. In the context of sport, it can be human interactions and the opportunities for surprise that can make sport events and services so interesting, such the interaction of fans, happy volunteers, or the dynamic instructor or coach, adapting to situations with energy, humour and empathy. Yet the human interaction element can also be a key source of customer frustration, such as inattentive or rude staff. The challenge is to try and maintain the positive variable elements, whilst smoothing out the inconsistencies in staff behaviour which can create customer frustration: a challenge that can be compounded in certain services, such as sport events, where there is a high throughput of new staff and volunteers, which can make consistency in customer care, harder to achieve. Here is a list of just a few of the problems which may create a negative customer experience:

- Rude or bored looking staff
- Staff who ignore you
- Staff who over promise and fail to deliver
- Staff who make mistakes in bookings
- Instructors or coaches who lack empathy

Braithwaite (2004) gives a reminder of the importance of HR to any business and organisation. A key part of any HR strategy is the need to ensure customer needs and satisfaction are synchronised with staff commitment, so this requires, as far as possible, a contented and satisfied staff. There is not the scope to fully explore all the necessary elements to ensure a committed and motivated staff, as again, that is a book in its own right, but here are a few simple tips for how the quality of a service can be maintained:

- Recruiting the right staff in the first instance
- Ensuring staff are qualified and trained to do the jobs
- Energising staff are motivated to do a good job
- Sustaining motivation of staff to carry on doing a good job
- Keeping staff up-to-date and informed of developments
- Developing effective and memorable training in customer care (see also Chapter 9)
- Empowering staff to take control of situations and make decision
- Ensuring there is enough staff capacity to deliver the service effectively, efficiently and safely

Obviously, these are only dealing with some of the issues on a superficial basis, as each will have numerous sub-tasks, which would need to be implemented and evaluated. In Table 5.3, a simple list of tips which can be blended into operational quality systems and staff training.

One tip which is given a star feature on the table is the principle of *'under promising, over delivering'* (see also Chapter 3). It is a simple principle but an invaluable one, if it is kept at the forefront of the managers and SDOs' mind. In essence, it relates to the idea that when dealing with both customers and staff, it can be tempting during a meeting or discussion, to over promise, such as when it is feasible to complete a task, only for the operational realities to mean that there may be a delay in when the task can actually be completed. The result can be frustrating and annoying for both staff and customers. Although some point to the dangers of adhering to this principle too rigidly, particularly in terms of marketing, where materials can become dull and not capture people's interest, in terms of operational practices and working with others and

Table 5.3 Customer Care Tips

Dealing with Angry Customers	Good Customer Care	Active Listening
How to deal with an angry customer: • Listen • Ask questions and empathise, but don't admit blame, or pass the buck • Propose • Check agreement • Do it and monitor • Note that the wrong phrase used can mean 'lift off' again in terms of customer frustrations	*Under promise, over deliver* - Use eye contact - Greet customers - Smile - Do not talk negatively about the organisation or other staff - Introduce yourself - Smart appearance - Ask 'am I treating this person the way I would like to treat myself?' - Everyone should have the authority to deal with complaints - Show people respect - Develop empathy - Active listening (see next column) - Remember, the customer is not dependent on us, but we are dependent on them! A customer is not an interruption of work: customers are the very purpose of work No one ever won an argument with a customer Customer is the most important person in the organisation Be calm and self-confident	- Non-verbal signs, such as nodding the head to show you are listening - Door opener questions - Restraint - Mirroring (posture) - Pacing (talk at the same speed, similar words)

Source: Piekarz adapting various practitioner tips and strategies.

customers, the art of not over promising, but over-delivering is a judgement call made by managers and SDOs.

5.4.6 Points of contact – technology and equipment

This section overlaps with the marketing contact subject (Section 5.4.2) and the discussion of the maintenance schedules of spaces (Box 5.6). Technology and good quality equipment have come to play an increasingly important role in the customer service experience. It can relate to the initial point of contact, such as booking a place for a service like a keep fit class, or purchasing tickets for an event. It can then go onto how new technological innovations have improved the quality of the playing and watching experience. This can include a huge array of factors, such as: the quality of mats used in fitness classes; the quality of the playing equipment such as the a racquet improving playing performance; and using VAR (Video Assistant Referees) in elite sport event. Here is a list of some common complaints from customers relating to technology and equipment:

- Booking systems are slow or too complex
- Booking systems crashing so customers have to upload and enter details again
- Forgetting passwords
- Poor quality and broken equipment creating a poor impression about the quality of the service

5.5 CONCLUSION

Managers and SDOs must consider quality and customer care on the grounds of morality, job satisfaction and achieving organisational objectives. An important part of customer care is understanding the customer encounter. The approach adopted here is to embed this analysis within a system and using theories and concepts from quality management to improve service operations and compliance with legal regulations. Customers may not always notice a clean sport space, but they certainly do a dirty one; customers may not always comment on good service from staff, but they quickly recognise staff who are bored or rude; customers may not notice all the elements which go into offering safe services, but they will certainly comment on unsafe practices. The customer journey should be an effortless one, free from frustrations, so they will return in the future and recommend others to do so, rather than post complaints which could be seen by thousands on social media.

References

AWID (2004). Intersectionality: a tool for gender and economic justice, women's rights and economic change, 9 August, available at: https://www.awid.org/publications/intersectionality-tool-gender-and-economic-justice

Bitner, M.J. (1992). Servicescape: The impact of physical surroundings on customers and employees. *Journal of Marketing*, 56(2), 57–71, available at: http://www.jstor.org/stable/1252042?seq=2#page_scan_tab_contents

Blakey, P. (2011) *Sport Marketing*. Exeter: Learning Matters.

Braithwaite, T.W. (2004). Human resource management in sport. In Beech, J.A. (ed.), *The Business of Sport Management*. London: Prentice Hall, pp. 93–126.

Buswell, J. (2004). Sport and leisure service encounter. In McMahon-Beattie, U. and Yeoman, I. (eds.), *Sport and Leisure Operations Management*. London: Thomson, pp. 3–15.

Carlzon, J. (1987). *Moments of Truth*. New York: Ballinger.

Deming, W.E. (1986). *Out of the Crisis: Quality, Productivity and Competitive Position*. Cambridge: Cambridge University Press.

Drucker, P.F. (1973). *Management: Tasks, Responsibilities, Practices*. New York: Harper & Row.

FIFA (2015). Stadium and event regulations, accessed 2 June 2016, available at: https://www.fifa.com/mm/document/tournament/competition/51/53/98/safetyregulations_e.pdf

Imai, M. (1986). *The Key to Japan's Competitive Success*. York: McGraw-Hill.

Kimberly-Clark Worldwide (2009). If you think safety is expensive try having an accident: Workplace injuries and illnesses can have a major impact on your bottom line, accessed 2 June 2018, available at: http://www.na.kccustomerportal.com/Documents/Upload/Application/2811/Learning%20Center/Article/K2750_09_01_If_You_Think_Safety_is_Expensive_FINAL.pdf

Kumar, V., Batista, L., and Maull, R. (2011). The impact of operations performance on customer loyalty. *Service Sciences*, 3(2), 158–171.

Leboeuf, M. (2000). *How to Win Customers and Keep Them for Life*. New York: Berkley Publishing Corporation.

Mitra, A. (2008). *Fundamentals of Quality Control and Improvement*, 3rd ed. London: Wiley and Sons.

Moore, R. (2019). Spurs new stadium: Let's call it a home win. *The Guardian*, 30 March 2019, accessed 2 June 2019, available at: https://www.theguardian.com/artanddesign/2019/mar/30/new-spurs-stadium-review-tottenham-hotspur-lets-call-it-a-home-win

Parasuraman, A., Ziethaml, V., and Berry, L.L. (1988). SERVQUAL: A multiple- item scale for measuring consumer perceptions of service quality. *Journal of Retailing*, 62(1), 25.

Slack, N., Brandon-Jones, A., and Johnston, R. (2016). *Operations Management*, 8th ed. London, Pearson.

Wakefield, K.L., and Blodgett, J.G. (1996a). The effect of the service scape on customers' behavioural intentions in leisure service settings. *Journal of Services Marketing*, 10(6), 45–61.

Wakefield, K.L., Blodgett, J.G., and Sloan, H.J. (1996b). Measurement and management of the sportscape. *Journal of Sport Management*, 10(1), 15–31.

Wilson, R., and Piekarz, M. (2015). *Sport Management: The Basics*. London: Routledge.

6
PROJECT SPORT AND EVENT MANAGEMENT

> **Challenges for managers**
>
> - What sort of sport projects do managers and sport development officers (SDOs) engage with?
> - How much difference is there between project and operations management?
> - How can a manager or SDO blend in the principles of operations management to help project manage and deliver sport events?

6.1 INTRODUCTION

Sport managers and SDOs frequently engage with a variety of projects. These can range from one-off sport events, fundraising projects, conferences, procurement of new sport facilities or working on specific target group campaigns, which are in addition to other mainstream day-to-day operations. Many projects begin at the strategic level of management in terms of the times scales and the breadth of resources which need to be planned for (see Chapter 1 for definitions); ultimately, however, all projects need to be operationalised, in order to deliver or complete the project by the set date. This is why project management appears in a book about operations management, as the two management areas utilise many key concepts and theories.

Just as with operations management, project management is a transformative process, changing input resources into outputs, which then offers opportunities to achieve outcomes, if, of course, they are properly leveraged (see Chapter 1). This chapter examines in more detail the similarities between project and operation management, in terms of the key theories, concepts and tools. It then develops a synthesised sport and event project planning process (Section 6.3 and its relevant sub-sections), which identifies the key project planning stages, offering additional discussion on sport event project legacy projects.

6.2 THE SIMILARITIES AND DIFFERENCES BETWEEN OPERATIONS, PROJECT AND EVENT MANAGEMENT

Project management is a discrete and distinct level of management, which has grown in importance in recent years. PMBOK (Project Management Body of Knowledge) is a professional body for project managers, which defines a project as:

> ... a project is a temporary endeavour undertaken to create a unique product, service or result ... And a project is unique in that it is not a

routine operation, but a specific set of operations designed to accomplish a singular goal.

(PMBOK, 2019)

In Table 6.1, some of the similarities and differences between operations and project management are examined. The key similarity between operations and project management is that they operate in systems, which transform input resources into outputs, where the intention is to achieve certain goals or objectives (Chapter 3), which is done by planning and keeping track of job tasks. They are also both, in essence, about trying to deal with future business uncertainty and managing risk. A core difference between the two is that projects have clear start and end points, which can utilise some specific project management tools, concepts and theories.

In sport, there are many possible types of projects, such as:

- **Sport event projects**: Events can be organised within an existing business or as special events which are bid for, such as the FIFA World Cup or the Olympics. They can also form an important part of SDO work, where it is vital to organise a variety of special outreach sport event projects to try and engage, encourage and animate communities to participate in sport and active recreation.
- **Funding bid projects**: The need to bring in revenue is a constant management pressure, whether this relates to private businesses looking for new sponsorship partners, or voluntary and public organisations putting in bids for lottery funding, grants and donations (see also Chapter 8).
- **Refurbishing projects**: It can be a vital part of the participant experience that sport facilities are refurbished, renewed or renovated, in order to maintain the quality of the customer experience, which helps retain existing customers and attract new ones.
- **Building new sport facilities and procurement**: Building new sport facilities might begin at the strategic level of planning, then the construction

Table 6.1 Similarities and Differences between Operations and Project Management

Similarities	Differences
- Underpinned by the use of systems theories - Tasks must be broken down into a series of sub-tasks or nested processes - Completing tasks is essential to ensure operations and projects progress or keep moving - Have aims, objectives or goals to give purpose and direction - Monitoring performance and KPIs is essential - All will need to manage the triple constraints of time, cost and quality	- There is a clear end of finishing point - Different concepts and terminology used to manage projects (e.g. milestones, Gantt charts, etc.) - Project management often starts at the strategic level of planning, in terms of time scales and the scale of resources which need coordination, and finishes with the operations level of management - Variations in the use of risk management practices in project management

Source: Authors.

project side is managed by architects and building contractors. Managers and SDOs, however, might have opportunities to influence parts of the project (e.g. design) and will be responsible for getting the facility up and running. These points of influence can be seen in a typical building project schedule which might run as follows: Preliminary planning and feasibility – funding – design – planning approval – commissioning – construction – operational systems set up – snagging checklists – hand over.

One important area of overlap between operations and project management is the use of systems theory. As a reminder, systems theory is about identifying job tasks and understanding how they integrate and relate to each other, which operate in an uncertain, ever-changing business environment, which has the potential to create crisis events that can disrupt continued operations or project completion (see also Chapter 9 on crisis management). For example, Gardiner (2005, p. 23), Cunningham and Maclean (2017) and Torkildson (2005, p. 549), in their approach to project management, use the concepts of *input* resources, which are then transformed though management processes (*throughputs*), to generate *outputs*. The limitations of their representation of the project management system, however, is that they do not consider the importance of outcomes (or, if you are focusing on a sport event, the term legacies might be used), which need to be leveraged. The operations system introduced in Chapter 1 is therefore adapted here to show the overlap with project management, shown in Figure 6.1, but with an added rationale box (projects must have a clear purpose and deadlines) with an example given in Box 6.1.

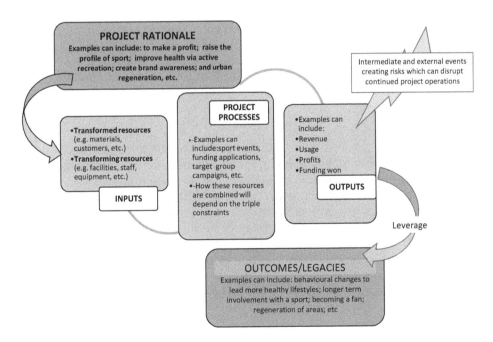

Figure 6.1 The Operational Project Management System.
Source: Author.

Box 6.1 Applying the project system concepts to a fun run event

Running events for charities and parkrun events have grown in global popularity. Parkrun, for example, is now a global limited company that has laid down a simple template for free fun running events, which take place on Saturday mornings, where people can time their runs (5k for adults, 2k for juniors). It began in 2004 by volunteers and is still dependent on volunteers for the operational delivery, where thousands of runs take place every week with millions of participants around the world. There are also numerous larger-scale city marathon events, which generate millions of dollars for charities around the world every year. These examples show the desire of people to get active and support charities.

If a village or town were to start their own charity fun run, here is a simple project outline which applies the project system concepts identified in Figure 6.1:

Rationale – A charity fun run is proposed by a small town which has the broad aim to raise money and awareness for a local charity. From this aim, three SMART objectives are set (see also Chapter 2):

- To have 1,000 people doing the run on 1 May
- Raise $3,000 from the event and supporting projects, by the 1st of June
- To increase the membership of the charity organisation by 5% at the end of the year

Inputs – A mix of input resources are then identified, such as:

- **Transforming resources needed**: volunteers, park space, equipment (e.g. road cones, barriers, tables, music speakers, etc.), publicity, etc.
- **Transformed resource**: people to participate in the running event; numbers of spectators who can support runners and offer additional charitable contributions; and calculation of the safe carrying capacity of the event

Throughputs – The project manager or SDO, even if they are volunteers, must take the lead in transforming and coordinating all these input resources, in order to stage the event, so this relates to the actual details of the event, such as starting time, course, distance and course route.

Outputs – This relates to the numbers who participate, the revenue raised for charity, the numbers of sponsors, etc., which all give a critical basis for forming SMART objectives and key performance indicators (KPIs) (see Chapter 2).

Outcomes/legacies – These are harder to measure but vital to achieve, particularly if any longer-term behavioural changes are to occur, such as more people take up running to improve their health, or helping to develop community cohesion.

Leveraging mechanisms – To achieve an outcome, there must be outputs (i.e. people participating) but whether outcomes are achieved, depends on the quality of leveraging or the intervening mechanisms, such as keeping in contact with participants to sustain their motivation. A crucial foundation is to give a fun and inspiring event, which can help fuel future motivation for participating running events. Continued communication strategies will be vital here, to make people aware of how they can support the charity and future fun run events.

Reviewed – Here analysis needs to be conducted to consider if outcomes and outputs have been met and how they meet the aim. With this evaluation, consideration can be given to how much impact it had on the organisation, people and community.

Discussion

Who should take responsibility of a sport event project, which is predominantly volunteer led?

Of the many types of project highlighted, sport events are particularly important and so need additional discussion. Sport event projects are often an integral part of sport managers and SDOs working portfolio, where they can be vital mechanisms to try and achieve a variety of outcomes and legacies (discussed in more detail Section 6.3.4). Bosscher et al. (2013) observe how frequently government justification of giving a large investment in elite sport is based on the arguments of positive benefits generated, such as improved national identity, pride, international prestige and their primary focus, on the claim that sport success brings an increase in sport participation via a demonstration effect. These are the theoretical legacies left behind. Critically, however, Bosscher et al. (2013, p. 334) observe that there is often a lack of hard, verifiable, statistical evidence to support these claims, whilst Byers et al. (2012) argue there can often be negative legacies left, such as additional tax burdens and expensive facilities that cannot find a proper use post-event. Indeed, Lensky (1996, 2000) argues that there are sometimes more legacy benefits from going through the process of bidding for an event, which can see an injection of money to improve facilities and infrastructure, but then lose the bid, so they do not have the expensive bill at the end of the event. Into this project event analysis should also go through the principles of the triple constraints, introduced in Chapter 5, Section 5.4 where an illustrative example is given in Box 6.2.

It is worthwhile noting that some sport events do not fit neatly into the event project category. Take, for example, the numerous, weekly games of football, netball, rugby, hockey, cricket, baseball, etc., that are organised as part of league structures or cup competitions. For these types of events, the distinctions between operations and project management will be blurred, which ultimately does not matter, as long as the key operations and project management tools and concepts are used to ensure a high-quality, safe service is delivered.

Box 6.2 The triple constraints of event projects and the risks generated

The theory of the triple constraints, whilst not always explicitly stated, is implicit in both operations and project management (e.g. PMBOK, 2019), which reminds managers and SDOs that resources are limited and compromises have to be made in terms of the price paid for the level of quality and safety desired, as the following examples illustrate.

As part of Japan's preliminary bid for the Rugby World Cup, the intention was to use the Tokyo Olympic stadium to stage the Rugby World Cup final. This was a particularly attractive part of the bid, as it meant that the final would be played in a new Olympic stadium. In 2015, however, it was announced that it would not be possible to have the Olympic stadium ready for the desired date and design specification, unless they doubled the cost of building the stadium. A choice therefore had to be made about where they would compromise. In the end, the Japanese government decided it was not willing to spend more money to develop the stadium within the Rugby World Cup deadline, with the quality and design standards specified; therefore, the decision was made to move the Rugby World Cup final to the Yokohama stadium, which had a smaller capacity of 72,000, but would be ready for the desired deadline.

For the 2014 Football world cup and 2016 Olympics held in Brazil there were also many examples of the triple constraint tensions. For example, in 2013, 200 days before the world cup was due to begin, a huge crane used to construct one of the stadiums collapsed, sadly killing two people and creating further delays to the project schedule. Some argued that the pressures to meet the deadlines meant that compromises had been made to meet quality safety standards. Similarly, for the Olympic outdoor water-based sport events, whilst the facilities were operationally ready for the event, they were not able to make all the improvements to the quality of water, so it in effect meant some events took place in polluted water.

Discussion questions

In order to comply with various safety at work legal regulations, it is not usually expected to remove all risks, but to keep the risks As Low As is Reasonably Practicable (ALARP principle). Considering this principle, how far can/should quality safety standards be compromised?

6.3 THE PROJECT OPERATIONS PROCESS

There is a huge array of literature on project planning and management. When scrutinising this work, it can sometimes feel very detached and separate from other areas of management. Whilst at times this can be appropriate, because, as PMBOK observes, project management 'is now seen globally as a separately recognized strategic competency, career path and a subject for training and

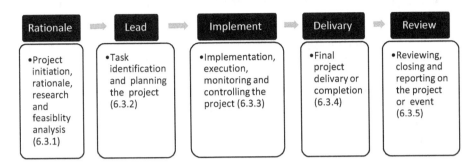

Figure 6.2 An Overview of the Key Project and Event Planning Process Phases.
Source: Piekarz adapting various approaches.

education' (PMBOK, 2019), this can, however, mean that it places too artificial barrier between the two. Yes, project management does have some distinct management tools and concepts, but it is still 'management', utilising the key management functions, roles and skills (see Chapter 1).

What will be done here then is to highlight the key process elements of project management, which are synthesised (i.e. bringing together) from a variety of project management approaches (e.g. Masterman, 2004; PMBOK, 2019; Torkildsen, 2005). It self-consciously uses some of the concepts already introduced in earlier chapters, to help emphasise the many areas of blended practice between operations and project management. Furthermore, the focus in this chapter is to show how projects and events are 'operationalised' and delivered as a result of the application of a management system and process. In Figure 6.2 an overview of the key planning project stages is represented.

It is important to briefly explain the difference between the system representation of project management (Figure 6.1) and the practical process diagram (Figure 6.2). Whilst the project system representation in Figure 6.1 gives a useful theoretical representation which can inform working cultures and planning approaches, it lacks details in terms of the practical steps for how to begin a project, hence the process model presented in Figure 6.2. The project management system (Figure 6.1) reminds managers and SDOs that they both are managing an interactive, dynamic business system (i.e. coordinating and transforming resources to achieve outputs and outcomes): The practical project process model (Figure 6.2), on the other hand, gives managers and SDOs insights into the practical process steps they need to start and complete a project.

For both students and practitioners who have come across different representations of the project management process stages, it is important to focus on the core underpinning concepts of each stage, rather than the descriptors used for each stage. Also, although the process is presented in a linear process, it is in fact more dynamic process, where there can be an inter-play between the different process stages. The process stages identified in Figure 6.2 are used to structure the rest of the sub-sections of this chapter.

6.3.1 Stage 1 – preliminary project rationale, research and feasibility analysis

In Figure 6.2, it should be appreciated that the broad process categories identified, whilst initially seeming quite simple, do in fact hide a great deal of complexity. This is because at each stage, there can be a multitude of nested processes, work breakdown structures (WBS) or jobs tasks, which will need to be broken down, delegated and resourced, then given a time scale of completion and monitored (see also Chapter 3 for how to do this). To help illustrate these features and how a project might begin, a creative thinking technique is used in Box 6.3, which begins by using the analogy of boiling an egg, to illustrate the basic underpinning principles of beginning a project.

Box 6.3 From boiling an egg to organising the Olympics: starting an event project

The technique used here adapts Gardiner's (2005, p. 249) post-it tab approach for beginning a project. This technique involves using coloured post-it tabs to represent different elements of the project event process, such as key stakeholders and partners (e.g. user groups, police, communities, sponsors, charities, etc.); key resources and equipment (e.g. staging, food, refreshments, lighting, etc.); tasks (i.e. what jobs need to get done) and location preparation (i.e. what can be done to the sportscape, discussed in Chapter 5, to enhance the event experience).

The 'boiling an egg' process is used as an analogy to illustrate techniques for beginning an event project and showing the complexities and interconnection of tasks and resources, where to miss just one task, or for an element in the supply chain to fail, can jeopardise the whole project and experience. The example works are as follows:

Project task – boil an egg for breakfast

Four different colour post-it tabs are used to represent the following categories:

- **Tasks** (e.g. Green post-it tabs) – What jobs or tasks to be done?
- **Resources** (e.g. Egg purple post-it tabs) – What materials are needed?
- **Preparation** (e.g. Yellow post-it tabs) – What additional tasks need to be done to the location to enhance the visitor experience?
- **Stakeholders** (e.g. Orange post-it tabs) – Who needs to be considered and involved?

It is possible to mind-map these areas, if post-it tabs are not available, where each category can be used as a key thought branch; the advantage of using post-it tabs is that they can be moved around, which is particularly useful in project scheduling.

These post-it tab categories can now be used to consider the project process for boiling an egg, which has the aim of:

To have a satisfying, relaxed breakfast, before setting off for work.

As this process is to represent a project, it must therefore have a clear end point, so the egg must be boiled, eaten and plates tidied (a representative bit of post-project work here), all by 8.00 a.m. Failure to do this means a missed breakfast, which can have wider implications in terms of work performance.

It is recommended that you have a go using the four categories, writing on an individual post-it tab for each separate job or resource (e.g. water goes on one post-it, egg on another, pan on another, etc.).

Here's an example of some of the jobs, tasks and stakeholder chains you might have produced in Table 6.1.

For such a simple task, there can be perhaps a surprising amount of system complexity. Looking at all the elements in Table 6.1, it can be used to illustrate the following points about project management:

- The resources represent the inputs, which go through a transformative throughput process, which can generate outputs (the boiled egg eaten) that can help achieve outcomes (e.g. feeling happier, better performance at work, etc.).
- If even one resource (e.g. pan to boil the egg) is missing, or task not done properly (e.g. failing to put the heat on or doing it late, meaning the egg won't be cooked in time before the person has to leave for work), the whole project again can be put in jeopardy.
- When one adds in the stakeholders, one realises that there is a whole supply chain, whereby one failure in this chain (e.g. no drivers to deliver eggs from the farm, to the packaging warehouse) means the project could fail again.
- Finally, the location preparation, although it overlaps with the task elements, can bring in a useful qualitative element, which considers some of the final elements for the 'relaxing element' that can better achieve the outcomes, such as having a clean space to eat or relaxing music.

So how can we go from boiling an egg to project managing an event like the Olympics? What differs is the scale and complexity of the interlinking parts, not the underlying principles. Whilst for the egg there are 11 interlinking tasks, for the Olympics there would be hundreds of thousands; whilst for the egg task, there are seven stakeholders, for the Olympics there would be thousands. And so one. To fail in one task can lead to delays and project disruptions; if a stakeholder supplier fails, this again can create delays and risks the project event delivery (something which happened for the London 2012 Olympics, when the private commercial contractor responsible for security failed, forcing the UK government having to use the military for stadium security).

(continued)

Box 6.3 (continued)

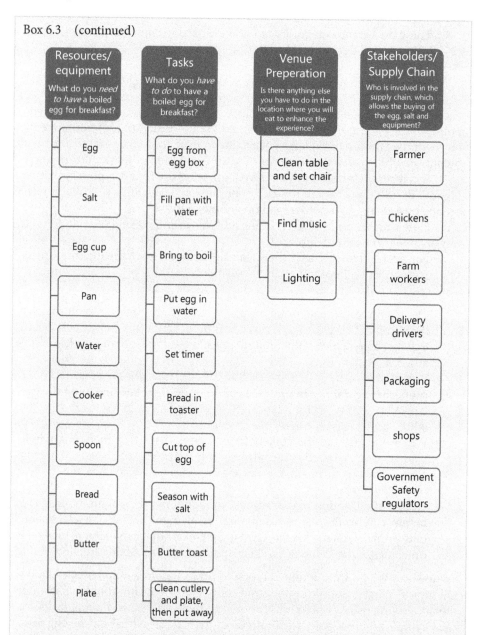

Figure 6.3 Post-it Tab Exercise: Identifying Key Tasks, Resources and Stakeholders.
Source: Author.

Just as the longest journey begins with the first footstep, so too can the largest event project begin with the first idea written on a post-it tab!

Task

Apply the four categories for a new sport event of your choice.

Project sport and event management **131**

Once some of the preliminary project tasks and resources are mapped out, this can help with the deeper exploration of its feasibility and whether it should be progressed. Here are a few examples of additional research and creative thinking tasks which need to be considered for deciding if the project is feasible or not:

- **Clarification of the project rationale**: Is it to make a profit, raise the profile of the sport or organisation, benefit the community or obtain more money from grant applications?
- **Researching the preliminary impacts and legacies**: These can range from looking at the economic benefits which could be gained, or how the local community or specific target groups could benefit in the future.
- **Preliminary budget, income and resource assessments**: This can have implications for gaps in funding in order to be able to get the project off the ground, or how much money has to be raised in order to get the event staged. Consideration of staffing and equipment can also be given here.
- **Preliminary risk assessments**: In the early stages of a project there will be more unknown elements and hence risks, but the financial risks should be less: As time goes on, uncertainty should be reduced; however, if a project is cancelled, the risk of financial loss or reputation can be greater (see also Chapter 9 on risks management).
- **Identification of any permissions and licenses**: For some projects, particularly for events and building projects, it may be necessary to check if any permission is needed, such as contacting the police and governments for any road closures, seeking licences for the permission to play music or even planning permissions to build on land. Failure to get these tasks done will mean the whole project could fail early on in the project planning lifecycle.
- **Consideration of the triple constraints**: It may be impossible to deliver the expected quality and safety, based on the money available, for the requested deadline (see also Chapter 5 and Box 6.1).

Remember each one of these broad areas will always be broken down into small tasks, which need to be monitored to ensure their completion.

If the preliminary research suggests that the project or event is feasible, then project planning can be continued. It then becomes absolutely critical to identify that the key deadlines or milestones of the project are identified and mapped out (remember the crucial distinguishing feature of a project is having a clear end point). Here are some examples of key deadlines or milestones which should be identified:

- **Project end point**: The end point could be date set for when, for example, the sport event might take place. If it is for a funding application, the closure date for when the grant application must be submitted sets the end point date, from which the planning process can be worked back from.
- **Venue preparation milestones for event projects**: This is when venues must be ready by, which for large-scale events can include pilot testing events.
- **Securing trained staff and volunteers**: First, it is about having people to deliver the event, but in order to comply with safety standards, it is vital that time is built in to ensure they are properly trained. This can be

particularly challenging when utilising volunteers, which are the life blood of many sport events.
- **Delivery of equipment milestones**: For some event projects, it is critical to have the necessary equipment delivered to run the event.
- **Market research and impact analysis milestones**: For some projects, having more substantive data is a vital underpinning which can affect whether the project can continue to progress.
- **Feasibility costing and pricing estimates**: This is vital part of the feasibility analysis, but is a dynamic ongoing process, and cost escalation can be a common feature of projects. This is also vital for sport organisations who bid to run sport services and events.
- **Project or event legacies**: This involves collecting data to report back on the post-event impacts.

Another important part of this first project planning phase is the development of the aim(s) and objectives, along with any KPIs which reflect the different areas of performance. In this sense, the principles behind writing aims, SMART objectives and performance evaluation have already been discussed in Chapter 3. It is therefore recommended that when engaging with this project process, that chapter is revised.

6.3.2 Stage 2 – leading, job task identification and developing plans

Leadership is a fundamental foundation for all management and SDO work. Obviously, all projects need to utilise the management functions and skills to be successfully completed. Yet this may not always be enough to ensure that project tasks and deadlines are successfully completed, which is where projects not only need management, but also leadership. This is because the managers and SDOs who lead on projects will need to:

- Articulate and communicate the vision and purpose of the project
- Energise project team members, such as engaging staff or volunteers to commit to the work and, crucially, to complete the work; sustain the motivation and energy in the project, in order to ensure its effective completion
- Adapting to situations as the operating conditions change, giving clear direction as to what needs to be done, by who and when

In the previous section, it was illustrated how some creative thinking techniques could be used to start a project. The work done at that early initiation stage, provided that it passes the feasibility analysis, should be built on here for this second process stage of job task identification, where more detail can be given for the *what, why, when, how, where* and *who*.

Whatever techniques are used to identify job tasks, these will at some point need to be formerly listed, linked and scheduled. Scheduling relates to the deployment of the input resources, such as staff and equipment, to the required order that they need to be utilised and job tasks completed. It cannot be reiterated enough that failure to identify or complete a job task, even if it seems on first glance unimportant, really can jeopardise the whole project, which can cost money, reputations and, even in some instances, lives (see back to Box 6.3 and the egg analogy). Scheduling is essentially about sequencing and allotting time for activities (Heizer, 2004, p. 58), by identifying and developing a network of tasks and their order of completion (or their critical paths). Forward scheduling deals with work as it arrives (Slack et al., 2016, p. 241), whilst backward scheduling means jobs are started at the last possible moment to prevent them being late (e.g. staff involved with non-urgent/important tasks).

Planning milestones should be built into schedules; these perform the function of checking where you are, in much the same way that road signs confirm your direction and if you are adhering to your planned journey route. As part of scheduling job tasks consideration to the triple constraints needs to be given, whereby managers must choose two from the following three: how quickly a job needs to be done; the level of quality and safety standards expected; and how cheaply it is delivered.

There are a variety of techniques which can be used to estimate time schedules, resources and the WBS or job tasks order of completion. Just two will be considered here: network diagrams and Gantt charts. First, network diagrams will be considered. There are a variety of networking techniques which can be used, such as PERT (Programming Evaluation and Review Techniques) and CPA (Critical Path Analysis). Consideration can also be given to the many software packages which can be found in relation to project management, such as Microsoft project management. There is not the scope to examine these in any depth, as the intention is to just focus on the key underlying principles of creating network diagrams, in order to show the relationships and the order that job tasks need to be completed. Reflecting back to Box 6.2, Figure 6.3 and the use of post-it tabs, what this technique also illustrates is the development of a simple, preliminary CPA, as the tasks are sequenced in the order of completion.

The second tool which can be used to identify relationship tasks and the schedule of completion is the use of Gantt charts. Gantt charts offer a simple visual representation and overview of some of the job tasks which must be completed, by a set date and in the required schedule order. They help identify the required resources and tasks for completion, which allow the estimation of costs and finish dates. When done properly, they also illustrate how different job tasks are linked or dependent on each other. For a simple illustration of Gantt charts, an example is given in Box 6.4. Gantt charts, whilst invaluable, do have some problems, such as the interrelationships of some of the tasks not being explicit enough, or being less suitable for larger, more complex projects. For our purposes, within an operational context, they are considered as a basic tool which managers and SDOs should understand and be able to apply, as their uses goes beyond the project level of planning.

In order to develop a Gantt chart for a sport project or event, it is vital that the key job tasks are identified in order to complete a project. To help illustrate

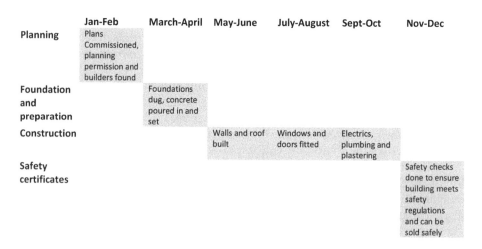

Figure 6.4 Simplified Gantt Chart and Schedule Using a Sport Building Analogy. Source: Author.

these points, a simple sport facility or building analogy can be used to show how these concepts can be applied (it also shows the generic nature of project management skills, which can be utilised to a variety of projects). A simplified project process might look like in Figure 6.4.

This figure shows how there needs to be a proper ordering or schedule of work. For example, there is no point getting a builder to start digging foundations, if there are no plans, or building permission given. Similarly, there is no point ordering windows and glaziers to fit them, if the facility walls have not been built! Other points to consider is how each of these broad task areas will in fact break down into numerous sub-tasks (e.g. researching, contractors bidding for work, getting the necessary money, submitting the plans, etc.). Furthermore, as each of these tasks is part of an interactive system, it would not take much for an external risk event to disrupt the schedule and the completion dates, such as poor weather creating delays, which in turn increases costs.

With some simple adjustments to this analogy, it is easy to see how it applies to various sport projects. Commissioning plans and permissions for a sport project could be the preliminary research to see if a sport service, facility or event is both needed and wanted; the construction phase for a sport project could relate to getting staff who are qualified and trained, then booking venues, purchasing equipment, developing a marketing strategy so people know what is happening. The key point to reiterate is the constant need to identify job tasks and their nested processes, to ensure they are tracked for completion, particularly if they are delegated. In terms of documentation, these tasks and schedules can be captured in more formal project plans, which are given their detailed operational refinement and delivery by the use of effective time management, discussed in Chapter 3. An illustration of these points is given in Box 6.4.

Box 6.4 Example of the preliminary job task identification and scheduling of job tasks: homeless rugby project

An innovative outreach project was organised by a number of UK Rugby clubs, such as the Worcester Warriors rugby club. There were two key rationales for developing a sport outreach project of getting homeless people to engage with rugby. The first was that engaging with this event project reflects the clubs Corporate Social Responsibility (CSR) commitments (see Chapter 7) to supporting the local community. The second was that it reflects both local and national concerns about the growing numbers of homeless people in certain towns. In turn, engaging with such a non-profit social activity creates an opportunity to leverage the stories which can help the rugby clubs brand. A preliminary mind-map using the *who, what, where, how* and *when* identified some of the following key elements to help start the project:

- **Why** – Help develop confidence in homeless participants to get jobs; raise money to support charities; raise club profile; have commitment to meet CSR objectives and its commitment to being a community club, who is sensitive to local issues
- **Who/stakeholders** – Worcester Warriors SDO takes lead, who coordinates a variety of volunteer coaches, charities and social services, both locally and nationally
- **When** – Weekly training events, to build up to a regional competition with other homeless rugby teams in six months
- **What** – Training sessions, opportunities for education and facilitation, to build confidence and health, leading to competing in a tournament
- **Where** – Training sessions to be organised in club training space

This preliminary analysis was used to develop some SMART objectives, which includes both outputs and outcomes (the last objective on confidence building):

- Twenty-two homeless people to engage with the project event (KPIs could be the average attendance each month)
- For this to form the basis of one competitive team to take part in the national tournament
- To attract two funding sponsors to support the team
- To have a partnership with homeless charities
- To build confidence in the homeless participants, to enable them to no longer be rough sleepers in towns by the end of the project

From this preliminary mind-map, the more practical operational details emerge which can be presented in a simplified Gantt chart (Figure 6.5), which establishes a key milestone for the one-off tournament. It should be noted that the visual layout of a Gantt chart can vary depending on the software used.

(continued)

136 Chapter 6

Box 6.4 (continued)

TASK	Month 1	Month 2	Month 3	Month 4	Month 5	Month 6	Month 7	Month 8	Month 9
Risk -Identification of key hazards and risk -Assessment forms completed -Control measures implemented	X	X X							
Research -Interviews with charities -Talking to homeless people about level of interest and challenges	X								
Finance -Cost estimation (staffing, equipment, marketing, etc.) - Bids put in to secure money		X							
Resources -Equipment purchased -Stored and checked			X						
Staffing - coach and volunteer job specs -advertised -interviewed -trained		X		X X	X				
Marketing -Participants found -Direct contacts kept - Press/social media release 1 (e.g. to generate interest to get volunteers) -Media release 2 (e.g. promote event and people to watch) -Media 3 (e.g. post event)		X	X	X			X	X	X
Transport -researched and costed -drivers who can drive mini buses -minibuses to pick up participants	X	X		X	X	X	X	X	
Venues -training and tournament venues researched -Venues booked _Venues inspected	X		X		X	X	X		
Coaching sessions -Fitness assessments - training				X	X	X	X		
Final mini-tournament								X	
Post Event -Data collected on outputs and any outcomes									X

Figure 6.5 Sample Gantt Chart for Homeless Rugby Event (Simplified).
Source: Author.

A couple observations should be made. The first is that some simple broad job task headings are given, loosely based around the classic headings of budgeting, staffing and risks, with each having a variety of sub-tasks or nested processes (greatly simplified, as there would in fact be far more in the WBS). It should also be noted, as with the building analogy, there is no point starting certain job tasks, unless earlier scheduled jobs are done, such as conducting a risk assessment and gauging the level of interest and commitment from the homeless people and various supporting charities.

Another example to illustrate the systems connectivity relates to transport, whereby the whole event could be jeopardised if they cannot find someone with the relevant training and eligibility to drive a mini-bus, in order to pick up the participants, to take them to the training venues. Finally, it must be stressed that if the outcome-related objective focuses on building confidence, to help the homeless rebuild their lives, then it is crucial that this event engagement is properly leveraged (e.g. contacts given to charities and educational programmes), which must be measured (e.g. the number who manage to stop being homeless).

Discussion

What sort of objectives and performance indicators could be built in to check if the project is progressing in right direction?

6.3.3 Stage 3 – impelementing and monitoring

The reason why this is a short section is because many of the practical skills and tools which can be used for ensuring jobs are completed on time, to the specified quality, has been dealt with in Chapters 3 and 5. With the key job tasks identified, mapped out and scheduled, this gives a crucial foundation for organising and coordinating the work in terms of time management, or whom the jobs tasks have been delegated to. At the most basic level, managing the project becomes about managing the checklist of 'to-do' job tasks. This checklist of actions or jobs for completion is a foundation for implementing and completing jobs. Having clear and specific designated action points or to-do lists, which have a clear person identified as owning the task, and a date of completion, which is tracked and monitored, is therefore a vital process of the implementation and monitoring stage. To reiterate, failure to complete even the smallest task – and this really cannot be stressed enough – can create project delays or even jeopardise the whole project itself.

Beyond the checking of job tasks being completed, it is also vital to build in a variety of indicators to check if the project is on course for its successful completion, to the quality standards expected. This is where the value of setting SMART project objectives comes in, where the targets can help inform a variety of indicators to check performance. Establishing the key milestones and SMART objectives, which include both outputs and outcomes, or even legacy objectives, means they can be reviewed on a regular basis to check if the project is on course to achieve its objectives and outcomes, within the designated time and budget.

6.3.4 Stage 4 – project delivery, completion and micro-leveraging positive outcomes and legacies

This stage relates to the delivery and completion of the project, such as the day of actual staging a sport event, submitting a funding bid or completing a sport building project. In these final stages, operational management is at the very heart of project delivery.

One area which may need particular consideration in relation to sport event legacies is the need to consider, what we will call, micro-leveraging. Micro-leveraging relates to the final operational decisions and actions taken on the day of event projects, which can be vital to help achieve outcome-related objectives and positive legacies. In Box 6.5, an illustrative example is given on micro-leveraging an event.

Box 6.5 Micro-leveraging the impacts from events – an observational study of the 2019 Rugby World Cup

In 2019, Japan staged the Rugby World Cup, which on numerous macro measures was very successful. The event was staged in 14 venues, across Japan. World Rugby (2019) reported a number of records broken in terms of previous rugby world cups: a record of 99.3% attendance, selling 1.84 million tickets; an estimated 1.13 million people filling the official fanzones; breaking past records for international fan engagement with 1.7 billion digital video views and an estimated worldwide broadcast audience of 400 million; a domestic all-time record television audience of 54.8 million for the Japan vs. Scotland pool game; and a decrease in the average winning margin between established and developing nations. Furthermore, off the pitch World Rugby claimed it was the most impactful, with more than 1.8 million new rugby participants across Asia as part of World Rugby's Impact Beyond legacy programme. Finally, there were the CSR charity programmes, which broke many records, such as raising more than £2million for the ChildFund Pass It, which benefitted over 25,000 under-privileged young people in Asia, using rugby to develop life skils.

In order to explore the operational impacts in more detail, it is useful to focus on just one of the venues. Kumagaya was unusual in the host cities staging games, in that it refurbished an existing purpose-built rugby stadium, with a capacity of 24,000. In theory, the rugby events offered Kumagaya a number of opportunities, which, if properly leveraged, could leave many positive legacies, such as: promoting their town and regional tourism attractions to Japan and the world; engaging and animating local communities in a variety of civic projects; and providing a boost to the local economy, by attracting thousands of visitors to use the hotels, spend in the shops and eat and drink in the many cafes, bars and restaurants.

As part of a research project examining the operational delivery of rugby games at the World Cup, a number of observational studies were conducted by Piekarz (2021) in Kumagaya, which held two Rugby World Cup games. One of the games observed was the USA vs. Argentina match, in the city of Kumagaya (the other game the City hosted was Russia vs. Samoa). The study observed the movement of fans and their flow to the stadium, in the fanzones and through the town and their interactions with different facilities and the host community.

It was clear that the City initiated many activities to try and leverage the event to achieve positive impacts, such as:

- Encouraging eating establishments to come up with themed food based around rugby and the event
- Engaging children and schools with various arts projects relating to rugby, with works displayed in various civic buildings
- Using banners, posters and decorations to create a sense of anticipation and occasion, such as banners on lampposts promoting the world cup event
- Taster rugby sessions of tag-rugby for children
- Training of hundreds of volunteers to help out on the day of events
- Getting children to learn the national anthems of the teams playing in the city
- Encouraging children and students to engage with visiting fans to practise their English and make them feel welcome

In addition to staging two games, they also had an official World Cup fanzones, which showed all the games on a large screen and included a small museum, food and various fun rugby development activities.

Both games ran smoothly in their operational delivery. Although restrictions were placed on bringing in bottled water to the stadiums and fanzones, as it was a hot day, volunteers were giving out free cups of water to visitors, welcomed by many fans, which also dealt with the risk of people dehydrating in the warm weather. The welcome by locals and volunteers was faultless and warm.

In terms of the economic impact, the decision to allow various local pop-up food stalls in the stadium perimeter and fanzone would be one beneficial to the local economy, as these businesses are more likely to source food locally, employ local people and re-spend profits in the local economy. In essence, it means that the additional money brought in by visitors is less likely to leak away, so more local benefits accrue. It can be a different story for the sale of alcohol, as these were restricted to the sale only of the official sponsors beer, Heineken. As Heineken is a multi-national business, it can mean that more of the money is likely to leak out of the local economy.

Clearly, there was a great deal that was done well in terms of leveraging the potential positive impacts and legacies, but it was still possible to identify some refinements to micro-leveraging the event for the benefit of all. Micro-leveraging refers to the operational decisions taken for dealing with fans on the day, in terms of maximising the benefits or minimising problems. For example, one observation made was how on the day of the games, fans were almost filtered too efficiently through the town to the stadium and rail station. As the stadium was a few kilometres from the rail station, a vast majority of the fans used the free shuttle buses. The problem, however, was

(continued)

Box 6.5 (continued)

that of the thousands of fans who came to the game from outside the City (its good communications with Tokyo meant it was feasible for fans to travel there and back in a day), they were directed from the train to the free bus service, with few opportunities to stop and look in shops or cafes; then, when the game was over, they were again very efficiently redirected back to the bus shuttle service and then directed back to the station.

Obviously, this directing of fans on designated routes, with roads closed, has many vital safety considerations. It did however mean that relatively few people, as a ratio of the total fans, broke free of the main mass of moving fans, which means that some of the potential economic and social interactions may not have been maximised for the local community.

In terms of micro-leveraging on the day, some smaller operational actions could have helped leverage more meaningful interactions, such as giving fans the choice of directions, to allow more interaction with local shops, cafes and bars. More refined signage – always a critical issue sport operation – could have helped many local businesses leverage more interactions, such as having more signs in different languages, which clearly informed fans of what they had to offer. It was noted, for example, that many local bars created some special dishes on themes around rugby, but if on the actual day, visitors are not reminded, or directed to the places, the opportunity is gone to sell those products.

What this illustrates is that leveraging outputs needs to be planned for at the strategic level of project management, but has to be driven all the way down to the operational delivery.

Discussion

How can the event be leveraged, to maintain children's engagement with rugby (i.e. a behavioural outcome) months and years after the event?

6.3.5 Stage 5 – reviewing, closing and final reporting

A crucial part of all projects is a post-project review, evaluation and the closing report, particularly if it is an event project which may have legacy or outcome-related objectives. Indeed, for sport events, this is work which can continue many years after the event, particularly with mega events. For this stage, it is vital that any key learning points are focused on and key stakeholders are communicated with (see Chapter 7). This is also the point whereby consideration is given to the project's success in terms of the different levels of performance, such as whether it helped the organisation operate more profitably, gained more brand exposure, public money was well spent or how effective it was in achieving a variety of outcomes (see Chapter 3).

For event projects, the consideration of the achievement of outcomes and legacies are particularly important, but it is beyond the scope of this book to fully discuss this vital and complex area. The key point to reiterate here (again) is that positive event impact and legacy outcomes are never automatic, but *must always be* leveraged, with Bosscher et al. (2013), arguing that they are dependent on 'why, when and how' sport success is used. What is also of value in their work are some of the speculative factors which can be considered as influential, such as amount of media attention, or the importance of having the supply opportunities for people to participate in (as they say, Olympic legacies need to be constructed or leveraged).

6.4 CONCLUSION

It will be near impossible for sport managers and SDOs to avoid engaging with some form of project, whether this is a sport event, building or funding project. A key distinguishing feature of a project is the need to have clear start and finish times. Whilst project management is a discrete area of management, it is important to reiterate that in order to complete projects on time, to the expected level of quality, it requires the utilisation of a variety of management skills, tools and knowledge, some of which are generic to all management, such as using time management and leadership. At other times, for complex projects it is vital that a range of additional concepts, theories and project management tools are utilised. What is always vital in both levels of management is the need to identify job tasks, nested process and WBS, which must be kept track of and scheduled, as to fail in the completion of even the seemingly smallest task can jeopardise the whole project.

In relation to sport event projects, it is important to note that they often have a variety of additional outcomes, which, in sport event literature, are increasingly framed and discussed around the concept of legacies. One of the implications of legacy analysis is that it can extend aspects of the project process, to many weeks, months and even years after the initial sport event has taken place. It is also vital that managers and SDOs never assume that positive outcomes and legacy impacts will accrue when outputs are achieved. Managers and SDOs must think carefully how they leverage the outputs, to avoid negative impacts and gain the positive ones.

References

Bosscher, V.D., Sotiriadou, P., and van Bottenburg, M. (2013). Scrutinizing the sport pyramid metaphor: An examination of the relationship between elite success and mass participation in Flanders. *International Journal of Sport Policy and Politics*, 5(3), 319–339.

Byers, T., Slack, T., and Parent, M.A. (2012). *Key Concepts in Sport Management*. London: Sage.

Cunningham, A., and Maclean, J. (2017). The role of the event manager. In Mallen, C. and Adams, L.J. (eds.), *Event Management in Sport, Recreation and Tourism Theoretical and Practical Dimensions*, 3rd ed. Oxon: Routledge.

Gardiner, P.D. (2005). *Project Management*. London: Palgrave.

Piekarz, M. (2020). Micro leveraging the rugby world cup, draft paper of research findings.

PMBOK (2019). What is a project, accessed 8 October, 2019, available at: https://www.visual-paradigm.com/guide/pmbok/what-is-pmbok/

Slack, N., Brandon-Jones, A., and Johnston, R. (2016). *Operations Management*, 8th ed. London: Pearson.

Torkildsen, G. (2005). *Leisure and Recreation Management*, 5th ed. London: Routledge.

World Rugby (2019). Rugby world cup breaks a number of records, 3 November 2019, available at: https://www.fbcnews.com.fj/sports/rugby/2019-rugby-world-cup-breaks-a-number-of-records/

7
STAKEHOLDERS, PARTNERSHIPS AND VOLUNTEERS

> **Challenges for managers**
>
> - Why are volunteers and networks so important in sport?
> - How can and should networks and partnerships be developed?
> - How can volunteers be recruited and trained?

7.1 INTRODUCTION

Volunteers, networks and partnerships are an essential feature for the effective and efficient delivery of sport services around the world. On a day-to-day basis a high level of communication and interpersonal skills are required not only to liaise with staff and customers, but also when negotiating and forming partnerships, developing networks and motivating volunteers.

There are three key theories used to structure this chapter, which are stakeholder analysis, partnerships and networking. Stakeholder analysis is the key underpinning theory used to explain the importance of partnerships, networks and volunteers. Particular emphasis is given to volunteers, who are so important in giving many sport services their vibrancy, creativity and a vital emotional charge, which can be leveraged to try achieve a variety of sport outcomes.

7.2 STAKEHOLDER THEORY

All business organisations will have a variety of individuals and groups who are impacted on, for good or bad, by the actions of that business. Initially, stakeholder theory focused on profit-orientated businesses, where the key stakeholders were simply identified as the owners and shareholders, where the purpose of business was to give a financial return on stakeholder investment, from any profits made. Today, this is far too simplistic an approach to stakeholder analysis, failing to describe the reality or reflecting the growing responsibility that all organisations have to workers, society and the environment – what is now sometimes described as Corporate Social Responsibility (CSR), which considers the Triple Bottom Line (PROFIT and financial performance; the PLANET and environment impacts; and PEOPLE and their human rights). The value of using stakeholder analysis to include CSR in operations is that it helps to identify the key constituents, groups or individuals the sport organisation has a financial and moral responsibility to – whether they use the services or not – or who can assist with effective and efficient service deliveries, such as potential volunteers, sponsorship partnerships and communication networks. The importance of CSR in stakeholder theory is elaborated on in Box 7.1.

Using stakeholder theory, then, is an essential part of the operations system managers and SDOs need to develop. In essence, it is the 'who' part of operations management, complementing the 'what', 'where', 'why' and 'how', discussed in previous chapters. As part of this system development and identification, managers need to consider the *to*, *for* and *need* which refer to:

- Who are they responsible **TO**? This relates to owners, stakeholders, trustees, local communities, governments, funders, etc.
- Who are they responsible **FOR**? This relates to who is impacted by the service operations, which can relate to staff, customers and all parts of the local community, whether they use the services or not. This has particular relevancy in relation to CSR and the duty of care organisations have for the health and safety of others.
- Who do they **NEED**? This relates to investors, community support, charities, local volunteers and governments (local and national), which should be combined with the concept of leverage, as partnerships and volunteers can be the critical factor in turning outputs into outcomes, as illustrated later.

The primary task which must be done by managers and SDOs is to identify and map out all the key stakeholders and their degree of power and influence, which will form a web or system network of constituents (see next section for more elaboration). Some of these groups will be clear and obvious – what Clarkson (1995, cited in Byers et al., 2012) describes as primary stakeholders, such as shareholders, customers and suppliers. Less obvious can be the secondary stakeholders, such as people in the wider community, but who Clarkson (1995) argues do not make or break a service, and can help enhance it. This simple demarcation between primary and secondary, whilst initially useful, helping to broaden out the groups who need to be identified, is less satisfactory when framed within the prism of CSR, where there can be instances where secondary stakeholders *can* in fact make or break a service, contrary to Clarkson's (1995) argument and as illustrated in Box 7.1. Although there are many other ways for classifying stakeholders, such as using the term internal and external stakeholders, for our purposes, using primary and secondary stakeholders is felt to be sufficient.

There are a variety of analogies which can be used to represent stakeholders, such as using a universe system (i.e. different groups represent stars, planets and satellites with different degrees of influence); for ease however, our preference is to use the ice-berg analogy, illustrated in Figure 7.1, which helps identify the variety of groups or stakeholders which managers and SDOs, have responsibility *to*, *for* and *need*. Whilst the obvious primary stakeholders sit above the surface of the water in the diagram, below the surface are the numerous other secondary shareholders who can in fact be just as influential and powerful.

Stakeholders, partnerships and volunteers **145**

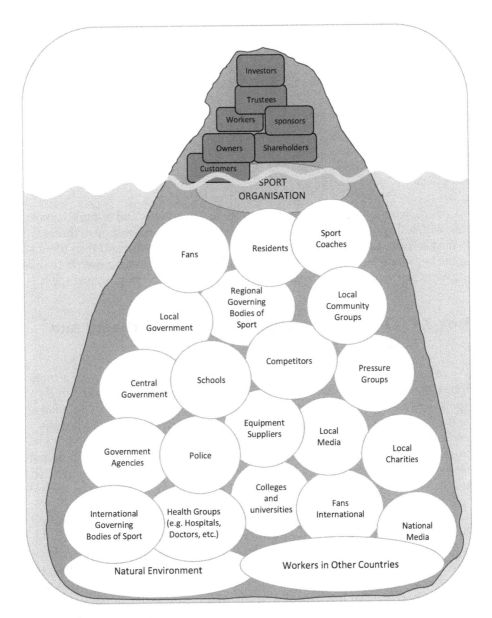

Figure 7.1 Generic Representation of Different Stakeholders.
Source: Author.

The many possible stakeholders, illustrated in Figure 7.1, offer a starting point, which can be represented in a network web diagram or table. In Figure 7.2, three simple further considerations are given to identifying different stakeholders which can help with operations management: the initial identification of groups (this can be done through a mixture of research and creative thinking); identifying their degrees of power and influence (power can come from 'within', 'with', 'to'

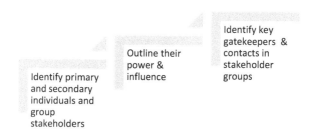

Figure 7.2 Three Simple Steps in Stakeholder Analysis.
Source: Author.

and 'over'), where encouragement is to adopt an ethical and CSR approach, where those with little power or influence are also considered (see new power theories in the next section, for more reasons why this can be important); and then identifying the key named individuals who can act as gatekeepers to their own networks, which can be invaluable source of communication, support or partnerships.

> **Box 7.1 The importance of stakeholder theory and CSR**
>
> When stakeholder theory is combined with notions of CSR, it allows a more robust analysis of the operations systems and the potential risks which a sport service might be exposed to (see also Chapter 9). In essence, CSR relates to the theory that businesses should behave in an ethical manner (i.e. to reflect on issues of right and wrong), where considerations need to be given not just to profit, but to their broader social, economic, political and environmental responsibilities they have, and the many stakeholders who can be impacted for good or bad by their business. It is an issue which is only set to increase in importance.
>
> Byers et al. (2012, p. 29), drawing on a variety of literature, emphasised the themes of integrity of the core values; responsibility towards stakeholders; a capacity for institutional reflection of their choices and the impacts on wider communities and environments. This principle of believing and acting ethically can also help enhance brands and guard against certain risks and crisis events; one just has to look at the cases of unethical behaviour sport of organisations accused of cheating, corruption, bribery or drug abuse to see the damage done to trust, reputations and brands, which in turn can test the continued viability of the business (e.g. issues of coaching abuse in Chapter 1, or the NFL and concussion discussed in Chapter 9). This is why good operation managers and SDOs should always have a key underpinning principle of ethics reflected in the mantra of:
>
> Ethics is doing the right thing when no one is looking.

Stakeholders, partnerships and volunteers 147

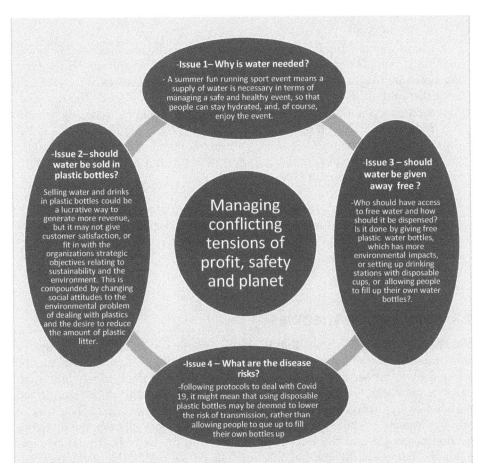

Figure 7.3 Example of a Stakeholder Paradox for a Fun Run Event.

In sport, the need to consider CSR can be of increased importance because of the many claimed beneficial outcomes of sport, highlighted in Chapter 1. In an operational context, managing the need to generate revenue and profit, managing safety and considering broader social and environmental issues can generate many paradoxical tensions, which need to be resolved. For example, a manager or SDO running a summer fun event would have to reflect and decide on the four issues, represented in Figure 7.3.

These examples of tensions for a fun run relate to what Goodpaster (1991) described as the 'stakeholder paradox', which refers to the constant system dynamic of conflicting tensions between the need to make financial returns and the needs of others in the business, local community and even the world.

Other similar tensions can be found when developing different types of sponsorship partnerships. It is a particular relevant issue related to sport

(continued)

> Box 7.2 (continued)
>
> events and sponsorship from companies who might be labelled as 'junk food' manufacturers. The tension created is that sport is often presented as having potential health outcomes; yet so many poor health issues are driven by poor diet and obesity, driven by the consumption of junk food. The result is that there is a paradoxical message, if not hypocritical one, sent out, which can undermine trust in those promoting the healthy living message. (It is an issue which has certain parallels with tobacco companies once there is a huge involvement in the sponsorship of sport events, until tobacco sponsorship was steadily banned in the 1980s and 1990s.)
>
> **Discussion**
>
> Using the example of the fun run, explain what decisions you would take to deal with the need to offer water and refreshments, considering how the decisions taken relate to CSR.

7.3 NETWORKING THEORIES

Stakeholder's analysis shows that there are a variety of individuals, groups or constituents who can have an interest in the sport organisation, or who may be affected by sport service operations and events. Using the imagery and analogies of networks – which is to say that there are a variety of interconnected parts or groups who can communicate and influence each other – is a way of refining aspects of stakeholder analysis. Network theory stresses the interconnection of people and the business environment, or the web of relationships, whereby changes in the internal, intermediate or external business environment can reverberate and impact on sport service operations. It is, yet again, using a form system theory to show the dynamic interactions of groups and individuals, in a VUCA world (See Chapter 1).

When a manager or SDO is able to map out their network of stakeholders, key gatekeepers or even super influencers, then it can prove invaluable in the effective and efficient delivery of services. Indeed, Weber and Kratzer (2013) argued that networks and networking are prerequisite for organisational survival and success, with Bjarsholm (2018) adding that sports organisation networks involve a wide range of contacts and links from all sectors of society, with the networks assuming many forms (e.g. social, institutional and reputational). Something should be evident back in Figure 7.4. Networks, therefore, allow organisations to extend their reach and gain advantage through mutual support. Using networks is also key marketing communication tool, where information and support can be disseminated through the network, whether this is via word of mouth, or using various social media platforms. An illustration of a communications network is given in Box 7.2 and in Chapter 8.

Stakeholders, partnerships and volunteers **149**

Box 7.2 Example of a communications network

In the past, before the growth of all the social media platforms, many SDOs and sport managers working in community sports might talk about their community family tree. In essence, the imagery of using a tree referred to how the roots and branches were used to show the importance of different stakeholders

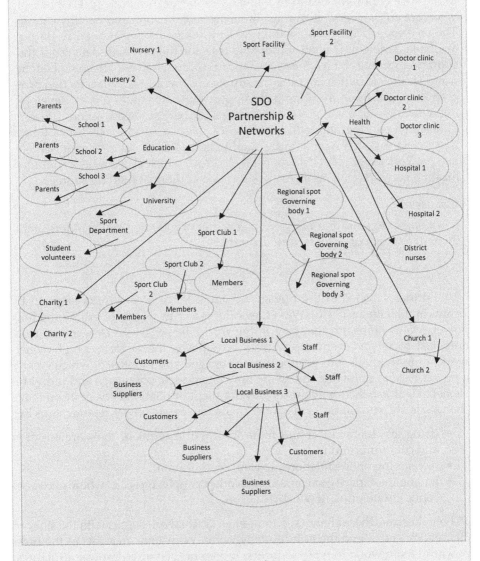

Figure 7.4 Example of Communication Network.

(continued)

> Box 7.3 (continued)
>
> (branches) and partners, who in turn could reach out to contact other groups (the leaves). Alternatively, it can be represented simply as a network connecting diagram, to show the web of interconnections between real and virtual communities, as illustrated in Figure 4.1, based on the example below.
>
> Here is an example to illustrate the importance of networks, using a simple scenario of a local or regional government, which has a broad aim to improve children's health in a town. As part of this strategy, a variety of SDOs are employed to encourage more active recreation and healthy eating. The challenge is the scale of the problem, whilst having limited resources available, whereby it is an impossible task for the SDOs to deliver all the sport programmes which the thousands of children in the town could benefit from. The key to both increasing the supply of sport and active recreation programmes and communicating these opportunities to children is by developing networks and a variety of partnerships. As part of the operations process of designing a programme (the *what, when, where, who* and *how* discussed in Chapter 4), research would be engaged to help identify the *who*, represented in a network diagram of different stakeholders, which also acts as a communication network, potential partnerships and additional funding sources.
>
> **Discussion**
>
> For a sport organisation of your choice, identify the key stakeholders, and then map them out in a network diagram.

Further salience to the power and importance of networks is given by Timms and Heimans (2018). What they offer is a critical lens for examining how power relationships are changing in the world, being driven by a mix of technological, social and economic changes. New power theory focuses on how networks of individuals and groups can be engaged and mobilised, which creates a power base to influence and shape how businesses, politicians and individuals behave. It is a theory about the development of relationships that can make changes in society. Timms et al. (2018) characterise new power relationships by:

- Being less hierarchical and more informal in terms of their organisation and communication
- developing online relationships and mobilisation
- having the capacity to connect with other people, on scale, where networks connect with other networks

To help illustrate these changes, Timms et al. (2018) work begins with the story of Harvey Weinstein and the #MeToo movement. Weinstein, once one of the most powerful Hollywood movie producers, represents classic old power structures: power was concentrated, institutionalised and underpinned by wealth, where power and wealth were accumulated over many years, which was then used to exploit and abuse women. In contrast, the rapid growth of the #MeToo movement typified new power relationships. This movement was a reaction to years of sexual harassment, abuse and violence experienced by women of all ages, around the world, where the pressures for change had built up, whereby the arrest of Weinstein acted as a catalyst to release all this pent-up frustration and anger that these abuses must stop. It was an example of a new power movement, which challenged old power values, and which was open, global, participative, and those who commented and acted had agency and value, which they used to mobilise millions around the world into direct action, demonstrations and demands for cultural and legal changes. Similarly, the #BlackLives matter campaign offers another powerful example of new power relationships, whereby the shocking killing of the black American, George Floyd, by police gave global impetus for demonstrations and demands for cultural and legal changes around the world. Timms et al. (2018) express new power as:

> Activity (e.g. sharing stories on social media, direct action, etc.) × numbers = power

New power, then, is about connecting networks, mobilisation and engagement. It is moving from passive consumption to more active engagement and shaping of experiences and services. Timms et al. (2018) say, 'new power is more flash mob and less general assembly'. They go onto say:

> The new power politics…is the management of relationships that allow agents (whether states, state agencies, companies, NGOs or individuals) to affect their fates and inclinations through collective mobilizations.
>
> (Timms et al., 2018, p. 2)

Another way of illustrating the differences is to consider how entrepreneurial projects are funded. Old power approaches might involve an entrepreneur having a few minutes to deliver a persuasive argument (i.e. the idea of the elevator pitch) to a small number of wealthy business people, as to why they should invest in their product or service (i.e. what is sometimes described the 'dragons den' type of investment scenario). In contrast, new power approaches attempt to mobilise people, usually through social media platforms, to invest in their idea or business – what is known as crowdfunding techniques, discussed in Chapter 8, in the discussion on fundraising.

In an operational context, utilising and mobilising networks can be of critical importance in terms of communications, mobilising support, animating volunteers or fundraising. The crucial foundation for doing this is to capture people's attention and interest, so they are willing to spread the idea. Here are some of the key points in terms of mobilising people in networks:

- Capacity to use a variety of social mediums, such as Twitter, Facebook, LinkedIn, etc.
- Need to be able to communicate concisely, a simple, powerful message
- You have seconds to capture attention, a few minutes to tell a story
- You need critical feedback loops for validation and to encourage engagement (e.g. using 'likes' and sharing the message with others)

- The capacity to harness the 'storms' (Timms and Heimans, 2018, p. 73), which relates to *creating storms* (e.g. releasing a media story to create controversy or publicity), *chasing storms* (i.e. using someone else's crisis event to your advantage) and *storm embracing* (i.e. you use it as an opportunity for improvement). See also Chapter 9 on crisis management for more examples.
- Creating the Ikea effect (the global Swedish furniture store, which sells furniture that people can build themselves) which means people can take more pride if they have contributed to building a movement, event or fundraising activity themselves.
- Ensure there is 'radical transparency' to help create a sense of trust and desire to be part of the group, which also links back to the CSR discussion, which is particularly important for the next generation of key consumers – Generation Z (those born from approximately 1996, following on from the millennial generation) – who tend to place more emphasis on the importance of CSR and a desire to develop more non-profit, social enterprises.
- Consider how people can move through a participation scale of involvement with sport projects, which involves:
   - Having few barriers to participation, so it is quick and easy to join
   - Capacity to scale up activism
   - Energise or inspire people to participate and spread the stories sideways
   - Focus on a key issue
   - Find connections and super participants, which relate to the people who have large networks and exposure, and can influence large numbers of people (note that this can also relate to the concept of the 'market maven' which relates to someone with a great deal of knowledge and market connections, who often wants to share their experiences, which when combined with trust can be very influential on other people's behaviour).

7.4 PARTNERSHIPS

As part of the stakeholder and network development, some of the individuals or groups identified can go onto form more intimate partnerships. In the contemporary sport business world, no matter what the sector operated in, partnerships have now become an essential part of the operational working environment. The theory of partnerships is founded on stakeholder theory, but has some unique attributes, with Simpson and Partington (2013, p. 157) making the crucial observation that the need to develop partnerships is in many job descriptions relating to sport (see Box 7.3).

Gillies (1998) describes a partnership as an association or voluntary agreement between two and more people or groups, who work cooperatively as partners towards a set of shared outcomes, with Yoshino and Rangan, (1995) emphasizing the importance of sharing some common goals. This belies the full breadth and complexity of partnerships which may be developed in sport operations. Perhaps the key point to focus on in relation to partnerships is the simple principle that more can be achieved together, rather than individually

(Corbin et al., 2016, p. 2). Partnerships can allow for the sharing of resources, expertise, communication networks, and sharing of staff, or bring in additional sources of revenue.

The nature of partnership varies. Some can be highly formal, with legally binding sponsorship contracts (see Chapter 8), whilst others may be more informal and ad hoc, particularly those relating to volunteers. There is also variation in their duration, type and scale (e.g. local, regional, national or even global). The following list gives examples of multiple types of partnerships a sport organisation can have during their normal operational delivery of services, with some applied examples given in Box 7.3:

- **Additional revenue sponsorship partnerships**: Sponsorship partnerships to bring in more money to sport organisation or club. Organisations such as FIFA or the IOC can generate millions from commercial sponsorship deals (see also Chapter 8).
- **Charity partnerships**: Charity partnerships can help raise the value of a sport brand, which for commercial sport operators, can help show a 'caring' side to their operations and publicise their CSR values. Large-scale sport events, similarly, may have charity partners which give opportunities to try and leverage the positive outcomes from participation, as illustrated in Box 7.3 (also see examples in Chapter 2 in relation to the Barca Foundation).
- **Equipment and supply partnerships**: Suppliers can raise awareness of their products, as people see their products used by the athletes, club or business, as illustrated in Box 7.4.
- **Working partnerships**: Some partners can have similar goals, but different expertise and skills. An example is how doctors and health authorities would want to encourage healthier lifestyles, or help people to rehabilitate from illness or injury.
- **Expertise partnerships**: In some instances, for sport facilities to be used more cost effectively, it can be far better to have voluntary clubs to manage some of the services. For example, a large leisure centre, which has a number of astro-turf pitches that can be used for hockey and football, may offer a mix provision of pay-as-you go hire (i.e. anyone can hire a pitch) and sport club time. These sport clubs would be in a better position to utilise their own coaches and volunteers for developing a variety of coaching sessions, for both children and adults.
- **Communication network partnership**: To communicate with others to share their networks can be done through formal networks or individual community users, as Box 7.4 illustrates.
- **Cross department partnerships**: Different people in an organisation might work jointly on a project to help with its successful delivery. An example could be someone working in the marketing department for a sport club, who could work in conjunction with an SDO, whereby the SDO can use marketing communications to get more local people involved with their new sport service; in return the marketing department gets opportunities to raise awareness about the positive work that they do, which helps raise brand awareness.

- **Cross sector partnerships**: This relates to public, commercial and voluntary organisations coming together for a common cause or project, such as any large-scale sport event will demonstrate.
- **Competitor partnerships and joint ventures**: Sometimes competitors can come together to help deliver on a project, particularly one which has wider community benefits. For example, local football teams might come together to help with some community outreach and charity programmes in deprived parts of a city.
- **Political partnerships**: Improved political power can be enhanced for potential lobbying via strategic alliances, with 'power in numbers' considered a key feature. For example, the Sport & Recreation Alliance, formerly the Central Council of Physical Recreation (CCPR), was established in 1935 to represent governing and representative bodies of sport and recreation, and provide a voice for the sports sector with government, policy makers and the media (Sport & Recreation Alliance, 2019, online).

Box 7.3 The growing importance of partnership work as discrete areas of operations management

Here are a number of examples to illustrate the variety of partnerships, in different sectors.

Case study 1 – Tottenham Hotspur Football Club: As part of the redevelopment of the stadium, they have developed and expanded the whole operational and commercial planning side to the organisation. As part of these changes, the work of partnership development has become a discrete form of specialised work, having a dedicated team of 15 staff who just focus on partnerships.

The partnerships developed not only relate to the staging of football games, but also a wide range of other events, such as corporate hospitality, social outreach work, NFL football, music concerts and many, many other activities. This partnership work requires working with many different types of partnerships, who have a local, regional or even global reach, such as:

- Main club sponsor: AIA (Lifestyle healthy living brand) are the key club sponsor
- Kit sponsor partner: Nike
- Bank Financial Partner: HSBC
- IT equipment partner: Hewlett Packard
- Gambling partners: William Hill (betting partner UK); FUN88 (Asia betting partner); Betway (African betting partner)
- Car sponsor: Audi
- Beer partner: Heineken

There are more club partnerships, which include video gaming, energy drinks, hotels and even dress suit partnerships. In addition to these club partnerships, there are also an additional 20 partners that just relate to the stadium, such as LG supplying over a 1,000 screens used around the stadium. Finally, into this mix, as part of their CSR objectives will go a variety of charity partners the club chooses to support along with many local community groups.

Case study 2 – UNICEF sport partnerships: UNICEF is part of the UN, which works around the world saving children's lives and defending their rights. It is a huge organisation, which involves dealing with some profound humanitarian crisis events resulting from war or natural disasters. Part of its strategy is to use sport to educate and rehabilitate children who have been affected by war and used as soldiers. It adopts (perhaps simplistically at times) a positive view about the power of sport to help change lives. As part of the operational delivery of the broader aim of protecting and educating children, it has developed a variety of partnerships, such as with Manchester Unities, FC Barcelona, the Special Olympics, International Cricket Council and FIFA, that are among its biggest named sport sponsors.

In terms of the actual operational delivery, it is crucial that they work with local partners. For example, in Chechnya, it supports the local non-governmental organisation, Laman AZ (Chechen for 'Voice of the Mountains'), which was part of the broader Min Action Survivor Assistance programme. UNICEF supplied the money and equipment, but it was in partnership with the local groups, who do the organisation and delivery of the non-profit sport services.

Case study 3 – Boston Marathon: The Boston Marathon is cited as the world's oldest marathon event, dating back to 1887. This annual event is one of the six world marathon majors (the others include London, Berlin, Chicago, Tokyo and New York), which has over 30,000 participants and hundreds of thousands of spectators. As part of the operational delivery, it has a variety of formal partnerships vital in the operational delivery of the event. In 2019 it had approximately 43 different types of partnerships, in a variety of areas, such as:

- Principal financial event sponsor: John Hancock investments
- Kit and apparel sponsor: Adidas
- Charity partnerships: Dana-Farber Cancer Institute and Jimmy Fund; Brigham and Women's Hospital and the Special Olympics Massachusetts.

In addition, they have many other subsidiary partnerships relationships, such as the supply partnerships of CITGO (official fuel sponsor); Poland Spring (official water sponsor); CLIF Bar (official sports nutrition supplier); Samael Adams (official beer sponsor); Gatorade (official energy drink supplier); Tata Consultancy (technology consultant); NBC (national television sponsor) and WBZ TV (local broadcaster partner). The list goes on to include airlines, vehicles and even a 'official leg cramp relief partnership' (Hyland's Leg cramps supplier).

Discussion

For a sport of your choice, research the key partners they work with and the type of partnership relationship they have.

For many community sport managers and SDOs working on limited budgets, and potentially working as lone deliverers covering large-scale areas or facilities, the need to work in partnership and develop alliances should be considered as essential to ensure successful delivery of sport services and the achievement of outcomes. The example given in Box 7.2 illustrates this, where identifying the network of stakeholders also acts to identify key partners who can assist in the delivery and communication of services. In order to achieve and deliver proposed services, as well as producing sound evidence of need, the SDO must 'sell' and promote the concept to key partners, which generally involves aligning their objectives and outcomes to their potential partner. Each organisation who forms part of the partnership remains independent of the other partners involved, so do not lose their strategic autonomy (Dussauge & Garrette, 1999), but are required to jointly work together to achieve collaborative delivery of a service or product.

7.5 THE THIRD SECTOR AND VOLUNTEERS

A crucial part of the stakeholder, network and partnership analysis is the identification and use of potential volunteers. The importance of volunteers is an essential component of many international sport systems, because without them it is unlikely that many sport activities would take place (Sport England, 2019). Indeed, Koutrou and Downward (2016) state bluntly that sports could not survive without volunteers. At times, volunteers are the generators of services, whilst at other times (See Box 7.3), they are necessary partners in the effective and efficient delivery of programmes and events (see Box 7.4). The reason why they are important goes back to the discussion in Chapters 1 and 2 on market failures (i.e. it is not profitable to provide sport services to all who need them or who could benefit) and government failures (i.e. governments do not have the money or expertise to deliver sport services to all those who need or could benefit from them). The result is that this gap in the need and want for sport services is often filled by individuals and groups volunteering their time and expertise to offer or support the delivery of services, which can range from: event marshalling; acting as trustees and committee members to help manage clubs; acting as a taxi services and washing dirty kit; and helping to raise funds and coach participants.

Box 7.4 Doha world athletics championship and the night of 10,000 metres personal bests (PBs)

Having millions of dollars to spend does not guarantee a successful sport event. The World Athletics Championship in September 2019, Doha, Qatar, showed that even though you have billions to spend, unless attention is paid to the operational and marketing details, any event will struggle. The Khalifa Stadium, first built in 1976, has been radically refurbished and considered 'state of the art' in terms of technology and innovative design, such as having an open-air stadium that is air conditioned. Despite this impressive stadium, the event organisers struggled to fill the 40,000 capacity stadium, which robbed the athletes competing at the World Championships of a competitive, atmospheric arena, to help drive their performances.

This failure to fill the stadium was due to a number of factors, such as: a lack of local population to generate domestic demand in the country, where athletics is not a significant part of their sport participation; the cost of overseas travel; and regional political tensions with Saudi Arabia and its allies. To deal with the problem of empty stands, the organisers put sponsorship flags over large parts of the seating to give a better visual impression for the global media and reduce the stadium down to 21,000. In addition, because of the lack of international travellers and domestic demand, the organisers were forced to give thousands of free tickets to the migrant workers from Africa and India, many of whom were working on the 2022 Football World Cup stadiums. In one instance, this meant that a decent sizeable core of Ethiopian workers was there to cheer on their long distance athletes.

Contrast this with an athletic event which was started by volunteers of an amateur athletic club in London, the Highgate Harriers. Ben Pochee noticed that there was a shortage of high-quality long distance athletic running events (Highgate Harriers 2020). He decided to organise an event which could attract elite runners, together with bringing in bigger crowds to help generate more interest and excitement, by having additional fun events for families and the community. From these small beginnings, in 2013, the event has now grown so that thousands of people attend the 'Night of the 10,000m PB's race', which runs over a few days. What is different about this event is that it has been compared with a music festival, full of joy and excitement, with a number of athletes eulogising about what an exciting atmosphere it is to compete in. As the event has grown, so too has the quality of athletes and competition, whereby, in 2018, Germany's Richard Ringer and Israel's Chemtai Salpeter posted the fastest European times of the year, describing it as one of the best 10,000 metres event they had experienced.

Why has it been so successful in attracting thousands of spectators and top-class athletes? It is down to the volunteers who love the sport and the imaginative ways they have tried to convey this passion, such as additional family fun events, music and a beer festival, which all combined to create a party atmosphere. Other innovations include having a bridge over the athletics track, so spectators can get close to the action and even more bold; having a beer tent (called the 'lactate tunnels of love') that straddles the race track, so the running lanes are filtered down to a couple of running lanes; and the athletes are cheered on by spectators who are literally standing next to the running lines. Add in the use of ringing cow bells, pyrotechnics and cheering on the athletes, and a very special atmosphere is generated for long distance running races, which had gained a reputation as being dull, 'metronomic experiences'.

(continued)

> Box 7.4 (continued)
>
> What this illustrates is that volunteers can play a vital lynchpin in both supporting and actually providing sport services that are designed for the participant, and to paraphrase the words of the Beatles song, 'they don't care to much for money, money can't buy you love' and that is what volunteers bring, which no money can buy.
>
> **Discussion**
>
> How can volunteers be used to create other, free exciting sport services and events to help attract people into a sport?

This filling of the gap in service provision by the third sector is perhaps not always given the credit it deserves. When looking at the history of sports, the establishment of countless sport clubs around the world is frequently started by groups of volunteers gathering together, whether it is for personal recreation, or to share the pleasure and benefits of their activity. Although many of these clubs and sports have now grown in terms of their scale and the breadth of the commercial exploitation, this has not necessarily seen the diminishing of the voluntary sector contribution. Indeed, as the sport has grown in its commercial appeal, so too has the importance of the voluntary sector, whereby there has also been a growth in social entrepreneurships, where individuals and groups exhibit the creativity, innovation and dynamism often shown in the private sector, but do this for no financial profit, but numerous personal and community benefits. (see Boxes 7.3 and 7.4).

> **Box 7.5 Volunteers and the Japan Rugby World Cup**
>
> According to the Rugby World Cup (RWC), the Japan Rugby 2019 organising committee launched its 'Team No-Side' volunteer programme, aiming to have over 10,000 volunteers across 12 cities. In the end they recruited over 13,000 volunteers, after receiving 38,000 applications, with 2,400 volunteers operating in Tokyo (Japan Times, 2019). They used the term 'No-Side' as a symbol of respect, hospitality and solidarity, which is rooted in Japanese rugby tradition going back to the 1920s. The recruitment programme ran from April to July in 2018, with the schedules of interviews and final notifications in January 2019, then staff assigned in the summer of 2019. The stipulation for applying was that people must be able to commit to 8 hours a day, be over 18 years old and be able to communicate in various languages (Japan Times, 2019; World Rugby, 2018). In addition, as each of the games was spread out, throughout the country, there would be a whole host of additional, local volunteers, helping out with a variety of activities and community events.
>
> The role of volunteering particularly stood out in one of the towns' staging games: Kamaishi. Kamaishi is city on the Northeast coast of Japan and

was known for three things: fishing, steel and rugby. That narrative, however, changed in 2011, when the town was destroyed by a Tsunami, in which an estimated 994 people died (not including the 152 missing), along with 3,656 homes destroyed, for a town with a total population of around 35,000. As the town recovered, volunteers were vital in the early stages of the disaster recovery programme. Volunteers would come from all parts of the country and even internationally, helping to rebuild communities, some delivering a variety of sport outreach programmes. It was also the work of many local volunteers who developed the idea to bid for the rights to stage a world cup rugby game, even though they had no stadium and there was so much damage to the local infrastructure. It was a bold move, but one which meant they could leverage the world cup to help rebuild the town and its sea defences more quickly.

After winning the rights to stage games, they set to work. On the site of the old school, which was destroyed by the tsunami, they built a new rugby stadium (the school was rebuilt on safer, higher ground) called the Memorial Stadium, and on the 25th September, Fiji played Uruguay. This game was perhaps one of the most emotionally charged and poignant games, not because of the game itself (even though it was a thrilling game, where Uruguay pulled off a memorable win), but it was because of the context. The game was attended by Prince Akishino, the brother of the Japanese Emperor, and opened with a passionate account from a young woman, who was a child at the time of the disaster, followed by a symbolic flyby from the Japanese air force.

In addition to all this volunteering that already taken place in the staging of the game and rebuilding of the city, there was still more examples of volunteering taking place. There were numerous outside charities, who leveraged the rugby tournament, to stage many mini-events, such as the fun rugby events and fun runs. Some of the fun runs for the children had an additional social outcome, in that they were designed to educate the children the importance of running to higher ground, if the tsunami alerts are sounded.

For the second game, between Canada and Namibia, sadly this ended up being cancelled because of the devastating typhoon that swept through the country. This again saw numerous volunteers come out, such as the Canadian rugby team who helped to clear the stadium of flood debris. The Kamaishi Seawaves rugby team, who helped the local community in the 2011 disaster, were also out on the Sunday, physically helping to clean up the roads from all the mud and flood debris (but getting less social media attention then their Canadian counterparts). Then there were the many locals who organised a spontaneous fishing boat flag ceremony near the stadium, for all the fans who would now no longer have a game to watch. Kamaishi, although it did not stage one of the big nation rugby games, was seen by many as one of the highlights of the tournament, helping to show the vital necessity of volunteers and how to leverage events to achieve a variety of outputs and sport event legacies.

(continued)

> Box 7.5 (continued)
>
> People volunteering not only makes many sport events and services possible, they also give it its heart and soul. As with many events, the volunteers in the rugby tournament were signalled out for the joy and sense of fun they brought, particularly at the end of games in both stadiums and fanzones, where they would line up, giving the fans high-fives, warm smiles and a big 'Arigatou' (thank you).
>
> **Discussion**
>
> Is using volunteers a way of providing sport services on the cheap, or do they give many sport events and services their integrity and joy?

Clearly then in terms of the historical importance and development of sport and the current supply of sport services, the voluntary sector is vital. For example, Sport England (2016) estimated that the sport and physical activity sector engages 5.6 million volunteers each month: putting the sector the third highest in terms of volunteer numbers behind education (including schools, colleges and universities) and religion, but ahead of health (and disability) and children's sectors (Sport England, 2016). If one looks at the mega-events, such as the Olympics or Football world cup, the numbers of volunteers can be quite astonishing. For the 2012 London Olympics, for example, it was estimated that over 70,000 people volunteered to help with the sporting festival, which some estimating it equated eight million hours of voluntary work. In Russia, for the 2018 Football world cup, it was estimated that they used 35,000 volunteers. Crucially, not only are these hours of work vital to the smooth operational delivery of an event, but it is also the energy and enthusiasm that they bring, which is why they so frequently get mentioned in closing ceremonies, as illustrated in Box 7.4.

7.6 OPERATIONS MANAGEMENT SKILLS AND KNOWLEDGE NEEDED FOR NETWORKING, PARTNERSHIPS AND MANAGING VOLUNTEERS

Clearly then, the identification of key stakeholders, the development of networks and partnerships and the effective use of volunteers is an essential part of the operations management process. In order that this work is effectively done, the following skills and knowledge are needed, but which can be explored in more specialist books and journal papers:

- **Leadership**: Confidence in leadership, reaffirmed by capacity to complete jobs and effectively delegate them (see Chapter 2)
- **People skills and emotional intelligence**: This can range from having a capacity to collaborate and work in teams, to having emotional intelligence to understand the needs and wants of potential or actual partners, or how to sustain motivation with volunteer groups

- **Research skills**: It is vital to be able to find out about the needs of potential stakeholders, partnerships and volunteers (see Chapter 10)
- **Communication**: The capacity to communicate key ideas is vital, which also overlaps with new power theories, negotiation and listening skills. Whilst a capacity to utilise social media is important, using traditional communication techniques, such as word of mouth should not be underestimated – in one survey for small sport clubs, it was estimated 66% of volunteers are recruited directly via word of mouth, via friends and family (Sport England, 2016).
- **Setting realistic expectations**: Simpson et al. (2013) observed how partnerships can go through lifecycles, such as starting with optimism, where they are full of hopes, but later tensions can occur, particularly if people are felt ignored (see also Chapter 5 and the key principles of customer care).
- **Training**: Organising proper volunteer and staff training is vital in terms of ensuring quality of service (see Chapter 5) and healthy and safe playing and working spaces (see Chapter 9).

Despite the importance of volunteers and the huge numbers of people around the world who volunteer, many clubs and organisations can still report that there are shortfalls in the numbers of volunteers required. The Sport & Recreation Alliance (2019), for example, reported that 7 out of 10 sports clubs do not have enough support and need more willing volunteers (Join In UK, 2014). There are therefore two critical questions, which relate to:

- Gaining and motivating volunteers to help support sport services
- Maintain involvement, motivation and satisfaction

To begin with, it is vital that volunteers are found and motivated to support. Here, it can be helpful to adapt some of the principles discussed in Chapter 4, about understanding the needs and wants of the participants and what motivates them. For example, according to one UK survey, people volunteer and give their time to sport mainly because they enjoy it (35%) and as a way to give back to their community (25%) (Join In UK, 2014). Much research has always been focused on those who benefit from volunteering, as opposed to what the volunteers get out of it. Volunteers provide time, energy and expertise, and support to those playing sport, but equally can gain benefits themselves. These benefits can be seen to align with current outcomes for sport, as proposed by Sport England (2016), such as: physical and mental well-being; individual development; social and community development; and economic development. Encouraging new volunteers should therefore begin by understanding their needs and wants, communicating to them, then attempting to remove the barriers to volunteering.

The gathering of volunteers is only part of the process. What is just as important is maintaining their commitment and motivation, and avoiding feelings that they are being exploited. Recruitment of such supportive and hard-working individuals is always a concern for many local sport clubs whose existence relies on their selflessness and generosity of time and attention. Indeed, three-quarters of those who volunteer in England do so in sports clubs, and yet a good number has shown dissatisfaction, being twice as likely to reduce their time commitment or stop completely, as to those in other sectors (Sport England, 2016), so it is vital that they are never taken for granted, their efforts are always recognised and communicated, along with offering opportunities for further skill enhancement and development.

7.7 CONCLUSION

Let us state it bluntly: Many services could not be efficiently, effectively and safely delivered without partnerships and volunteers. They are sometimes needed for their money, sometimes for the time, sometimes for the labour and sometimes for their experience. Into this mix must go the importance of understanding the wide variety of stakeholders who need, and interests must be considered, particularly if they have little power or influence. Some of these stakeholders can go onto form more formal partnerships, who are used for mutual gain and can provide anything from money and expertise, or to help with the brand image and CSR.

CSR is now of critical importance as new power relations continue to grow, whereby acting ethically with utter transparency seems to become more important, particularly as younger generations of consumers emerge, who can be more sensitive and responsive to organisations which they believe and trust to act ethically. Fulfilling the responsibilities a sport organisation has to different stakeholder can contribute to success far beyond financial monetary outputs.

References

Bjarsholm, D. (2018). Networking as a cornerstone within the practice of social entrepreneurship in sport. *European Sport Management Quarterly*, Volume 19, 2019 – Issue 1: Social Responsibility and the European Sport Context.

Byers, T., Slack, T., and Parent, M.A. (2012). *Key Concepts in Sport Management*. London: Sage.

Corbin, J.H., Jones, J., and Barry, M.M. (2016). What makes intersectional partnerships for health promotion work? A review of the international literature. *Health Promotion International*, 33(1), 4–26.

Clarkson, M.B.E. (1995). A stakeholder framework for analysing and evaluating corporate social performance. *Academy of Management Review*, 20, 92–117 cited in Byers, T., Slack, T., and Parent, M.A. (2012). *Key Concepts in Sport Management*. London: Sage.

Dussauge, P., and Garrette, B. (1999). *Cooperative Strategy: Competing Successfully Through Strategic Alliances*. London: John Wiley. ISBN: 978-0-471-97492.

Gillies, P. (1998). Effectiveness of alliances and partnerships for health promotion. *Health Promotion International*, 13, 99–120.

Goodpaster, K. (1991). Business ethics and stakeholder analysis. *Business Ethics Quarterly*, 1(1), 53–73.

Highgate Harriers (2020). 'Night of the PBs' 10,000 m race at Parliament Hill? available at: https://www.highgateharriers.org.uk/hh_aa_interviews.php?i=284

Japan Times (2019). Rugby world cup organisers recruit more than 13,000, *Japan Times*, 15 January 2019, accessed 20 September 2019, available at: https://www.japantimes.co.jp/sports/2019/01/15/rugby/rugby-world-cup-organizers-recruit-13000-volunteers/#.Xb6mXS2cbUo

Join In UK (2014). Hidden diamonds: Uncovering the true value of sport volunteers, accessed 5 February 2020, available at: http://sramedia.s3.amazonaws.com/media/documents/0ebbd77c-bdf1-4568-b63d-156164550539.pdf

Koutrou, N., and Downward, P. (2016). Event and club volunteer potential: the case of women's rugby in England. *International Journal of Sport and Politics*, 8(2), 207–230.

Simpson, K., and Partington, J. (2013). Strategic partnerships. In Tobson, S., Simpson, K., and Tuck, L. (eds.), *Strategic Sport Development*. London: Routledge, pp. 148–174.

Sport England (2016). Volunteering in an active nation strategy 2017–2021, accessed 5 February 2020, available at: https://www.sportengland.org/media/11323/volunteering-in-an-active-nation-final.pdf

Sport and Recreation Alliance Club Survey (2019). accessed 5 February 2020, available at: http://sramedia.s3.amazonaws.com/media/documents/809016c4-9819-49ee-8dd7-d32e6070d05d.pdf

Timms, H., and Heimans, J. (2018). *Newpower*. London: Picador.

Weber, C., and Kratzer, J. (2013). Social entrepreneurship, social networks and social value creation: A quantitative analysis among social entrepreneurs. *International Journal of Entrepreneurial Venturing*, 5(3), 217–239. doi: 10.1504/IJEV.2013.055291.

World Rugby (2018). Volunteer programme RWC 2019, available at: https://www.rugbyworldcup.com/volunteers

Yoshino, M., and Rangan, U.S. (1995). *Strategic Alliances: An Entrepreneurial Approach to Globalization*. Boston, MA: Harvard Business School Press.

8 FUNDRAISING, SPONSORSHIP AND DIGITAL TARGET MARKETING

Challenges for managers

- Why do sport organisations need to generate revenue from a variety of sources?
- What techniques and tools can be used to fill funding gaps?
- How have new power relationships changed the funding environment?

8.1 INTRODUCTION

The funding of sport, around the world, is full of paradoxes and inequities. For some elite athletes, sport clubs or governing bodies, they can receive quite astronomical amounts of money: in contrast, there are numerous examples of athletes in less popular sports, or small community sport clubs, or even sport development officers (SDOs), who will find themselves in a perpetual struggle to fill gaps in funding, in order to ensure their continued operations. Little surprise then that having the skills and knowledge to seek and secure money from a variety of funding streams has grown in importance for sport operations.

Although financial management is one of the core business functional areas, the specific skills of finance and accounting are not discussed here. Instead, this chapter examines the subject of funding gaps and how they can be filled to ensure organization are competitive and service operations remain viable. This chapter focuses on some of the practical approaches to bridging funding gaps, or gaining additional income streams to enhance profit and competitiveness. It examines the different funding sources, ranging from submitting grant applications, crowd funding campaigns and other methods of fundraising. Considerations are also given to how new power relationships and social media, discussed in Chapter 7, continues to transform the sport funding environment.

8.2 THE FUNDING GAP

Sport contributes to the economic health of any nation through direct and indirect employment, income from taxation and money flows from events and sales of sports goods and services. Sport as a global economic activity can generate some quite staggering amounts of money. Consider some of these statistics:

Fundraising, sponsorship **165**

- Commercial investment in sport, evidenced by sponsorship revenues, has increased year-on-year to a worldwide spend of $66.4 billion in 2018 (Statista, 2019).
- The American NFL team, the Dallas Cowboys, is among the richest sport clubs in the world, where it was able to generate an estimated $340 million in sponsorship and premium-seating revenue at the AT & T stadium (note the stadium having sold the naming rights to a sponsor to generate more revenue). The Cowboys has been ranked as the world's most valuable sports franchise for four years in a row, worth $5 billion, with recorded profits in 2017 being $365 million, operating in the world's richest league (Badenhhausen, 2019)
- The Spanish football team, Real Madrid ranked third in Forbes 50 richest clubs, was worth an estimated $4.2 billion, operating in La Liga, where it earned over $100 million for winning La Liga in 2018.
- Some sport stars can be worth huge amounts of money, which can come from salaries/prize money or sponsorship deals, as the following examples of the most valuable athletes in the world, according to Forbes (2019), show: Lionel Messi, a football player for Barcelona earned $127 million ($92 million in salary and $35 million in sponsorship endorsements); Canelo Alverez, a boxer, earned $94 million ($92 million in salary/winnings and $2 million in sponsorship and endorsements); Roger Federer, a tennis player, earned $93.4 million ($7.4 million in salary/winnings and $86 million in endorsements and sponsorship); and Russell Wilson, a American Football, earned $89.5 million ($80.5 million salary/winnings and $9 million in endorsements and sponsorships).

Whilst these are some striking amounts of money in the top echelons of sport, it is far from an equitable distribution. First, depending on the economic sector worked in (i.e. public, private or voluntary) can influence the type of funding challenges faced. For the commercial private sector, money will come from primary spend (e.g. the ticket to watch a sport event), where a price will usually be set to make a profit (see Chapter 4 for examples of pricing services) and secondary spend items (e.g. money spent on food and drink at an event). In addition, commercial sport organisations will also look for ways to try and reduce input costs, such as staffing or raw materials, which can further enhance profit margins. Other funding streams, such as selling advertising space or developing a range of sponsorship deals, offer (increasingly) vital additional sources of revenue, which all contribute to give a profitable return for owners and shareholders. Yet even with all these funding streams, it can perhaps be surprising how many sport clubs can actually still make a loss, such as Barcelona – one of the most valuable football clubs in the world, with strong global brand appeal – still managing to post a loss of $37 million in 2018, because of excessive player wages (Badenhhausen, 2019).

One other vital observation to make about the list of the richest teams and athletes is that they are all male, which is an indictment of the glaring gender inequities in the distribution of money in sport. Whilst there is no doubt that women have made considerable inroads in the equity of opportunity and participation, there is still a long way to go in terms of equity of money, media coverage and gaining senior management and coaching positions in sport organisations. All of which can be framed as important issues, which can be partly changed through operational practices.

In the public and voluntary sectors, there are a different set of funding challenges. For sport organisations operating in these sectors, because the rationale for sport services is based on sport being considered as – to use the language of economists – a merit good. This means that sport is viewed as having a capacity to generate many positive externalities or spin-offs outcomes, such as improving people's physical, mental and social health and well-being. These claimed beneficial outcomes, outlined in Chapter 1, together with the arguments of equity of provision, go some way to explain why governments around the world are willing to fund and subsidise non-profit making sport services (see back to Chapter 1 and Box 1.1 for a fuller discussion of the claimed benefits of sport). Sport services offered in these public and voluntary sectors, whilst they can still generate income via primary spending on services, the price charged may only help the provider break-even (i.e. just cover the operational input expenditure costs). Indeed, it can be quite common to set the price below the BEP (Break Even Point) to encourage more users, particularly those on low incomes. The result is a gap in the funding which helps explain why fundraising has become a growing, vital knowledge and skill set for sport managers and SDOs.

What has compounded funding gap challenges for sport services in the voluntary and public sector is that in many countries, after the 2008 global financial crisis, governments around the world cut back spending on sport, as they attempted to try and reduce government debt. For example, in the UK, spending on sport was initially protected because of the commitment to the 2012 London Olympics in 2012, but afterwards, public expenditure on sport declined from £984 million since 2014/15 to £3.013 billion in 2018. For comparison, the UK in 2017/18 Governement spent: £4.339 billion on prisons; £4.66 billion on roads; £38.7 billion on defence (Statista, 2019). This meant funding for some sport reduced, programmes was, such the funding for Sport England went down 33% over four years, whilst for UK Sport, funding was reduced by 28% (Slater, 2010). The policies of austerity after the global 2008 financial crisis have seen deep public sector cuts in funding (not just within sport) across the Eurozone, including public sector job losses, increased retirement age and government spending reductions.

Additional funding, then, will be sought for a variety of reasons, which can be summarised as:

- **Competitiveness**: This focuses on securing sponsorship deals can increase profit and money for investment to maintain competitiveness, such as developing a winning team, or better shareholder returns.
- **Continued operations**: This relates to ensuring sport services with social objectives are able to continue.
- **Improvements**: Additional money is often needed to improve the quality of experience and achievement of outcomes, which is important to maintain or rejuvenate demand in the product life cycle (e.g. purchasing new equipment or playing areas, discussed in Chapter 4).

- **Create**: There is often a need to create new sport services (e.g. to meet identified target group needs based on community research).
- **Morality**: This focuses on the arguments of equity of opportunity and provision, whereby those who may not be able to afford to participate in sport should not necessarily be denied the right to participate.

The rest of this chapter explores the practical operational aspects of finding and securing different revenues and sources of funding to maintain competitive advantage, or to fill a funding gap, to ensure the continued viability of the sport organisation. Remember, this chapter focuses on the alternative sources of revenue beyond primary spend and secondary spend.

8.3 OVERVIEW OF FUNDING TECHNIQUES AND THE ART OF PERSUASION

When examining the operation and project processes which may be engaged with for generating funds beyond primary and secondary spends, many of the theories and concepts discussed in other chapters need to be blended into the operational practices of fundraising. For example, putting in a grant bid can be considered as a project (Chapter 6), which will need a capacity to set SMART objectives (Chapter 2), identify potential outcomes (Chapter 1) and then be managed using both project and time management skills and techniques (Chapter 3). In addition, a key part of many funding bids is often the need to identify key stakeholders and partnerships (Chapter 7). Implicit within this process is the need to understand basic marketing concepts (Chapter 4) and consideration of the many other external environmental challenges (Chapter 1). Finally, there is a need to be able to utilise a variety of communication methods, ranging from writing emails, producing sponsorship packs, making videos, completing grant bids or doing short presentations to a live audience, all of which is underpinned by evidence collected from research (Chapters 4, 5 and 10).

In addition, using new power theories give further critical insights into fundraising activities. To recap from Chapter 7, new power is defined by its use of extensive networks and partnerships, and how these relationships are developed and mobilised, usually via social media, whereby the numbers involved create a power base to help bring about change, or, as it is used here, to help create a funding platform via the process of crowdfunding. New power relations are given further impetus by the Generation Z group (i.e. those people born from 2000 onwards), who have been described as the true digital natives (i.e they have used digital technologies for all of their lives), characterised by being more socially aware and sensitive to ethical issues, that influence their purchasing of goods and services. New power reflects how technology has created new funding opportunities, which are combined with willingness to engage with these activities, but where changing social attitudes – particularly in terms of ethics – has become vital underpinnings, particularly where younger generations are reached out to.

When looking at the subsequent specific sections on fundraising techniques, various theories on the art of persuasion can be helpful for the operations manager and SDO to develop convincing and powerful arguments, to persuade

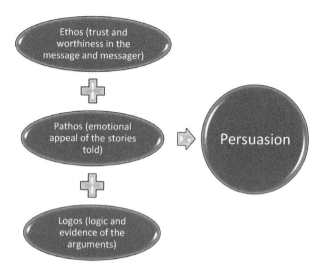

Figure 8.1 The Foundations of Persuasion.
Source: Adapting Aristotle's three classic elements of proof, cited in Borg (2008).

others to give financial support. Borg (2008) examined the art, not the science, of persuasion. He begins his work by looking at Aristotle's three classic types of proof, which form the foundations of persuasion. They still offer a simple and easy way to approach the art of persuasion, where the three types of proof are summarised in Figure 8.1.

These elements need a brief elaboration. Ethos refers to the credibility and the trust that people have and that their values and opinions are viewed as credible. Logos is the appeal to logic, which relates to the words, facts and evidence produced. Finally, pathos is the emotional part of the message, which can appeal to a variety of emotions. There can be many variations of these principles in the business functions. Although Aristotle placed logic as the most important factor in persuasion, Borg (2008) and many others disagree, arguing that it is often the emotional appeal which can be the critical ingredient for changing behaviour. He says facts are not enough, arguing that 'contemporary persuasion is now rarely done through argumentation. It seems to operation outside the edge of reason' (Borg, 2008, p. 24). It is not that facts are unimportant – examples given in this chapter point to them being very important – but it is often the emotional appeal which generates the energy for action.

Here is simple example of how some of these elements of persuasion can come into play, which can nudge people's behaviours to achieve both social objectives and brand enhancement. It relates to Nike's (2012) video called '5 extra years'. The 'logis' arguments relate to the forecast that young people's longevity was acknowledged as being five years less than their parents due to lack of physical activity and poor lifestyle choices. The short video asks a variety of children what they would do if they had five more years, with answers ranging from "I'd buy more hamsters" or "I'd build a helicopter – a wooden helicopter – but I don't have any wood". In terms of the pathos or emotional arguments, these were very powerful, mixing humour, sadness, shock and even perhaps guilt. The degree of trust in the message can be strengthened by the use of children describing these things. In terms of Nike, some would see it as a trusted company, whilst others might see it as a cynical ploy by Nike. Whatever position taken, it is a video worthwhile scrutinising to see how to tell a powerful video story in a couple of minutes. In terms of the 'nudge' and changes of behaviour, this video can act as leverage to encourage more physical activity.

In Table 8.1, a summary of some of the factors which can be leveraged to try and persuade people and organisations to give money is given. It should be noted that ethos is particularly important in relation to new power theories, whereby there must be trust in the people and organising requesting funds, which can come from endorsements, testimonials and a scrupulous track record in behaving responsibly, transparently and ethically (Timms & Heimans, 2018). In terms of emotions, some will be obvious, such as instilling pride and passion, but some might be surprised to see more negative elements, such as guilt or anger. The reason why these are put in is that they can provide legitimate emotions to appeal to, helping people to reflect on their own positions of privilege, or

Table 8.1 Sample Factors Which Can Be Leveraged for Persuasion

Ethos (Ethics and Trust)	*Pathos (Emotional Appeals)*	*Logis (Factual Arguments)*
- Demonstration of empathy - Clarity of communications and utter transparency - Listen to people's concerns - Establishing codes of best practice - Outlining CSR values - Ethical commitment (i.e. doing the right thing when no one is looking, such as not accepting bribes, cheating, engaging with drug doping) - Using partnership endorsements of trusted individuals, such as athletes, or trusted organisations and quality benchmarks	- Sense of pride - Collectivism and belonging - Inspiration and hope - Embarrassment and shame - Sense of injustice - Telling individual stories to outline the needs for support, or how they have benefited	- Output data based on past services or comparative examples; evidence of benefits based on academic research; using statistical data on community profiles - Evidence of outcomes, where behaviour has changed, or impacts have been made on the community - A capacity to cost out a service, plan it and map out how it can be delivered - Capacity to write SMART objectives - Develop and show plans for how the project will be achieved

Some principles of good communications
Tell a story; do not overwhelm with too many facts; just try and use a few 'killer' statistics; focus on brevity and clarity of message; relate stories and messages (i.e. people can relate to the story and the concepts used); rehearse live presentations; proof read all copy which is outward facing, getting others to read and check it; capture using photos, videos, banner headlines and quotes; get testimonials

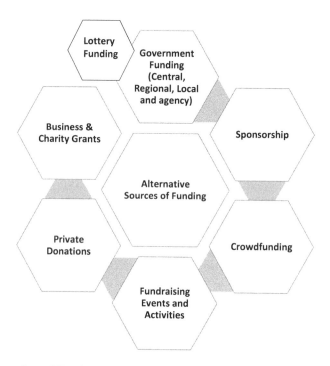

Figure 8.2 Overview of Funding Sources.
Source: Piekarz.

to sting people into action through guilt or even anger and injustices. Finally, the logos factors draw on gathering proper research and evidence of the numbers who can benefit or how they benefit (see also Chapter 10). Here a mix of data can be used, which could be generated by the sport manager and SDO, such as using any output data or using more detailed academic research of the benefits. One observation to make is that depending on the fund applied for can influence the type of persuasion focused on. You will see that often for government-based grants, there can be more emphasis on the *logos* elements (i.e. the hard facts and data); in contrast, for grants made available by private companies or crowdfunding campaigns, the pathos elements can be more important.

These theories of new power relationships and the art of persuasion should be considered in relation to the more specific, practical aspects of fundraising, outlined in Figure 8.2.

When looking at Figure 8.2, a few observations should be made:

- Those providing the additional sources of money can be based in government, the charitable voluntary sector or commercial providers.
- Organisations from any sector can seek additional revenue from these different sources of money.

- Funding can form a mix or cocktail of different funding sources, so it is possible for commercial organisations to seek money from government and charities, or voluntary organisations seeking money from commercial organisations, government and charities.

For the rest of this chapter, each of these different funding sources is explored in more detail.

8.3.1 Government funding and grant applications (including lottery funding)

Most governments around the world will award money to support a variety of sport services.

The amount governments give to support sport services and the mechanisms for distributing money is far more variable. There is not the scope here to explain all these variations in government funding rationales and mechanisms for distributing funds; there is, however, opportunity to identify some of the core features of putting in bids for money, to support sport operations, services and projects. The ubiquity of governments from around the world giving grants of money allows for a simple comparative analysis to be conducted, in order to identify a few key principles when bidding for government money, whether it is done directly to governments or via a government agency. In Table 8.2 a number of examples of grant money for sport projects are compared, based on different countries who may distribute money via government departments, regional governments or government agencies (in theory using government agencies can allow the allocation of money to be distributed using the 'arm's length principle', which means money can be given without government interference – a theory that does not always match the reality).

There are countless other examples of grants made available by governments around the world, but even from this simple comparative analysis presented in Table 8.2, it is possible to distil some key principles of good practice which the operations manager and SDO should consider. When comparing approaches, whilst the terminology may vary, the following key points can be observed:

- **Budgeting**: An ability to cost out the sport project (see Chapter 4 for how to do this)
- **Output data**: Identifying who can be targeted (community groups or market segments) and benefit (see Chapter 10 for examples of data), which can be found from a mix of databases
- **Outcome data**: Identifying how people will benefit, which MUST be related to the criteria specified in the grant applied for. This might require additional research, to evidence the effectiveness of the programmes and its impact and legacies
- **Leverage mechanisms**: An ability to explain how the outputs and outcomes can be achieved

Table 8.2 Examples of Different Government Grants Available for Sport

Name of Grant and Country	Description	Key Measures and Processes
Legacy Partnership, made available by New South Wales Government (NSW, 2019), New Zealand	NSW have made a variety of grants available as part of the 2022 UCI World Cycling Championships (September 2022). This is described as the 'pinnacle event in the international road cycling calendar' (NSW, 2019), which involves both men and women's races, and different age groups. They have made a variety of grants available to non-profit organisations, designed to achieve a different objectives, such as: - Increase opportunities for participation in cycling - Support initiatives that increase opportunities for participation in cycling - Provide a platform to galvanise the community interest and support to deliver legacy as part of the W2022 (NSW, 2019)	Any bid put in must address at least one of the previously described objectives, which will form a key part of the assessment criteria These criteria involve producing evidence relating to input data (e.g. number and types of users of the service or project); output data (how they will benefit); a costed budget of the project is produced; demonstration of the capacity and experience to deliver the project; evidence of partners; demonstration of new and innovative ideas; geographical spread; evidence of legacy; and the reach, diversity and scale of the increase in participation Once a bid is submitted, this will be scrutinised by a panel, and if passed, the submitters will be invited to do a 20-minute presentation, where they can pitch their case for why they deserve the money
The International Sports Programming Initiative (ISPI), Bureau of Educational and Cultural Affairs, USA	The Federal Government Department has an annual open competition for U.S. public and private non-profit organisations to bid for sport grants. The grants are designed for underserved youth and/or their coaches/sports administrators who manage youth sports programs. It is also quite openly used as a tool for sports diplomacy, or soft power, as an extension of 'U.S. foreign policy goals through interaction with hard-to-reach groups such as at-risk youth, women, minorities, people with disabilities, and non-English speakers'. It also aims to 'build and promote values of inclusion and open opportunities for people to contribute fully to society' (Bureau of Educational and Cultural Affairs, USA 2020)	In order to be successful, a number of criteria had to be met, which can be described as outcome-related objectives, such as: demonstrating how the sport project can instil the principles of leadership; responsibility, teamwork, healthy living and self-discipline; to encourage youth to stay in school; prevent substance abuse and violence and mitigate extremist voices; and demonstrate the value of sport as a tool to promote tolerance and understanding through organised activities that appeal to youth and youth influencers and that focus on conflict prevention/resolution There are a number of other outcome-related objectives, such as those focusing on improving the quality for people with disabilities, building self-esteem and confidence, enhance active participation and improve health In addition, it was also necessary to demonstrate and explain how the proposed sport project can achieve these outcomes – the need to show the resources you have in terms of the experience and expertise – and demonstrate the partnership organisations who will be worked with. Finally, there also had to be a clear budget of the key expenditure items

- **Expertise**: What is the experience of people involved in delivering the project, to help demonstrate competence, which in turn can help give confidence that the money won't be wasted
- **Partnerships**: Consistently, a demonstration and understanding of the network of partnerships will be crucial, as discussed in Chapter 7
- **Plans**: Having a capacity to work out the planning time scales, key milestones, etc., as discussed in Chapters 3 and 6.

Looking at these points, hopefully, any sport manager or SDO worker should be perfectly comfortable with these concepts, as they have all been discussed throughout this book. It is information and data which is embedded in the operations process and system. In addition to these key pieces of information, for some countries, particularly the UK and New Zealand, there are additional pieces of information, which can be framed around ethos or trust that may be required, such as:

- **Governance**: Clear evidence that the organisation is properly governed, such as having a clear constitution and a business plan
- **Safeguarding**: This is particularly true for the UK, where issues of child and athlete safety are crucial to provide (see also Chapter 1)

Whilst having good quality, specific data and information gives a solid foundation for building a successful bid, it does not guarantee it. This is where the written and sometimes oral communication skills come into play. When completing forms, there is usually a limited number of words with which to make the case for why your organisation deserves the money. The writing must be concise, and focus on using the language, terms and key criteria highlighted by the body awarding the grant. For example, for the Sport EnglandSmall Grants fund, highlighted in Table 8.1, focuses on encouraging 'active recreation' and targeting particular community segments, so it is essential that any bid should try and reflect these issues and use their terminology. For some of the grants, there may be a second or third round, where a team presentation may have to be given, which requires a different communication skill set. Here, focusing on some 'killer statistics' and some personal, emotive stories and images can be effective here. In Box 8.1 a more detailed example is given of the grant application stages.

Box 8.1 Completing a grant application: small grant application, Sport England

It is often relatively easy to find potential sources of funding that can be bid for, but it is far more complicated to complete. To illustrate these points, a UK example is focused on, to show points of best practice which can be used in any grant application, in any country.

Sport England's (2020) Small Grant fund gives small amounts of money between £300 and £10,000 to sport clubs. On the application form, it begins

(continued)

Box 8.1 (continued)

with the usual preamble questions, such as asking for details on the club: if it is a registered charity, contact details and nominating a referee, with the additional open question asked of 'How does your referee know your organization?' After asking all these background questions, the form asks more complicated questions such as:

Your project description

- What is the title of your project?
- In up to 100 words, please describe your project.
- Which sport(s) will your project involve?
- Select the national governing body (NGB).

Tell us more about your project

- Why is your project needed? (Why the project needs to happen and what evidence you have gathered to support this in 500 words.)
- What difference will your project make? (The impact your sport project will have on sports participation in 500 words.)
- How will you make this project happen? (Tell us your project plan in 500 words.)
- What will happen after the project ends? (How will participants continue their involvement in sport at the end of this funding in 500 words?)
- Will you work with anyone else to make your project happen?

People taking part

- How many people have taken part in sport at your project in the last 12 months, counting each person only once?
- When will the project start and end?
- Please tell us a bit more about the background of these people entering the number or the % of the people from the specified groups.
- How will you collect the information (i.e. methods of evaluation)?

Your small grants budget

- Please provide a detailed breakdown of the total costs of your project.
- Do you have any other cast funding for your project?
- Total Project Costs include amount requested and any other funding.

Application review

- This provides a series of checklist questions, which also ask for additional verification documentation, such as bank statements, child protection polices and safeguarding vulnerable adults.

This form requires some vital specific data – perhaps more than is required in comparison with grant applications in other countries around the world – but if the manager or SDO has a capacity and knowledge to answer these questions, then it would give a solid foundation for completing any grant application, in any country. These are some of the key elements which should be considered for *any* grant application:

- **Create an exciting pitch**: You should name and describe your project in an interesting, dynamic exciting way (this is also relevant for crowd-funding techniques). In later stages, emotive stories, case studies and testimonials can help here, but it is vital that the person scrutinising the form is engaged with it, which is why even simple things such as the sport project title can be important.
- **Collecting evidence to show value and measure success**: You need to collect relevant output data, relating to your existing users and potential users, which can be broken down into different segments or communities (see Chapters 2, 4 and 10). Showing other mechanisms for collecting data how performance will be measured is also important here.
- **Explain how you will achieve the outputs and outcomes**: This relates to the planning and mechanisms of leverage, to show who use the service (outputs), then how their behaviours will change (outcomes) when the project finishes (legacies). Project planning is important here, in terms of the who, what, when and where (Chapters 3 and 6).
- **Can you demonstrate that you are trustworthy**: The information provided in previous sections will help demonstrate competence, which in turn enhances trust. The capacity to identify partnerships is also important here (Chapter 7).

We would argue that all these basic competences should all be within the realms of any sport manager or SDO, which would create a foundation for a successful application. It weaves in the basic principles of persuasion, with basic operational practices which must be engaged with all the time.

Task

For a country of your choice, look for the grants which they can make available for sport projects and what are the key criteria which must be met, or the data which can be collected?

8.3.2 Private business and charity grant applications

Another source of grant application are those made available from commercial businesses and charities. For charities, offering grants to groups is an obvious mechanism to operationalise and achieve their charity objectives. For commercial businesses the reason for offering grants may be less obvious, but is usually related to CSR agendas, discussed in Chapter 7. Many large commercial businesses will often have a range of grants available for community groups, which

Table 8.3 Examples of Different Commercial and Charity Grants Available for Sport

Name of Grant and Country	Description	Key Measures and Processes
ANZ Netball Grant, ANZ Bank New Zealand, New Zealand	This money can be used for equipment, court makeovers, coaching sessions and, in their words, they encourage the organisation to: Think big and we may just make your ideas come true. As this is a bank, this relates more to their broader commitments to CSR and supporting communities. When scrutinising the information they ask for, it is clear it is less about meeting tight-specific criteria and more about good news stories They state simply that they are proud to help netballing Kiwis at every level to achieve their ambitions (ANZ, 2020)	To be successful, they stipulate that the organisation submitting the proposal must explain why they are a worthy recipient in 3,000 words, which needs to consider: - How your team/club/centre/school will benefit from ANZ - Why you feel your team/club/centre/school deserves help, which includes relevant supporting information on the profile of players, history, town etc. - Consideration to the lasting impacts or legacy given within the community, school or team, or to an individual fan or player In addition supporting messages, videos and enthusiasm and commitment to make things happen
Coca Cola (2019) Thankyou Fund, Ireland, in partnership with the Irish Youth Foundation	Coca-Cola, in order to try and enhance its brand, supports a variety of charities and makes available a number of grants, for charities or community groups to bid for around the world The Thankyou Fund, started in 2011, is one of the grants they make available for non-profit organisations, which focuses on community projects focusing on young people, healthy lifestyles and environmentalism in Ireland The funds can be accessed initially via an online application form, where they encourage applicants to know their projects, to be innovative and to be clear how the money could make a difference	The Thankyou Fund makes a variety of small grants of €5,000, €10,000 or €20,000 available to groups. In 2019 they had 260 entries, which will be shortlisted by a panel to 20 groups Applicants have to submit a 50-word summary and then invited to present to a panel, which if successful, the 50-word summary will go forward to a wider audience who vote on it in the People's Choice Award. The shortlist is leveraged for maximum publicity by Coca-Cola, using national media to announce shortlists, with the winners announced at a youth conference One of the winners in 2019 was Monkstown Boxing Club, who won money to support programmes, aiming to achieve 'sustainable positive change in the lives of marginalised young people, in one of Northern Ireland's most deprived communities

help them meet any CSR objectives and offer many good new stories which they can be leveraged to help enhance their brand image. In Table 8.3, some examples of grants made available by commercial businesses are given to highlight the core features of the application process.

In terms of the elements of persuasion, whilst *logos*-related arguments (e.g. providing hard data to substantiate claims) can be more important for government grant applications, the elements of *ethos* (ethics and trust) and *pathos* (the emotional appeal) can be more important for grant applications made to charities and commercial businesses. Commercial organisations in particular like to leverage the positive and inspirational stories which the groups bidding for money can generate. That is why they often place less emphasis on some of the hard facts and quantifiable data in comparison with government grant applications, as illustrated back in Table 8.3. This is not to say that the quantifiable data is not important, rather, that for commercial grant applications they are often more interested on the supporting messages, videos and demonstrations of 'enthusiasm and commitment to make things happen'. For example, on the ANZ netball site, highlighted in Table 8.3, they provide a variety of video examples and stories of how they have helped different clubs and athletes. For the Coca-Cola example in the table, they make great play about maximising the media attention and community involvement, going through many stages of application, but which can generate many interesting and emotive stories.

8.3.3 Sponsorship

Sponsorship, as it is used here, relates to a formal partnership, which gives both parties some type of reciprocal gain. It can at times be confused with advertising and donation giving. Advertising is a paid-for mass communication medium that utilises multiple channels to reach its audience, whilst donations are given without (in theory) any strings or additional reciprocal actions, beyond those of thanking the donator. Sponsorship contains features of advertising and donation given, but it is more clearly an exchange process, with what is 'given' or 'gained' can be highly nuanced, which goes beyond just money. In Figure 8.3, an overview of the types of sponsorship and benefits is represented, along with who can seek to develop sponsorship.

The first observation to make about this figure is that there are no restrictions as to 'who' can seek a sponsorship deal, where voluntary, public and commercial sport organisations can all seek to form sponsorship partnerships, although for perhaps different goals. Whilst for the public and voluntary sector, sponsorship is used to help bridge funding gaps, or generate more revenue for charitable causes, for commercial sponsorships, it relates to profit and competitiveness, particularly for professional sport clubs.

In terms of the types of gains or benefits represented in Figure 8.3, these are perhaps more varied then might initially be expected, which importantly needed to be considered as existing for both parties. The obvious benefits for many commercial clubs, stadiums, athletes and sport competitions are the additional financial revenues which can accrue. In others instances, the benefits might be the provision of certain equipment, food and drink, or the main provider of services,

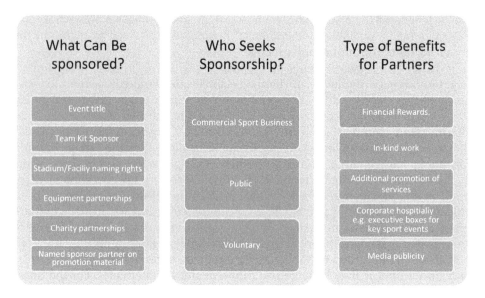

Figure 8.3 Overview of the Types of Sponsorship Relationships and Benefits.

such as with transport or IT services (see also back to Chapter 7 and Box 7.3 for more examples). In return, what these sponsors might expect are opportunities for displaying their logos and brand, which helps people make positive associations and attachment to their products or services. Another important part of the sponsorship benefits is the opportunities created for hospitality, which is particularly important for large scale, elite teams and live events. For the sponsor, these corporate hospitably events, which can also feature visits from the sport stars themselves, offer additional leverage opportunities for the corporate sponsor to develop other commercial deals.

In terms of just what can be sponsored, there are many variations. For example, stadiums around the world can often strike lucrative sponsorship naming rights, so the stadium can be known by the sponsor's name, such as:

- Emirates stadium, London, UK
- City Mazda Stadium, Richmond, Australia
- AlccorHotels Arena, Paris, France
- Cadillac Arena in Beijing, China
- Coca-Cola Stadium in Xian, China
- Allianz arena in Germany (Allianz sponsors a number of stadiums around the world)
- PalaWhirlpool multi-purpose indoor arena in Italy
- Toyota stadium, Toyota City, Japan
- Shonan BMW football stadium Japan
- Pepsi Arena in Warsaw, Poland

The list can go on for some considerable length. One interesting observation from this list is how corporate businesses will sponsor stadiums in other countries, to gain more brand awareness, such as the American car manufacturer, Cadillac, sponsoring a stadium in China. A similar pattern of selling the naming rights of sport events has also grown over the years, whilst kit sponsorship certainly for the top sport performers, can also be fiercely competitive, where different parts of the athletes kitted body can be sold off (for example, in Formula 1 motor racing, the racing drivers arm, which can be seen waving in the onboard cameras, can have separate sponsorship deals in comparison with other body part apparel, such as the hats worn on the winning podiums).

One interesting growth area for sponsorship is the use of charity partner sponsorships. For many large-scale sport events, having charity partners can be a key part of the brand exposure for a business, which commercial sponsors want to be associated with. For example, from 1996 to 2009 Flora sponsored the London marathon, whose main sponsor was the charity, the Heart Foundation. Flora – a spread made from sunflower oil, which claims to help reduce cholesterol and was marketed as being good for the heart – meant that they could leverage the positive association of the potential health benefits of its product. During this time, the London marathon become one of the largest charity fundraising events in the world, raising millions not just for the heart foundation, but for many other charities as well.

For the largest stadiums, top sport clubs, events and athletes, they will not be short of potential sponsors. Sponsorship at the non-elite level, however, is very different. Here, part of the operations process for non-elite sport organisations and clubs is as much about the seeking of potential sponsors, as the work of maintaining the partnership relationship. This process of seeking out sponsorship deals could easily fill multiple chapters, so what is done here is a simplified identification of some of the key operational tasks which a sport manager or SDO might be required to engage with. It synthesises a variety of approaches and practical guides (e.g. Eventbrite, 2017; Eventmobi, 2017; Practical Sport Sponsorship Ideas, 2020). Although there can be many different sub-tasks and processes, for simplicity, the key tasks are organised around three key themes, which are summarised in Table 8.4.

Looking at that table, it is particularly important to recognise how there has to be a clear understanding of the nature of the sport organisation, its service and its key communities, and how these elements can be presented (sold even) and matched to the needs of potential sponsors. If a sport manager or SDO was to utilise some of the basic marketing principles, discussed in Chapter 4, this would give a sound starting point with its focus on understanding different potential sponsorship partner's needs and wants, to show how the sport facility, service or event fits in with the potential sponsor's products, services or brand. Whilst some of the elements of sponsorship are familiar, in Table 8.4, there are some additional distinct activities identified, particularly in relation to the contact strategies and promotional materials sent, such as how to use networks, and identify gate keepers and the presentation of sponsorship packs.

Writers, such as Skildum-Reid and Grey (2014), describe sponsorship deals as a WIN-WIN-WIN situation, because rights holders benefit from an income stream into their organisation; the sponsor benefits from being able to access and communicate with an audience that would otherwise have been much more

Table 8.4 Key Tasks for Seeking and Winning Potential Sponsors

Organisational Audit	Develop Sponsorship Packages and Documentation	Develop Contact Strategies and Relationship with Potential and Actual Sponsors
This reviews what is needed, such as a review of equipment and supply partners who could be approached for potential sponsorship - Costings and planning out the project so it is clear the amounts being looked for - Identifying strengths and what you have to offer, which can be presented to potential sponsors - Review of customer bases and targets which can be presented sponsors - Outline communication channels - Identify potential stories to leverage and access to media and partner networks - Identify core values, ethical principles and CSR commitments - Be clear what you have to offer Note that utilisation of SWOT, PESTLE or Porter's five forces tools can be of benefit here	- Simply put, two types of sponsorship deals can be offered: Tiered sponsorships, which means different levels and packages, such as platinum, gold, silver and exhibitor. The listed benefits can be given according to the level of money - The other alternative is the selected sponsorship deal, or a La Carte, which focuses on specific areas, such as equipment, food and transport. - Remember also that scarcity can create value - Present information in a sponsorship pack which utilises all the information gathered and can be sent out to potential sponsors	- Identify sponsors in terms of the match to equipment, target audiences and ethical principles - Provide proof in terms of statistics, data, testimonials and stories - Get the right person to talk to, avoiding cold calling (i.e. the idea of a gatekeeper, discussed in Chapter 7), but email can be what they call 'lumpy' in that it contains a package which might stimulate their interests - Using word of mouth networks and partnerships; use emails and networks to make contacts - Agree measures of success, such as writing SMART objectives

Communications: Clarity of letters and packages; ability to produce powerful infographics which sells the course; ability to develop trust and understanding; ability to develop a clear sponsorship pitch, being clear what you wanted

Research: using data to underpin information to support persuasive arguments

---

difficult to reach; and the audience benefit from being provided with an opportunity to consume a product/service more easily that can enhance their everyday life. This view is perhaps a little too simplistic as there can be downsides, which in some instances have also been a source of crisis situations (discussed in Chapter 9). In Chapter 7, examples were given of non-profit organisations accepting financial sponsorship from businesses who were not in fact a good match in terms of the values and their products (e.g. sport charities dealing with children's sport, accepting money from sweet and fizzy drink manufactures). Similarly, when sport has been engulfed in issues of corruption and cheating, it can mean sponsorship deals can be broken off, such as the cyclist Lance Armstrong reputedly losing a $75 million sponsorship deal with the sport manufacturer Nike, after he admitted bullying and drug taking to enhance his sport performances. The list of possible examples here can be a long one. In Box 8.2, some practical case studies in sponsorship are examined.

Box 8.2 Examples of sponsorship

Sponsorships vary considerably in their size and who and what is sponsored. For example, for a small club, such as a university or college sport team, sponsorship can be as simple as receiving money from local hair salons, nightclubs or retailers, who might sponsor kits and transport, and can have their logos displayed on portable banners, when the team plays.

Alternatively, many large businesses will often look to develop some different types of sponsorships, which they can use to leverage their brand and generate stories. For examples, the European budget supermarket, Aldi, sponsors a variety of sport providers, such as the Irish Rugby Football Union and the far larger commitment to the GB 2020 Olympic team. Another example is the American car manufacturer, Chevrolet, who sponsors Manchester United, which allows them to leverage the appeal of the football club and the English premiership in Asia, to generate greater brand awareness in countries such as China, South Korea or India.

Alcohol and sport have a long association. For sport, it can bring huge amounts of money into the sport, whilst for the alcohol companies, it provides an opportunity to target key audiences. For example, the European beer manufacturer, Heineken, is involved with many sport events. The overriding purpose of Heineken sponsoring sport is to reinforce its position in the premium beer market: a competitive business strategy to defend, as well as to increase market share worldwide (Sports Promedia, 2020). To this end, it has been a long-term partner of UEFA football Champions League and has a significant presence in Formula 1 and rugby union, being the key beer sponsor of the Japan Rugby World Cup. Indeed, Heineken has history with rugby union and likes to leverage how its own core business/brand values align to those of rugby. Heineken has also leveraged various sport events to build market share in countries around the world, such as non-European countries growing interest in the UEFA Champions League. For Formula 1, it offered the potential of reaching an additional 200 million people, whilst also organising additional events, such as the 'Heineken Saturday' events (live band performances), established at three GP events to create more excitement and appeal to fans, but with the potential to attract a new audience to F1 and Heineken beer.

Increasingly, questions are being asked about how ethical these certain types of sponsorship are, particularly in terms of alcohol, betting companies

(continued)

182 Chapter 8

> Box 8.2 (continued)
>
> and fast food, snack and high sugar drink manufactures. It is a paradox and tension which is only set to grow, where managers and SDOs will have to walk the tightrope of trying to promote a message of the health benefits of their sport services, yet manage the criticisms of receiving sponsorship from products, which have the potential to create a variety of health problems, in much the same way as tobacco sponsorship of sport events also created in earlier decades.
>
> **Discussion**
>
> For a sport or team you are interested in, identify the key sponsors and what the benefits are for the two parties? Are there any ethical concerns about the brand association for the sport organisation?

8.3.4 Crowdfunding

Crowdfunding exemplifies a paradigm shift in the funding of sport. The growth of digital technologies, new power relationships and changing social attitudes has created new ways of funding sport activities and services. When looking at the methods of fundraising discussed in the previous sections, they tend to represent an old power relationship, where power is concentrated in the few. The communications materials developed or the 'pitch' will need to persuade a small panel of people, who will have their own interests, preferences and even prejudices.

Crowdfunding is different, where ideas, projects and enterprises can be opened up to the many. In addition, it should be appreciated that crowdfunding also gives a way of gauging demand and interest in potential services, where the numbers (e.g. the number of 'likes' received) can be used as evidence to support other bids. Crowdfunding techniques for sport have been used in a variety of ways, such as helping raise money for individual athletes, teams, people completing challenges, purchasing new facilities and equipment, or even competitions. In Table 8.5, it synthesises some of the key features of the factors which can be considered when developing a successful crowdfunding campaign, drawn from a variety of writers and websites (e.g. Cornell, 2014; Mollick, 2014; Timms & Heimans, 2018).

Whilst there should be some elements of familiarity in terms of doing the background work, such as costing out the project, clarifying who will benefit or identifying key partners, there are some distinct attributes. Looking at Table 8.5, the importance of stories with strong emotional appeal (i.e. pathos) and using the medium of video are key stand out differences with the previous methods. Utter transparency and honesty should also (again) be emphasised (i.e. ethos). Remember, as Mollick (2014) noted, projects succeed by narrow margins or fail by large amounts. Success is linked to project quality, where the most successful campaigns include a personal narrative or a 'wowsome' video. Highly

Table 8.5 Key Features of a Successful Crowdfunding Campaigns

Project Stage	Description
Idea generation and engaging descriptions of the need for funding	As with all the other forms of fundraising, this is underpinned by research, costing and planning, together with being clear with what is needed, who it is needed for, why it is needed and how it can be achieved. Whilst all this information may not be utilised in terms of, for example, the video pitches, there must be clarity in the project, such as the amount needed, by a set date
Clear funding goals and rewards	Crowdfunding should be treated as a project, where clear targets and completion times are set. Having these milestones and targets is – in fact – a classic underpinning for all fundraising, developed by Charles Sumner Ward, over 100 years ago, such his development of a campaign clock to create a sense of urgency and action even though the dates could be quite arbitrary Clarifying some of the rewards is also important, which can range from posting thankyous to businesses, shout-outs, wrist bands, T-shirt, training sessions, meet and greets, commemorative photos, etc.

Identification of clear partnerships	Crowdfunding requires three types of actors:
	
	- A project initiator – the person/team/organisation requiring the funding
	- Supporters – individuals/groups of willing donators
	- A mediator (the 'platform'), such as the following platforms:
	
	    Sportsfunder, Pledgesport, Indiegogo, Justgiving, Kickstarter, Crowdfunding Campus, or Rockethub
	
	It is this interplay between a worthwhile cause, targeted at sufficient supportive backers via (hopefully) a vibrant digital platform that generates a successful outcome. The most common mediums which can be used to distribute and share these stories can be via:
	
	    Facebook, Twitter, Instagram, WhatsApp, WeChat, Tik Tok.
	
	Remember, using existing partnerships, such as friends and familiar, is the obvious starting point for sharing stories of the fundraising cause. Partnerships can also help create a sense of trust and give supportive testimonials

Video and a social media campaign designed to engage supporters and attract funders	Video messaging is vital, where clear, interesting and engaging pitches must be done in a few minutes. A featured image and video, with music and simple images and supporting graphics, can be vital here. Crowdfunding Campus noted that once on the platform website the backer is drawn to a campaign by its widget (the picture headlining the campaign), then the backer watches the video, followed by considering the rewards, and finally reading the description about the project. So, in essence, the video sells it! Some important considerations here relate to using banner headlines, great pictures, simple messages and tag lines, and telling engaging stories In terms of the stories to tell, personal stories of people who have benefited, or using the history of the club, or some provocative exciting fact, can all be useful here

Project Stage	Description
React and utilise feedback	Crowdfunding allows for valuable 'real-time' feedback from the market, thereby, supporting a reflective learning opportunity for the development of this "wholly different set of skills" (Benderley, 2013) and their implementation. Evaluate/reflect upon the relative success or failure of the project. Ask why did the campaign succeed and/or why did the campaign fail and how can it be improved? This 'dialogue' also forms an important part of the content which can be used to generate more contacts with people, which helps keep the cause alive in people's consciousness. The challenge is to try and get a message that can go viral and get thousands of likes which continue to be shared. Give lots of thanks and praise, and use pictures and videos clips which can help with the sharing. As Pledge sport says '…Don't forget to thank people: do it on social media, do it in person, do it everywhere, all the time'.

personalised connections on social networks is also a key to success. Furthermore, there can often be a strong geographical link to project success indicating where time and effort to reach a wider audience could be focused beyond those potential backers already known to the project (Macht & Weatherston, 2014). In Box 8.3, some examples of successful sport funding campaigns are given.

There are a variety of ways that crowdfunding campaigns can be organised. To begin with, using an established crowdfunding platform can help save time and generate ideas for inexperienced mangers or SDOs in this area. There are a wide variety of platforms to choose from, some of which have different areas of specialities, a number of which are highlighted in Table 8.5, such as Sportsfunder, Pledgesport or Crowdfunding Campus. These platforms facilitate

Box 8.3 Examples of sport crowdfunding campaigns

Here are few examples of successful crowdfunding initiatives, which draws out some points of good practice and where the actual campaigns and videos should be examined online.

Case study 1 – Girl Scouts Association of America, using the Indiegogo crowdfunding platform: This example, whilst not a pure sport example, is the one relevant in terms of active recreation and many important learning points, used as an illustrative example of new power theories by Timms and Heimans (2018). The Girls Scouts of America was given a generous gift of a $100,000 dollars by a single donor, to be used on disadvantaged girls. It was an example of classic old power relationships, of a generous award of money given by a single person. It was a gift the Association was initially delighted with, but there was a condition attached: it could not be used for any transgender issues. After much consideration and reflection of their own aims and values, the Association returned the money and launched a crowdfunding, where the two-minute video had some simple, clear messages leveraging the story of how they had to return the money and some emotive images of girl guides engaged with a variety of projects. It went viral, and they soon reached their target amount of $100,000, then going onto achieve over $300,000. Instead of 1 backer giving 100,000, 7,950 backers gave over $300,000, which is a prime example of new power relationships.

Case study 2 – Luz Grande professional body board surfer: Luz Grande is a professional Puerto Rican body board surfer, who has won various top competitions over the years. In 2019, because she was unable to secure any sponsorship or sport agent support, she used www.sportfunder.com as a crowdfunding platform, in order to fund her professional competitive participation in the world circuit, with the money used for such things as transport, equipment, accommodation, etc.

She leveraged a variety of stories and appealed to different emotions to help encourage people to donate money, by telling the story of how she got involved in the sport as a young girl, her sport successes and the community outreach and legacy work she does, such as the organising the 'Eco-sports Day' in the community of La Perla (San Juan), which has outlined various educational outputs and is free to the young in the community. She also leveraged how she would be a representative of Puerto Rico, to raise the profile of the country and help attract future competitions. These were presented on the page, along with a short, professionally produced video, which was linked to YouTube. In all, she managed to raise over $10,000 from 290 contributors, with people pledging anything from $10 to $600, in one-off contributions or monthly contributions.

Discussion
Examine the crowdfunding platforms, and identify the most appealing campaigns considering what factors create the attraction and appeal.

this process by showcasing the project idea, the athlete or the team seeking money. The advantage of these platforms is that they provide a simple structure with which to set up a crowdfunding campaign. When looking at these many platforms, there are again some common themes which emerge, such as the now familiar establishing targets, developing engaging headings and descriptions and creating interesting videos, which identify key partnerships, to help get the crowdfunding campaign going. Interestingly, some crowdfunding platforms only release the donations once the pledge target has been surpassed; alternatively, others give over all the money once the date deadline has been reached – so the recommendation is to choose carefully which platform to utilise.

8.3.5 Fundraising activities

The list of additional fundraising activities is considerable. In Table 8.6, four broad categories are given, with the fundraising events having the longest list of possible ideas. Many of the examples given in that table should be familiar, such

Table 8.6 Overview of Fundraising Techniques

Techniques	Description
Fundraising event ideas	Event challenges (e.g. danceathons, walkathons, fun runs, Santa runs at Christmas, etc.); car washes; cake sales; social events; coach punishments, such as dunking in gunge; kids camps and skill development; rubber duck racing; face painting; charity auctions, lotteries or quiz evenings; athletes hired/rent-a-athlete to do work in communities, etc.
Branded fundraising merchandise	This is in addition to secondary spend items, such as T-shirts, caps, mugs, branded wrist bands to show support
Peer-to-peer funding, partnerships and 'Give days'	Asking people to utilise their networks, try and create viral fundraising activities; give Tuesdays, where people donate money which might have been used elsewhere, such as for Black Friday sales; text to give; using partnerships to help raise money, such as using restaurants to have socials
Pay-roll giving and gift aid	People can donate money on a monthly basis, in addition to any club subscriptions. Using gift aid, which allows charities to claim back tax or gain government tax exemptions

has cake sales have a long and rich history, but in recent years, there has been a growth in more fun and novel events being organised. As with crowdfunding, new power relationships are offering some interesting new events, such as getting large groups of people together to take part in large flash mob events, or organising challenges which go viral, such as the ice-bucket that began in 2013 and went global in 2014.

In turn, these more novel forms of fundraising offer additional stories which can be leveraged to generate additional media coverage of what the organisation is trying to do in terms of their funds. When combined with crowdfunding techniques, these stories provide further stories to generate social media traffic, whilst in the same instance, crowdfunding can be used to share the stories and the events for people to attend. As with all of the other funding streams, the utilisation networks and partnerships are again vital for using these different types of fundraising techniques.

8.3.6 Private donations

Asking for donations from individuals or businesses can take a variety of forms and be particularly useful in sport building and renovation projects. There are plenty of examples of philanthropic gestures from rich business people, who can give money to help fund projects or refurbish community facilities. The contact strategies for seeking money are just as important and all the principles of good communication as crucial here, as in all areas of funding. If large amounts of money are asked for, then conducting the research, for example, on philanthropic entrepreneurs and how your project fits in with the potential donor's values and beliefs is vital. Other popular examples can relate to donation packages which mix arge individual donations and many smaller donations from stakeholders or fans, such as sponsoring a building brick campaigns, where people can buy bricks and have their names written, literally, into the fabric of the sport structure.

8.4 CONCLUSION

Fundraising and grant applications have become an increasingly important part of operations management, and any sport manager or SDO who has a track record of securing money from different funding streams is likely to be highly regarded and much sought after. When looking at the key skills and knowledge needed to be successful in this area, all the other elements of operations management discussed in this book can be drawn upon. What is needed in addition to these skills and knowledge is a capacity to communicate in a variety of formats, ranging from persuasive, fact-filled forms to telling emotive, powerful stories using the written word, the spoken performance or woven into a video presentation. What can help refine and target the communication method used is the consideration of the different elements of persuasion, relating to pathos (emotions), ethos (ethics and trust in the message) and logos (the facts used to persuade). Although a little simplistic, it is clear that all these elements have to be considered, but used in different mixes, such as being more fact (logos) driven for government grants, whilst for crowdfunding and grants from commercial businesses, emotive (pathos) storytelling can be more important, both of which will be underpinned by trust (ethos).

References

Benderley, B. (2013). Going online for research funding. *Science Magazine*, 10 June 2013 (online), accessed 25 February 2016, available at: http://www.sciencemag.org/careers/2013/06/going-online-research-funding

Borg, J. (2008). *Persuasion*, 4th ed. London: Pearson.

Bureau of Educational and Cultural Affairs, USA (2020). International Sports Programming Initiative (ISPI), available at: https://eca.state.gov/programs-initiatives/initiatives/sports-diplomacy/sports-grants

Coca Cola (2019). Thankyou fund, accessed 2 November 2019, available at: https://www.coca-cola.ie/stories/thank-you-fund/thank-you-fund-faqs

Cornell, C. (2014). Crowdfunding: More than money jumpstarting university entrepreneurship. *Proceedings of the Annual Conference* of the National Collegiate Inventors & Innovators Alliance, accessed 2 March 2016, available at: http://venturewell.org/open2014/wp-content/uploads/2013/10/CORNELL-2.pdf

Eventbrite (2017). 10 types of sponsorship packages brands love, available at: https://www.eventbrite.com/blog/sponsorship-packages-ds00/

Forbes (2019). The world's highest paid athletes, accessed 2 April 2020, available at: https://www.forbes.com/athletes/#17476a3955ae

Macht, S., and Weatherston J. (2014). The benefits of online crowdfunding for fund-seeking business ventures. *Strategic Change*, 23(1–2), 1–14.

Mollick, E.(2014). The dynamics of crowdfunding: An exploratory study. *Journal of Business Venturing*, 29, 1–16.

Nike (2012). 5 extra years, accessed 12 June 2020, available at: Nike 5 More Years video from 2012: https://www.youtube.com/watch?v=_3D7xFrZ8mI

NSW (2019). Legacy Partnership Program, available at: https://sport.nsw.gov.au/sites/default/files/2022%20UCI%20road%20-%20grant%20guidelines%20v4%20-%20without%20event%20logo.pdf

Practical Sport Sponsorship Ideas (2020). Winning a sponsorship proposal, accessed on 3 March 2020, available at: https://practicalsponsorshipideas.com/create-a-winning-sponsorship-proposal/

Skildum-Reid, K., and Grey, A. (2014). *The Sponsorship Seeker's Toolkit*, 4th ed. London: McGraw-Hill Education.

Slater, M. (2010). Community and school sport bears brunt of spending cuts, accessed 25 October 2019, available at: http://news.bbc.co.uk/sport1/hi/front_page/9111865.stm

Sport England (2020). Small grants funding, accessed 2 November 2019, available at: https://www.sportengland.org/how-we-can-help/our-funds/small-grants

Statista (2019). Public sector expenditure on recreational and sporting services in the United Kingdom (UK) from 2013/14 to 2017/18 (in Million GBP), accessed 23 February 2019, available at: https://www.statista.com/statistics/298898/united-kingdom-uk-public-sector-expenditure-recreational-and-sporting-services/

SportsPromedia (2020). Engaging early: Heineken's Hans-Erik Tuijt on the rugby world cup renewal and more, accessed 5 March 2017, available at: http://www.sportspromedia.com/quick_fire_questions/engaging-early-heinekens-hans-erik-tuijt-on-the-rugby-world-cup-renewal-and

Timms, H., and Heimans, J. (2018). *Newpower*. London: Picador.

9
CRISIS MANAGEMENT, RISK AND DYNAMIC RISK ASSESSMENTS

> **Challenges for managers**
>
> - How far is it reasonably practicable to prevent crisis events?
> - How can crisis management practices be blended in with mainstream project and health and safety risk management processes?
> - How can time-pressured crisis situations be analysed, and management actions taken?

9.1 INTRODUCTION

A crucial part of operations management is decision-making at a time of crisis. In Chapter 2, it was highlighted that much of a manager's or SDO's work arrives on the day, which if they threaten the continued operations of the organisation, they can be considered as potential crisis events. These events become the priority for the manager to deal with immediately, where actions need to be taken to prevent the crisis escalating in the severity of the outcomes, then later, managing the recovery process.

The approach taken in this chapter is to frame crisis management within a broader risk management process. It begins by defining the terms of 'crisis', 'risk' and 'dynamic risk assessment', to show how the concepts and practices overlap. The 'crisis' elements relate to the extreme risks identified during the risk management process, which can have serious impacts and consequences in terms of people's health, the reputation of the organisation and its continued operational viability. Practical operational insights are given by explaining how to develop crisis manuals, – which consider the actions needed to either prevent a crisis, or manage a crisis if it does occur, – then finally how to recover from a crisis.

9.2 DEFINING RISK, CRISIS AND DYNAMIC RISK ASSESSMENTS

Sport managers and SDOs will find it impossible to ignore risk and crisis management concepts and practices. There are a variety of reasons for this. The first is that risk is an inherent part of sport, which must be properly managed.

The second is that all managers should consider it a moral responsibility to ensure customers, staff and even the organisation itself are kept safe. Third, utilising risk and crisis management theories and practices can represent best management practice, in order to deliver high-quality, safe sport services. Finally, there are the various legal regulations found in different countries around the world, which require businesses of all forms to engage with risk management as it relates to operational health and safety assessments, or corporate governance.

There is a problem, however: the many variations in the risk practices and concepts found between countries, the levels of management and even within individual organisations. The result can mean duplication of work, poor communication and confusion. To deal with these issues, what is proposed here is to use a single risk definition and risk management process for different types of risk assessment, relating to operational health and safety assessments, project risk management and strategic risk planning and governance. The proposed definition is presented in Table 9.1, which also includes definitions of crisis

Table 9.1 Comparing Definitions of Risk, Crisis and DRA

Risk Management	Crisis Management	Dynamic Risk Assessment (DRA)
Risk management is the **process** of identifying and analysing **hazards**, which are sources of **potential** risk events. These risk events are assessed in relation to their **likelihood** of occurrence and the positive or negative **outcomes** or impacts on people, equipment, money and reputation of the organisation. Risk management is not about the removal of risks – to do that can be to remove the essence of the sport activity – but the control of risks to maximise the benefits, or to transfer, reduce, or avoid the potential negative impacts	A **crisis event** represents the **extreme risk events** which have a **probability** of occurrence and are **severe** in their **outcomes**. This severity relates to the **disruption** of continued service operations, or the dangers and threats to life, or even the future operational viability of the whole business organisation. These crisis events can be internally or externally generated, threatening people, buildings, equipment, finances and the reputation of the business. Whilst it is common to frame crisis events in a negative prism, good managers and SDOs should also be alert to the opportunities that might be created	DRA is the **'live'** operations decision-making process, where situations, such as crisis events, are constantly evaluated and acted upon. It is relevant for all employers and at *all* levels of management and through training and experience, is about making the **best decisions** to first protect the people, then the reputation and financial health of the business

Source: Author.

management and dynamic risk assessments (DRA), discussed later. They are definitions based on synthesising a variety of definitions (e.g. Glaesser, 2003, p. 3; Government of South Australia, 2009; London.Gov.Uk, 2015; Piekarz et al., 2015; Sport and Recreation Alliance, 2015), which show both the distinct and shared attributes of each concept.

A number of important observations need to be made to help clarify what these definitions mean in terms of operational practices:

- **Symmetric definition of risk is used**: This means that rather than just define risks and crisis events in terms of loss, dangers and injuries (an asymmetric definition), there is consideration given to how taking risks can also create gains or be opportunistic.
- **A hazard is distinct from a risk**: It is not unusual to find examples where risks and hazards are used inter-changeably. This should be avoided. A 'hazard' is often described as the *cause* of the risk, but we prefer to describe it as the *source* of the risk, with examples given in Box 9.1.
- **The concept of hazard can be used in all forms of risk and crisis management**: Whilst in health and safety risk definitions it can be common to use the concept of a hazard, in other areas of risk management, such as in project risk management, it can be less common to use the term. Absence of use does not however mean lack of relevancy; it is perfectly possible to apply the concept of hazards to other areas of risk management, such as how external PEST factors can be framed as hazards, as they are a source of risks for sport operations.
- **Two core pillars of risk are used**: Risk should be considered in relation to the 'probability' of occurrence (variations of 'probability' may be to use the terms 'chance' or 'likelihood') and the 'outcomes'. An asymmetric definition would usually use the term 'severity of outcome' (e.g. injuries), but because we adopt a symmetric definition, 'outcomes' are framed as offering both gains and losses.
- **Crisis events are framed as the extreme risks**: When analysing and assessing potential risks which are severe in their negative outcomes, whether this relates to life, finances or brand reputation, they can be considered as the key crisis events which can be given separate, more detailed management attention and documentation in crisis manuals.
- **DRA is the operational part of crisis management**: Although managers and SDOs will in effect constantly analyse risks in their day-to-day operations, DRA is focused here in terms of how it relates to the processes engaged with when a crisis event is encountered.

It is worthwhile briefly elaborating on the differences on symmetric and asymmetric definitions of risk. Conducting operational health and safety assessments in work places is a legal obligation in many countries, whereby it is common practice to adopt an asymmetric definition that focuses on the probability of harm occurring to people. In other areas of risk management however, such as when it is used in project management or strategic planning, it can be more

Box 9.1 Applying risk and crisis management concepts to swimming pools and swimming

Swimming pools have a variety of hazards and risks, some of which are inherent in all pools, whilst others are unique to certain pools and so will require different risk control measures. Here are some of the benefits of swimming, then the generic hazards, risks, controls and crisis management scenarios:

- **Risk benefits**: Physical, mental and social health benefits; community bonding; the ability to swim can save a life; it is an enjoyable recreational activity, etc.
- **Hazards (source of the risk)**: Water in the pool; wet surfaces; steps and edges; other swimmers; and pool chemicals. If the pool is outdoors, then weather hazards should also be considered, such as summer storms.
- **Risks**: Drowning; neck injuries from diving in shallow water or colliding with other swimmers; cuts, bruising or breaks from slipping on hard surfaces; chemical burns or poisoning; illness from bacteria in poorly treated water (e.g. Cryptosporidium infection); physical and sexual abuse; and sunburn for outdoor pools.
- **Examples of control measures to reduce likelihood of risk occurring**: Rules or codes of practice, such as no running on pool sides, or diving in the shallow end; trained life guards who can enforce rules; restrictions placed on number of swimmers who can be allowed into the pool; and rules that young children must be accompanied by an adult, etc.
- **Control measures to reduce severity of outcomes**: Trained life guards who can rescue people and perform lifesaving first aid, such as: CPR; using defibrillators to start a heart; and alarms to call for help and ensure trained emergency staff can quickly deal with the situation.
- **Examples of crisis scenarios used for training**: Drowning scenarios and process for rescue; cardiac arrest; chemical spill or leak; equipment failure forcing closure; heating system failure; and structural building failure, etc.
- **Example of a DRA (gas leak scenario)**: Although modern pools are much safer, they still utilise a variety of chemicals, some of which can produce dangerous gas, such as chlorine. One of the crisis training scenarios to prepare for is gas leak. Staging this crisis event as a live scenario can test such things as: if the safety equipment (e.g. breathing apparatus) is fit for purpose and in the right location; if emergency evacuation processes work; and if staff are properly trained, etc. The hope is that by going through these crisis training scenarios, it will refine and improve the DRA abilities, helping them make better decisions if they are unlucky enough to be faced with this crisis (see Table 9.1 for more performing cardiopulmonary resuscitation (CPR); examples of scenarios).

Discussion

What are the pros and cons of utilising a symmetric definition of risk in health and safety risk assessments?

common to adopt symmetric definitions, which consider the probability of negative losses or harm AND the positive benefits and gains which can accrue from engaging with hazards and taking risks. For example, the ISO (International Standard Organisation) offers a definition which has global application, defining risk simply as: 'the effect of uncertainty on objectives' (ISO, 2018), whereby the effects or consequences on objectives of a risk event have the potential to be 'positive or negative, direct or indirect'. Other writers, such as Bernstein (1998, p. 9), argue that risk has increasingly been seen as a 'friend' rather than an adversary to be battled, whilst Waite (2001, p. 3) makes the concise argument that 'without risk, there can be no profit for businesses'.

The preference in this work is to adopt this broader symmetric definition of risk, in *all* the management spheres (e.g. project risk management, governance and strategic planning and health and safety assessments). It is an approach more commonly used in countries such as Australia and New Zealand, which shows that although it may not be adopted in some countries, it is in fact possible to use symmetric definitions of risk at all levels of management. The advantage of using a symmetric definition is that it develops a broader, single risk culture which can be used for all risk management practices, whereby the analysis of risk can not only be given to *who* will be impacted (i.e. staff, customers, other stakeholders), but also *what* can be impacted (e.g. financial losses and gains, risks to equipment, impacts on reputation, etc.). An illustration of some of the cultural and country variations is given in Box 9.2.

A further advantage of adopting this asymmetric risk definition, which focuses on the duality of gains and losses, or opportunities and threats, is that it better links with current crisis management theory and practice. This view argues that the best performing businesses will be ones who adapt when crisis events occur, looking to turn a crisis event into a critical learning opportunity, to improve services and practices in the future. In the case of accidents and health and safety, this idea of winners and losers may seem initially distasteful, but it is vital that organisations adopt this approach. It is after all a critical underpinning of Syed's Black Box thinking approach (discussed in Chapter 1, Box 1.4) in terms of using failures as critical points for reflection, analysis and learning (look back to Chapter 1, Box 1.5 of the dangers when this *is not* done). Adopting a cultural outlook where crisis events are framed as opportunistic learning events is by no means an original idea, having a long cultural history, used to build resilience. For example, Pilling (2014, p. xxii) discusses the old Japanese proverb about *Bending Adversity*, which refers to transforming bad fortune into good. Another example relates to Timms and Heimans' (2018, p. 73) new power theories, discussed in Chapter 7, where they discuss how successful organisations are the ones who can 'harness the storms' (i.e. the crisis events), whereby they are capable of:

- **Creating storms** (e.g. releasing a media story to create controversy or publicity)
- **Chasing storms** (i.e. using someone else's crisis event to your advantage)
- **Embracing storms** (i.e. you use it as an opportunity for improvement, which also relates to how the glide path to recovery is managed).

Box 9.2 Contextual variations in risk management

Case study 1 – Oasis leisure pool, Swindon, UK: This leisure pool was opened in 1976 and was a highly innovative pool, not just in the UK, but in all of Europe (its other claim to fame is that the British music band, Oasis, named themselves after the venue, when they played there in the 1990s). The pool demonstrated a highly innovative design, which created a glass biodome, where the intention was to recreate a tropical environment, with green planting and a pool that is entered like a beach. It even had one of the first recreational wave machines in Europe, to further recreate a sense of a tropical environment. Over the years, it has remained innovative, such as the 1990s getting some of the biggest flume rides in the UK.

This innovative design, the addition of a wave machine and flumes created some additional hazards and risks in comparison with more traditional pools. For example, the beach shelving steadily into deeper water means people enter in at a shallow level, but they can easily find themselves out of their depth. These difficulties can be compounded when the wave machine is switched on, which can mean that young children or weak swimmers can get into difficulties. The slides or flumes also create a variety of additional risks, such as abrasion burns, cuts, breakages and bone dislocations.

Despite these risks, this pool has for decades given huge enjoyment to millions of visitors, who have experienced the pool safely because of the additional risk controls put in place such as: timed controls on the number of users; timed controls of people going down the flume slides; lifeguard monitoring of splash tanks; supervision of all blind spots and deep ends; extra lifeguard supervision during the use of the wave machine; alerts to tell people when wave machine is being used.

Case study 2 – Parc Wodny, Krakow, Poland: This indoor water park was opened in 2000 and is a popular family recreational facility. It has a variety of leisure flume rides and slides, some of which can be done with mats, or inflatable rings, along with having adventure climbing areas and a pirate island play area. One of the design changes for some of the flumes is to have a longer, shallower splash tank at the end of the flume ride, to slow people down, but who can't be submerged.

The pool has many similarities with the Oasis leisure pool, but has approached the control of some of the risks in different ways. This shows how there can be different cultural interpretations and evaluations of what is deemed as 'reasonably practicable' to deal with hazards and risks. For example, in this pool, on the poolside, it has a small café, selling snacks, some hot food and even beer; these are hazards, which can create the risks of food, contaminating water or even people getting drunk. They are, however, deemed as low risk and one which staff can easily monitor and control, where the benefits – such as trying to create a more relaxed family environments, getting people to stay longer and generate more revenue – outweigh the likelihood of the negative consequences occurring. Furthermore, in one of the water-play areas, themed around a pirate ship, they allow parents to take pictures or film their children using their phones, which perhaps would not be deemed as an acceptable risk in other countries. The decision to take this risk again reflects their desire to create relaxed family experiences and their confidence in controlling this risk, whereby staff feel confident that they can discern if the person taking a picture is a family member or not.

Case study 3 – Jackie Robinson open air pool, Harlem, New York: The Jackie Robinson pool was renamed in 1978, after the first black professional baseball player in the major league, who broke the colour line, playing for the Brooklyn Dodgers in 1947 – one of the breakthrough moments in the long struggle for breaking down colour segregation in the USA. It is was also one of the 11 pools, opened in 1936, mentioned in Chapter 4, Box 4.3. Because it is an outdoor pool, it will be subjected to a variety of additional hazards from the natural environment, where the summers can be very hot in the City, where electrical storms are not uncommon. Its public funding status has also meant that over the decades it has been exposed to a variety of external environmental crisis events, such as the threats of closure when governments reduce spending.

To deal with some of the additional operational hazards and risks, it has developed a variety of risk controls, such as: users must bring a padlock to use on lockers, so they can secure their possessions safely; babies and toddlers need to have swim diapers or nappies; men's shorts may be checked for linings, if they can't tell they are wearing a bathing suit; coloured t-shirts may not be allowed, in case the colour dyes run in the pool; and no food, glass bottles, electronic devices, or newspapers (tendency to blow away).

One particularly interesting control is how the pool offers free sunscreen via dispensers on walls. This is done in partnership with the American Academy of Dermatology's SPOT Skin Cancer programme, which allows an opportunity to educate people about the risks of skin cancer and hopefully change behaviour – an example of using outputs to achieve outcomes, as there are opportunities for educating people about the risks of skin cancer and changing their behaviours accordingly.

Discussion

What variations in the risk controls can be found between private health club or hotel pools and publicly owned swimming pools?

9.3 OVERVIEW OF THE RISK AND CRISIS MANAGEMENT PROCESS

This section focuses on the practical operational steps involved in risk and crisis management. This is done by adapting Piekarz et al.'s (2015) synthesised operational risk process model, represented in Figure 9.1. The salient point argued here is that when the risk management process is engaged with, then it can make

Figure 9.1 Synthesised Risk and Crisis Management Process.
Source: Adapting Piekarz et al. (2015).

sense to also begin planning for crisis events, which can be complemented by additional, separate documentation, if necessary, discussed in later sections.

These stages are given a brief elaboration here:

- **Stage 1 – Context**: This should clarify *who* and *what* is at risk and *how* they are at risk. This can relate to both the key stakeholders, the brand of the business and the nature and objectives of the organisations (see Chapter 3). By doing this, it gives further insight about the *risk exposure* (e.g. the people, money, brand or reputation) and potential crisis events.
- **Stage 2 – Analysis**: This involves deeper exploration of causation factors and how hazards are interacted with, along with any possible trigger events which can lead to crisis. In relation to crisis management, analysis can be given to how extreme risk events may come about, which can affect life, money and reputation, or continued service operations. When the key causation variables are understood, then this also allows for better controls to try and prevent crisis events occurring.
- **Stage 3 – Assessment**: This involves giving a measurement to the risk, such as rating how likely a risk event is and what the consequences may be. In relation to crisis management, any activity which may have a high probability of occurrence and high negative impact should be avoided. There will, however, be many instances where activities will be engaged with, which have a low probability of occurrence, but a severe negative impact (i.e. a potential crisis events), so considerations need to be given to what should be done in separate, crisis planning documentation.
- **Stage 4 – Controls**: This relates to the measures or actions taken, which allow the benefits of interaction with some hazards and taking risks, and to continue with the service operations. Controls can focus on reducing

the likelihood of occurrence or reducing the severity of their outcome. One important consideration here is the principle of ALARP, which stands for keeping risks 'As Low As Reasonably Practicable'. What should also be appreciated here is the theory of nudge, discussed throughout this book, whereby people can be encouraged to make small changes in behaviour, but which can have a big affect on risks.
- **Stage 5 – Monitoring**: Risk should be considered as a dynamic process which always needs monitoring and reviewing. In relation to crisis management, operational environmental conditions should be constantly monitored, as the risks and potential for a crisis can change month-by-month, day-by-day, even minute-by-minute.

It should be appreciated that in practice these steps can be more fluid and overlap, but they help convey the key elements of what must be done in risk management and lay the foundation for developing separate, more detailed crisis plans and checklists, discussed in the next sections.

9.4 DEVELOPING CRISIS MANAGEMENT PLANS

In essence, what needs to be distilled from the risk process are those key events which can have a low probability of occurrence, but have a high assessment rating in terms of the negative impacts for life, equipment, buildings, reputation, finances and continued operations. These types of events can be framed as the potential crisis events which are considered in more detail in what are variously described as either Business Continuity Plans, Crisis Preparedness Plans, Vulnerability Audits or Crisis Manuals.

Fagel (2014), using his experiences of dealing with the huge crisis events which can affect the USA (and we are talking the real big ones, such as hurricanes, floods and forest fires), stresses the importance of a number of themes which should be considered in crisis plans, saying that emergency planners MUST (his capital letters) focus on PLANNING, PREPERATION and PRACTICE. Integral in this process for both preventing a crisis and dealing with it more effectively is 'COMMUNICATION, where everyone must be OPEN to communication at every level, at all times' (Fagel, 2014). What is therefore needed is to guard against failures of IMAGINATION and develop a CULTURE OF PREPAREDNESS (Fagel, 2014, p. xvii). These are important points and are embedded not only in the subsequent sections of this chapter but throughout this whole book, particularly the aspects of developing fit for purpose working cultures.

When engaging with risk and crisis management, one question which frequently arises is how feasible is it to prepare for all the possible crisis situations which could occur? What is argued here is that whilst it may not be possible to plan for every key crisis event, it is however possible to prepare for some of the key crisis situations and some of the generic responses. For example, it is not possible to predict all the different ways that a service is cancelled, or customers being severely injured or dying, but it is possible to work out

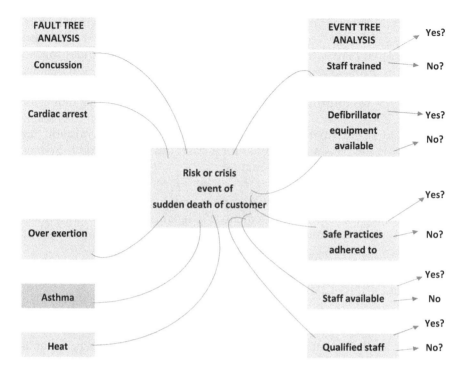

Figure 9.2 Examples of Fault and Event Tree Analysis for Sudden Death of Sport Participant.
Source: Author.

what is the crisis response to these events. The point of more detailed crisis planning, therefore, is to:

a. **Prevent**: Put in controls to avoid crisis situations occurring in the first instance.
b. **Reduce severity**: If a crisis event does take place, then having controls in place try and reduce the severity of consequences.
c. **Recovery**: To outline actions to help individuals and the business, recover from the crisis event.

The process of crisis management begins with the preliminary risk assessment process stages (Figure 9.1), which try to identify the key crisis events that can disrupt service operations. As before, this process can involve a variety of creative thinking techniques (Chapter 3) and more research (Chapter 10). Piekarz et al. (2015) outline the many creative thinking tools, which can be used in risk management, to try and guard against catastrophic failures of imagination. One of the techniques discussed is the use of fault and event tree analysis, illustrated in Figure 9.2. In this example, it explores the crisis scenario of someone collapsing and dying, combining both fault tree (what causation factor can lead up to this event) and event tree (what are the consequences of the event). (Note: when these two tools are combined, it is sometimes also described as bow-tie analysis, because of the shape produced, as shown in Figure 9.2).

Crisis management, dynamic risk assessments 199

The point of this exercise is to focus on the controls or management actions that need to be taken to either reduce the likelihood of occurrence or the severity of the impacts. For example, one of the causation factors identified for sudden death or collapse can relate to over-heating, so management controls can be put in place such as timing the event at cooler parts of the day (or in some instances at night!); ensuring there is plenty of water and shade and monitoring levels of exertion. In Figure 9.2 it also begins to map out the consequences of a collapse (the event tree analysis), where further scenarios can be mapped when different controls may or may not be available, such as having first aid qualified people who can intervene and save a life (i.e. reduce the severity of outcome). These scenarios can also form a vital part of staff training to help with Fagel's early point about PREPAREDNESS. The importance of research and crisis planning is given in Box 9.3.

Box 9.3 When a bat flaps its wings: crisis management, chaos theory and global pandemics

The list of sport events facing a crisis because of events generated in the external environment is a long one. For example, terrorist attacks (e.g. the 9/11 New York attacks; the 2005 London Underground and transport attacks; the 2013 Boston Marathon bombing; and the 2015 attacks in Paris on the Stade de France and the Bataclan theatre) have seen thousands killed or injured and numerous sport events cancelled. The natural environment too has resulted in a long list of sport event cancellations, when volcanic eruptions, earthquakes and typhoons have occurred.

All these examples, however, pale into insignificance when considering the impact of the pandemic, COVID-19, has had on sport and leisure around the world. It offers many lessons for learning about the value of understanding both systems and chaos theory (discussed in Chapter 1), where, in this instance, it was perhaps not the butterfly that flapped its wings, but the bat.

The COVID-19 virus spread around the world, seeing an unprecedented post-war impact on economies, businesses and sport events. It graphically illustrates how the global, interconnected VUCA world (see Chapter 1) brings countless opportunities, but also many risks, which can generate crisis events that can threaten continued operational business viability. Runciman (2019) discusses the fear of interconnectedness, saying, that whilst global interconnectedness has brought great wealth, there are some who feel the world has become vulnerable to collapse, 'because everything is joined to everything else (p. 112).' He discusses how the global systems of finance, energy, communication and transportation are complex, interconnected network systems, going onto say 'what makes networks frightening is the thought they could collapse without warning'.

(continued)

Box 9.3 (continued)

And in 2020, that is just what happened. Was it, however, without warning? It was an example of what could be described as a 'known/unknown' crisis event rather than an 'unknown/unknown' event (also sometimes described as a black swan event). The evidence is that it could have been anticipated: this means it is a known/unknown event, which means if it had been identified, so known, but what we don't know is when it could occur, which is an unknown element. For example, Runciman commented that a pandemic could circulate around the globe in a few hours thanks to mass air travel (p. 112), which would disrupt the running of the global economy. It is a scenario that had been discussed for many years in in the scientific community. Then there has also been outbreaks of other diseases, such as Eboli in West Africa, which in 2014 saw the African Football Cup being cancelled in Morocco, and was moved to Equatorial New Guinea.

So, there was plenty of evidence and cases that could have been used to feed the imagination of possible crisis events, which could have allowed governments and businesses to plan for the effective measures to deal with the crisis event (which some did, others not). For sport organisations, there is no doubt that many could also have done more. What is clear, however, is that in the future, dealing with pandemics will now be seen as a vital part of their crisis planning manual, or business continuity plans, such as how to maintain streams of income, or allowing some form of service operation.

What the COVID pandemic example of 2019–2020 reminds us is that that humans are often poor learners of the past. Clarke's (2013) observation about how countries drifted into the First World War gives a useful analogy:

> No one sought it. No one understood how to stop it. Nothing was pre-ordained. Contingent choices, shaped by particular circumstances, drove individuals to make what would only emerge in hindsight as catastrophic mistakes. These politicians were not simply in some hypnotic trance, doing what the system demanded of them.
> (Clarke, 2013, p. 115)

Replace First World War with COVID-19, and these sentiments are just as applicable.

A key way to deal with this weakness is to therefore adopt transparent open learning cultures, underpinned by integrity, humility and ethics, that try and analyse systems that inter-connect in complex ways, trying to avoid those catastrophic failures in imagination. All sport organisations will also need to consider crisis management contingencies, which blend in social distancing controls, issuing protective clothing to staff, improve cleaning practices and sanitisation after events, to have different ways to participate in services (e.g. online fitness classes).

What is also of interest is how some sport organisations have attempted to leverage the opportunities from the crisis events – such as supporting charities and health workers to enhance the brand, or offering more bespoke, personalised sport services – and examples which show the value of thinking creatively to try and embrace crisis storm events.

Discussion

Focusing on disease-related crisis events, elaborate on some of the key crisis measures which sport organisations need to consider to: reduce the likelihood of diseases spreading; deal with the severity of the impact of pandemics; and how they can try and ride or embrace the storm, as part of new power theories.

In order to further help stimulate the creative thinking processes of analysing and assessing risks and crisis situations, other research techniques can be used. For example, it is possible to use typologies of crisis events and conduct research on past incidents, which can be analysed and learnt from. In Figure 9.3 a simple typology is given of potential crisis event sources (the descriptions surrounding the overlapping circles) and examples of their consequences (the descriptions which appear in the boxes surrounding the crisis events). These categories are based on synthesising a variety of source materials (e.g. Business Links, 2012; Curtin, 2005; Piekarz et al., 2015).

Looking at the typology of crisis events, it can be observed that some of these events emerge from different layers of the business environment, such as the internal layer (e.g. equipment failure, staffing issues, etc.), the intermediate environment (e.g. the actions of competitors) and some from the external business environment (e.g. extreme weather, political changes, acts of terrorism, etc.). It is self-consciously adapting the techniques of SWOT and PESTLE analysis to show how these processes can be blended in naturally with risks and crisis management practices. To further help with the identification and analysis of crisis events, more elaboration is given in Table 9.2, which can be used to help prompt deeper exploration and use of creative thinking techniques.

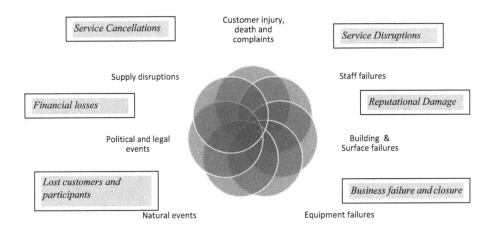

Figure 9.3 Sources of Crisis Events and Key Consequences.
Source: Author.

Table 9.2 Description and Examples of Key Sources of Crisis Events

Category	Description	Examples of Crisis Scenarios to Plan for
Internal Environment		
Customer crisis events	Customers can be injured or die whilst doing an activity, which may be related to other external factors, such as weather conditions and acts of terrorism, or relate to their own personal health problems. Customer complaints can also escalate and become more serious, whereby technology and social media have the potential to make a complaint go viral	Severe injury, death of participant, accusations of abuse, etc.
Equipment failure or playing environments not fit for purpose	This could relate to a huge number of issues, such as equipment failing which means people cannot play the sport, to larger equipment failures, such computer system failures, which can mean bookings cannot take place, or data is lost	Cancellation procedures; back-up equipment scenarios; IT booking system failures and data protection breaches; heating and air condition systems to allow safe participation of activities and back-up procedures (e.g. hiring temporary heating or air condition systems)
Staffing failures and scandals	Staff have the potential to create crisis events, which can range from illness of a key member of staff to poor behaviour which requires their suspension and could attract media attention. For elite athletes, their actions are constantly scrutinised by the media, which can raise challenges for how agents, clubs and the governing bodies of sport should respond. The ripple effects of scandals can tarnish a whole sport, which the manager and SDO may need to try and manage to rebuild trust in the sport, even though they may not be directly involved	Rude staff or abuse of customers; staff engaged with inappropriate behaviour; staff cover for illness and absence; demonstration of the ethical underpinnings of your sport services in case of broader sport scandals, which can damage the reputation of the sport
Building and playing surfaces	There can be a variety of causes, from natural disasters, acts of vandalism or even terrorist attacks. The risks of fire are a particular important consideration here, where, in conjunction with fire services and compliance with fire regulations, various controls should be put in place to initially try and prevent a fire (e.g. smoke alarms), having mechanisms to prevent fire escalating (e.g. having fire extinguishers placed around the building) and fire escapes to help people to ensure people are alerted and can evacuate safely, thus reducing the severity of the consequences and a bigger crisis, where the trauma of loss of life is avoided. Playing surfaces can also be prone to change and create more risks, such as frozen pitches, which are too dangerous to play on	Building evacuation procedures; testing of alarms and communications systems; systems to protect pitches to keep the safe and playable (e.g. heating systems, protection from rain, etc.)

Crisis management, dynamic risk assessments 203

Intermediate

Supply failures	Supply failures may be considered as more important for manufacturing (i.e. if you do not have the raw materials, you can make the product), but they can be crucial for some sport services. There are many instances where events have had to be cancelled, or participant's health exposed to unnecessary risks, when water supplies have failed to be delivered for competitive events, such as marathons and athletic meetings	Back-up suppliers of equipment, food and (for events) water; scenarios for supplying water in key areas of running courses; risks for dealing with food contamination or quality issue scandals (e.g. food sold as organic turns out to be a lie)
Actions of competitors	The actions of competitors can affect the business in a variety of ways, such as a competitor budget gym, opening up near more established facilities, which can mean that core customers may be lost	Prices change scenarios and impacts on revenue; impacts of key loss of income, such as sponsor deal, or government funding cuts

External Environment

Political instability and legal changes	Events rooted in the political and social environment can be disruptive. These can range from the actions of governments, such as changes in policy – changes in legislation – or more dramatic political acts, such as war and civil unrest. Terrorism has also become a key problem to consider	Dealing with protestors and disruptions; terrorist attack scenarios for prevention and post-attack recovery
Economic crisis events	At times there can be a slow economic decline that can prose numerous challenges for sport memberships, such as rising unemployment. Gym membership can be particularly prone to the economic fluctuations. At a local level, the closure of a key employer, such as a factory, can have quick immediate impacts	Scenario impacts for local and national economic downturns; threats to key market segment if a key local employer or factory closes.
Social changes	Attitude changes in society can raise the potential for a crisis. Although sport is often presented as a progressive force for change, it should also be appreciated that it can at times be a negative one, where entrenched views hold back change	Ensure responding to changing social attitudes (e.g. dated, sexist marketing campaigns); responding to negative stories for sport to rebuild trust and brand image
Natural environment, disease and natural disasters	This has to be done in the context of the country and the location the sport events and services are taking place, which can impact in a variety of areas, such as damage to buildings and equipment, or changing the risks of the event for participants (e.g. extreme heat impacting on participants doing endurance events)	Context dependent, such as dealing with extremes in heat or cold, or if they are prone to natural disasters, such as earthquakes, Tsunami and volcanic eruptions.

9.5 DEVELOPING A CRISIS MANUAL OR BUSINESS CONTINUITY PLAN

Whilst crisis events can have a complex pattern of causation, whereby it is impossible to anticipate every possible crisis event which could occur, it has been argued that it still feasible to anticipate some of the broad crisis events and how they can disrupt activities (see back to Table 9.2). The application of the various risk process stages, which can also be used to identify, analyse and assess different crisis situations, will act as the key foundation for producing a crisis manual or business continuity plan.

Whatever its title, this manual should contain the following elements:

- **Prevention**: Identifying controls to try and prevent a crisis, or reduce its escalation (see back to Figure 9.2 and the fault tree analysis). This is sometimes described as the pre-crisis planning phase.
- **Managing**: Putting in controls to deal with the crisis as it unfolds to try and mitigate or reduce the severity of consequences. This relates to DRA discussed later.
- **Recovering**: Developing measures for the organisation to recover from the situation, which moves into the strategic level and is important part of managing reputational risks and brand management.

In order to make an operational crisis manual easy to use, it is recommended that it presents information concisely, often using checklists of actions which deal with different scenarios, in order to prevent, deal with, or help recover from a crisis. Gawande (2010), drawing on examples of how the aviation, engineering and the events sectors have dealt with complexity, provides an invaluable text on the importance of developing operational checklists for everyone, in all fields of work. The work is based on the challenge he was given by the UN for developing a simple, one-page checklist for surgeons to use all over the world, which could help save lives. Based on this work, here are a few of Gawande's (2010, p. 43) adapted principles of good practice for developing checklists:

- Checklists can range from **DO to CONFIRM** (i.e. confirm you have done an action) and **READ to DO** (i.e. read what has been written and do it).
- If it is an operational checklist, identify points where verification can be confirmed.
- Ask what or will go wrong?
- Check chains of command for clear communication.
- Select staff/train and prepare.
- Contacts – are they clear and up to date.
- Ask yourself this – "How could I justify this decision in courts?"
- Develop a checklist manual which is easy to understand (or links into other checklists).
- Date and sign any forms with any subsequent amendments or reviews.

Aspects of these elements of checklists have already been explored in earlier chapters (e.g. Chapter 3 and the underpinning principles of time management and quality systems discussed in Chapter 5); hopefully it is recognised that checklists are not only a vital part of risk and crisis management, but in fact ALL management. In live crisis events or dynamic risk situations, they can play a pivotal role in helping to make clear decisions, during potentially stressful and emotionally charged moments. Elements of crisis checklists are also explored in Box 9.3.

The final parts of the crisis plan can deal with the medium- to long-term actions which may need to be taken post-crisis event. This is part of the glide path of recovery and needs to consider how the business begins service operations again, such as the actions to rebuild trust and confidence in the service and brand, such as promotional schemes, price reductions, supporting charities and helping those who were affected by the situation. Whatever actions are taken, what must never be forgotten is that operational practices are constantly reviewed to try and improve upon.

Here is a summary of some of the key points of crisis manuals or continuity plans should include, drawn from a variety of literature (e.g. Bernstein, 2015), for both electronic and hard copies, made available to key members of staff who are identified as having responsibility and leadership roles in crisis events:

- **Background information**: This should include key roles and contact details, particularly the key spokesperson to lead on the crisis, or the Crisis Communications Team – who may have to deal with the media and other key stakeholders (e.g. families); preliminary outline of what to do in early stages of a crisis event, contextualised around the broad scenarios (e.g. sudden death of participant or staff member); and ensuring staff know where the manual is – and include details of key suppliers (e.g. IT support, glaziers for broken glass, plumbers, electricians); include maps, if appropriate, of key buildings; specify who is the key spokesperson; include audits of what is vulnerable (see Figure 9.1) and how; ensure key quality standards and regulations are complied with.
- **Prevent**: Outlined here should be the measures taken to anticipate or prevent a crisis occurring. The key crisis scenarios should be mapped out to create awareness of situations (see back to Table 9.2 for examples). Measures taken to identify key training need to prevent or reduce severity of outcomes; methods of communications to staff and key stakeholders about the crisis manual and creative thinking activities, outlined in various stages of this book, can be used to avoid any 'catastrophic failures in imagination.'
- **Managing the crisis**: Different crisis events will require different responses and access to information. As part of the key crisis planning stages, key operational checklists should be identified, which are clear and easy to understand (see back to the Checklists and Box 9.3). Write key holding statements for people to state, if necessary.
- **Post-crisis management**: This can be just as important as the other stages, where failure to manage this can result in the business failing. Continue to maintain Crisis Communications Team, ensuring messages are clear and accurate. Avoid 'cover-ups.' Organise investigation using an open learning culture (see Black box thinking in Chapter 1 and the importance of ethics discussed in Chapter 7). Keep communications simple. Have no more than three main messages that go to all stakeholders and, as necessary, some audience-specific messages for individual groups of stakeholders.

Box 9.4 The operational challenges of managing the risk of concussion in sport

Part of the attraction of sport for both watching and playing is the physical contest between people. This does however create many risks, which, if not properly managed, can result in both short- and long-term health impairments or even death. Sadly, there are many instances where players' health has been sacrificed by the governing bodies of sport and clubs, in the misguided attempts to try and protect the reputation and brand of the sport, by covering up or simple denial, whether these relate to issues of corruption, drug abuse, health risks or coaching abuse (see Box 1.5 for other examples).

The dangers of behaving unethical is graphically illustrated with how the American NFL handled the risk of concussion to players of the game, which became a costly and long-drawnout crisis event, costing billions of dollars in compensation, a damaged reputation and worst of all, many ruined lives of former players. It is a salutary lesson for 'what not to do' in a crisis, when commercial interests are put before the moral and legal responsibility to health and safety. Rather than dealing with the health risks from concussion can cause (e.g. early onset of dementia and other brain diseases) the NFL, for decades, chose to deny, cover up (e.g. paying doctors to contest the medical evidence emerging of the risks of brain disease) and even in some instances resorting to intimidation. As evidence continued to build and the extent of the covering up was exposed, the damage to the trust and reputation was all the greater (you are encouraged to explore the issue in the book by Fainara-Wada and Webster (2012), the journalists who exposed the scandal, and how the NFL made the fateful decision of denying the risks, rather than accepting them).

The issue of concussion and the mishandling by the NFL is just as relevant in many other sports, such as boxing, ice-hockey, soccer, rugby and even cricket. For example, the governing bodies of rugby union, although initially slow to deal with the risk of concussion, in recent years, have been more proactive in dealing with the risks, clearly attempting to learn from the NFL experience. Their actions demonstrate how in order to deal with the risks and prevent short-, medium- and long-term crisis events, the issue needs to be managed both at an operational and a strategic level. Here are some examples of risk control checklists, framed around the earlier outlined principles of prevent, manage and post-crisis event management based on the RFU (2015) guidelines:

Examples of preventative actions and controls (for all participants, designed to reduce the likelihood of serious injury taking place which precipitates a crisis):

- Not allowing players to be tackled in the air
- No high tackles to the head or neck
- Padding on goals posts
- Rules for how scrums must be engaged with in terms of binding to reduce the likelihood of scrums collapsing and spinal injury occurring

Manage crisis events (designed for coaches, referees and medical staff, after a serious injury has occurred)

- **DO NOT** move the casualty.
- Keep calm, reassure casualty and keep them warm.
- Summon the first aider/medical personnel to scene.
- Remain with the casualty until first aider arrives.
- Move other players away from scene, and ensure they are supervised and protected from the weather.
- Arrange for next of kin to be notified if not present.
- Arrange for the injured player to be accompanied to hospital if no next of kin present.

Post-crisis checklist of actions (designed for senior club officials, outlining some actions to take after a serious injury or death has occurred):

- The club should contact their RFU Regional Press Officer who will be able to assist in terms of media management and putting in place arrangements with the RFU.
- Legal counsel is likely to lead on the RFU support in the management of the incident which will include the following:
  - Notification of the RFU Insurers
  - Notify the press office
- Co-ordinate any formal safety investigations that may be required:
  - Where appropriate, arrange for the appointment of external advisers to any investigation initiated by the RFU. Clubs should not appoint experts to investigate an incident without legal advice being obtained first.
- Co-ordinate the preparation of any RFU lead investigation report.
- Advise on any communications received from third party's lawyers.

Discussion questions

For a different sport, explore the guidelines which have been issued for dealing with serious injury and what sort of operational crisis checklists can be developed.

9.6 DEALING WITH THE MEDIA AND THE NEED FOR INTEGRITY

Reputations and brands can take years to build, but destroyed in days, hours and even minutes. This means a critical part of crisis management responses *must* be dealing with the media, which the growth of social media platforms has only accentuated. Indeed, in a sport context, some writers, such as Bernstein (2012), argue that sport crisis events can receive a disproportionate share of media attention. This is not perhaps too surprising as scandals, issues of corruption or the juxtaposition of a disaster occurring for people who are having fun and enjoying themselves can add to the power of the stories. It must be stressed that how the media dealt with during and after a crisis event can affect the future viability of the business itself, where if it is mismanaged can result in business closure, people losing their jobs and even people going to prison. What has compounded the complexity of handling the media has been the growth of social media, which Cross (2011) argues further help shape crisis events in terms of the speed of the communications and the quantity of people who can access it.

It is beyond the scope of this chapter and book to give the full details of media management and public relations. All that can be done is to outline some simple measures that can be considered by managers who may have to deal with the media, whereby a key part of the crisis manual is identifying the key media spokesperson(s):

- The classic, standard response to a crisis when talking to the media is:

    - **Pity**: Extend and state your sympathy for the family or those people directly effected by the event.
    - **Praise**: Comment on the good work done by emergency staff and key staff and workers.
    - **Promises**: State that every effort will be made to find out why it happened and lessons will be learnt.

- Additional points of good practice are as follows:

    - Appoint a senior media spokesperson.
    - Never say "no comment" as this suggests you are hiding something.
    - Never put your hand over the camera.
    - Never speculate about the cause of the event.
    - Never give 'unguarded remarks'.
    - Be prepared to talk to the press and pool interviews.
    - Consider setting up an incident rooms/team if necessary. This can help control the flow of information. A vital component in the incident team is clear and concise communication, where daily briefings take place and a single point of contact is established.
    - In early stages of a crisis event, send some people home to rest, as they will be needed later, even though the temptation may be to have everyone there.
    - Media can be both a friend and an enemy. For example, emergency services use the media as they can disseminate information and warnings very quickly. Others, however, who have been involved with crisis events have found their experiences as very difficult, even traumatic.
    - What can help in the response or dealing with the media is to understand what they want, such as having story deadlines and a desire for emotive stories.

The final point to consider is the vital importance of utter integrity when approaching crisis events. When crisis events occur, there can be at times a temptation for people to cover up. Ultimately this can be more costly in the long run, as Text Box 9.3 illustrated, or various other examples of operational failure used in this book have also shown. It is morally wrong to do this, and if that is not persuasive enough, it can be costly financially where the future viability of the organisation can be called into question. Remember, reputations are built on trust and belief, which younger generations of consumers seem set to give even more credence to (i.e. Generation Z). By maintaining integrity, this will help harness the crisis storms and potentially turn them into an opportunity.

9.7 DYNAMIC RISK MANAGEMENT, ASSESSMENTS AND CRISIS MANAGEMENT

DRA represents the operational part of crisis events operating in real time. DRA has grown in importance and is rooted in the emergency and social services, who have to deal with a variety of incidents and disasters, where they constantly need to review and evaluate the risks to themselves and others, as they engage with the event. In one sense, good managers and SDOs should always be engaging with DRA, as they should be alert to hazards, analysing them (e.g. changing weather conditions), assessing the risks, then making decisions about how to deal with them; the difference, however, with dynamic risk management (DRM) is that it takes place in more time-pressured, dynamic, ever-changing situations.

The reason why DRA is combined with crisis management is that if certain key crisis situations are identified, then managers, SDOs or anyone else involved with decision-making can have their decision-making improved and refined through training and using operational crisis management checklists, discussed in the previous section (i.e. PREPAREDNESS). Assessing a situation and taking the right action really can save lives, money and reputations. For example, it is possible to adapt some of the emergency services procedures, such as the STAR system some use when faced with a crisis event, which stands for:

- **STOP** (stop what you are doing to face the new situation faced)
- **THINK** (assess the situation before acting, in order to proceed safely and not put others and undue risk)
- **ACT** (take actions as appropriate, ensuring good communication with others)
- **REVIEW** (after taking actions, review and continue to communicate)

Crisis manuals and risk assessments can initially help identify key areas of training and qualifications (e.g. having people who are first aiders), which can be refined with scenario training (e.g. bomb alerts, sudden death of participants, pandemics, etc.). The lists of checklist actions can further help with the decision-making, in much the same way that pilots will use a manual and go through a series of checks during crisis situations.

9.8 CONCLUSIONS

Crisis management stretches across the management levels of strategic planning and operational decision-making. The recommendation here is to blend in crisis management and planning with existing risk practices which must be engaged with as part of a moral obligation and legal compulsion. As part of the process of identifying and managing risks, those that are deemed as low probability, but severe in their potential impacts, which can disrupt continued service operations, can be identified and used for the basis of crisis management plans. These plans do not need to identify every possible crisis event, but can focus on certain key event outcomes, whereby the plans should be concise, clear and identify initially how to prevent the crisis. They can then identify how to deal with the crisis to reduce the severity and loss. Finally, how to recover from the event. All of which should be underpinned by having a learning culture that is open, driven by acting ethically, and has a humility to accept criticism and look to learn from the past.

References

Bernstein, P. (1998). *Against the Gods: The Remarkable Story of Risk*. Chichester: Wiley and Sons.

Bernstein, B. (2012). Crisis management and sports in the age of social media: A case study analysis of the tiger woods scandal. *Journal of Undergraduate Research in Communications*, 3(2), 1/31.

Bernstein, J. (2015). Sports crisis management, accessed 29 January 2015, available at: http://www.bernsteincrisismanagement.com/sports-crisis-management.html

Business Link (2012). Crisis management & business continuity planning, accessed 29 January 2015, available at: http://webarchive.nationalarchives.gov.uk/20120823131012/http://www.businesslink.gov.uk/bdotg/action/layer?topicId=1074458463

Clarke, C. (2013). *The Sleep Walkers: How Europe Went to War in 1914*. London: Penguin.

Cross, M. (2011). Bloggerati, Twitterati: How Blogs and Twitter are Transforming Popular Culture. Santa Barbara, CA: Praeger.

Curtin, T (2005). *Managing a Crisis: A Practical Guide*. London: Palgrave Macmillan.

Fagel, M.J. (2014). *Crisis Management and Emergency Planning: Preparing for Todays Challenges*. London: CRC Press.

Fainara-Wada, M., and Webster, M. (2012). *League of Denial*. London: Penguin.

Gawande, E. (2010). *Checklist Manifesto*. London: Profile books.

Glaesser, D. (2003). *Crisis Management in the Tourism Industry*. London: Elsevier.

Government of South Australia (2009). Risk management resource for recreation and sports organisation. Report, accessed 2 September, 2019, available at: https://orsr.sa.gov.au/__data/assets/pdf_file/0021/7815/Risk_management_resource.pdf

ISO (2018). 3100: 2018, accessed on 2 August 2019, available at: https://www.iso.org/obp/ui#iso:std:iso:31000:ed-2:v1:en

London.Gov.Uk (2015). Preparing your business, accessed 29 January 2015, available at: http://www.london.gov.uk/mayor-assembly/mayor/london-resilience/preparing-your-businessPiekarz, M., Jenkins, I., and Mills, P. (2015). *Risk and Safety in Adventure, Sport, Tourism and Events Industries*. Wallingford: Cabi Publishing.

Pilling, D. (2014). *Bending Adversity*. London: Penguin.

RFU (2015). Guidance to CBs, clubs and schools on serious injury management, available at: https://www.englandrugby.com/mm/Document/General/General/01/31/66/47/160229_GuidancetoClubsonSeriousInjuryManagement_English.pdf

Runciman, D. (2019). *How Democracy Ends*. Croydon: Profile Books.

Sport & Recreation Alliance (2015). Crisis management plans, accessed 29 January 2015, available at:http://www.sportandrecreation.org.uk/smart-sport/communication/communication-strategy/crisis-management

Timms, H., and Heimans, J. (2018). *Newpower*. Croydon: Macmillan.

Waite, B. (2001). *Managing Risk and Resolving Crisis*. Harlow: Financial Times Prentice Hall.

10 RESEARCHING AND CONSULTING COMMUNITIES

Challenges for managers

- How do you find out about what sport services people need and want?
- What databases can be used for research about communities?
- What practical methods can be used to collect data and information?

10.1 INTRODUCTION

Managers and SDOs need data and information. They are the foundation for good decision-making in operations management. Data refers to the unprocessed facts and figures that managers and SDOs can collect, which, once they are organised, analysed and assessed, then becomes information. This information is needed to ensure that: managers and SDOs are market orientated; to ensure services are delivered to the expected level of quality for customers and clients (Chapters 1, 4 and 5); to help answer the questions 'how are we doing?' and 'are we going in the right direction?' (Chapter 2); to evaluate if sport service outputs are effectively being leveraged to achieve a variety of outcomes (Chapter 1); and to ensure public money has been used efficiently and effectively (Chapters 2 and 8).

This chapter explores some of the practical tools and techniques for collecting data and information. It begins, by giving a short discussion of communities, to give an insight into what sort of information may need to be collected from them. It then gives an overview of the research process, considering the *why*, *what*, *when* and *where* of data collection and research, for effective and efficient operations management.

10.2 RESEARCHING COMMUNITIES AND OUTCOMES

Sport services should be embedded in communities. This is important not only from a marketing perspective, to ensure service efficiency and effectiveness, but also because of the broader responsibilities to non-user stakeholders, discussed in Chapter 7. It is worthwhile, then, to clarify what is meant by the term 'community'.

In essence, a community refers to a group of people who are linked and connected in some way, whether this relates to geographic location, culture, religion, language or numerous other possible connecting values. Etzioni (1993) has been an influential writer on communities and the theory of communitarianism, which, simply put, outlines ways that communities can become better connected and supportive of their collective interests (a little simplistic, but it is sufficient for now). He argues that communities are made of many different blocks, where people can have multiple and overlapping connections. For example, some people could be part of a community which is shaped by their work, but who could then belong to different communities based on their religion, or the local neighbourhoods they occupy, or even the sport and recreational activities they pursue. Etzoni's theory of communitarianism offers, a way to try and deliver healthy, strong and safe civic communities (the term 'third way' is also sometimes used). As part of this approach, sport and recreation has sometimes been viewed as a useful resource to develop a sense of attachment and collective identity (i.e. leveraging sport outputs to achieve outcomes). This work is not without criticisms, such as the argument that governments have used these theories to remove themselves from some of the financial and moral commitments to provide key welfare services; whilst important criticisms, they should not however stop managers and SDOs making genuine attempts to leverage sport participation and services to help support and nurture communities.

Utilising the concept of social capital helps to give further insights into the subject of sport and communities. In essence, social capital refers to the 'glue' that connects and binds individuals to other groups in the community, which relates to Putnam's influential work (2000) about how the demise of traditional communities was leading to decline of social capital. In essence, Putman argued that modern economic relationships could place more emphasis on the individual, rather than the collective, which can lead to a weakening of social capital, where the problem was encapsulated by his book "Bowling Alone". This was the analogy used, where Putman described how bowling clubs were once hugely popular social groups, which many would participate in; the decline of these groups, Putman argues, is an indicator of wider social changes, which sees people becoming more insular and isolated (hence the 'bowling alone' analogy). It is not surprising that sport has been viewed as a useful potential mechanism to try and improve social capital, because of the opportunities to bring people together, where the emotional shared moments can help act as a bonding agent to develop identity and collective action.

From a practical operations management perspective, it should also be recognised that exploring communities and the many different groups who exist in the community are intimately related to marketing and the theory of market segmentation. There is not the scope to explore all the different ways people can be segmented and targeted, so it is recommended that more specific marketing books are used for this subject area. For now, the following points help highlight some key attributes of a community which sport managers and SDOs need to research, based around:

- **Geography**: Communities, traditionally, have been defined in a geographical context, such as a village, town, city or region, which is particularly important part of SDO work. Although social media has changed the

dynamic, in sport service operations, the geography that communities are located in is still important.
- **Attachment**: There is a sense of attachment to the area that the groups live in, which can be further strengthened by a variety of factors, such as ethnicity, work occupations, religion and sport and recreational interests and facilities. This sense of connection and attachment can come from actually having sport and recreational facilities people can share and utilise, or from the support of sport teams rooted in the area.
- **Need**: There can be the twin notions of 'Being part of' a space or group (sociological), or 'identifying with' a group or area (psychological). When connected to theories of needs (e.g. Maslow's hierarchy and the human need of belonging, status and self-actualisation, discussed in Chapter 4), this gives an insight of the importance of communities and the value of sport to achieve these forms of outcomes.

One observation which should be made is that the traditional focus on communities belonging to specific geographic locations has changed. This is very evident in the how the elite sport teams around the world have sought to broaden their appeal and communities beyond their towns, regions and even the country itself. For example, for many of the top European football teams, their initial foundation and growth was rooted in local working-class communities, with many stadiums built near workplaces, so that workers would work a half-day Saturday shift in a factory, finish work, then walk to the stadium to watch the afternoon game. The service experience and identities created were firmly rooted in the physical geography and the limitations of communications. Today, technology has meant that these physical limits have been removed, which means it is possible to create football team communities, in other countries, around the world.

10.3 OVERVIEW OF DATA COLLECTION METHODS

Many managers and SDOs may have encountered research methods in former academic studies, particularly when studying for a university degree course. The value of the subject is not always appreciated at the time of study: yet once the realities of work hit, where managers and SDOs constantly need data to inform and justify decisions, the importance becomes clear. Managers and SDOs will find gaps in their knowledge, which can hinder effective decision-making, whilst also struggling to find the time to collect and analyse data. In this section, the key terminology and methods used in data collection and research are outlined, summarised in Figure 10.1. This process considers *why* data is collected, *what* type of data is collected, *when* it is collected and *how* it is collected, finishing with a brief consideration as to *how* it can be analysed. These stages form the subsequent sub-sections of this chapter.

To gain a sense of why data is important and the variety of ways it can be collected, an illustrative case study is given in Box 10.1.

Researching and consulting communities 215

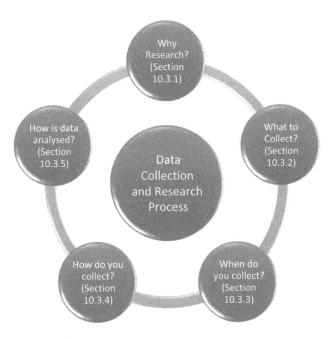

Figure 10.1 Overview of Research Process.
Source: Author.

Box 10.1 Performance evaluation and data collection for a sport *for* development: slam dunking aids out

There has been a growth in popularity of sport *for* development projects around the world (see Chapter 1), whereby sport is used as a vehicle to educate and create awareness about a variety of issues, such as combating discrimination or educating children about diseases. The proposition is that because sport activities can be popular with children, if their participation (outputs) can be properly leveraged, then more profound changes in heath behaviours can occur (i.e. the outcomes).

An example of a sport *for* development project is 'Dunking Aids Out: Learning About AIDS Through Basketball Movement Games' (Davies et al., 2005). This basketball sport project was developed to try and reduce the spread of AIDS and deal with the issues of stigmatisation and discrimination. To this end, Davies et al. (2005) produced an invaluable practical manual for coaches, teachers and SDOs, to show how they could use basketball to teach broader lessons about the disease of aids. Although it was initially

(continued)

Box 10.1 (continued)

developed within the context of poor communities in African countries, with limited sport infrastructures, the activities can easily be adapted and applied in other situations and countries, no matter what the level of economic development, or used for other health messages. This practical manual gives many instances of how to try and leverage outputs, into outcomes, by playing a variety of basketball games, then building in some reflective learning points (i.e. the mechanisms of leverage), as the following examples illustrate:

- **DAO triple cool position** – The ball is presented as the problem, where you have a number of options for what you can do with the ball, such as dribbling, passing or shooting. These three options are then used to represent three options: abstain from sex; be faithful with one partner; or use a condom. The game is then played with three players, where players practice these options and score points. Crucially, in terms of leverage, a key part of this activity is the follow-up activities and discussion about the analogy of the game and the three options.
- **21 Wins – AIDS kills** – Two teams are formed, who form a line in each corner of the free throw line. The first player shoots, then follows up with their rebound, scoring 2 points for every basket or 1 point for catching the ball from a rebound, before it hits the ground. When a player misses and the ball hits the ground, they collect a Letter A, the I for the second miss, D for the third and S for the final miss. When AIDS is spelt, a video is showing AIDS is the real killer.

So how does research and data help with this work? Remember, because outputs are achieved, this *never* means positive outcomes automatically accrue – this is dependent on other variables, such as how the coach or teacher uses the session, which, if it is fun and enjoyable, can create a memorable moment to learn from. To begin with, data can be collected to find the pockets of need for a sport *for* development project. In essence, this adopts a marketing approach, but instead of looking for new markets for sport services based on affluence and disposable incomes, the focus is on the social needs of the community and how to deal with some of their complex health problems. For example, WHO (2020) provides a wealth of invaluable quantitative secondary data in terms of health and the incidence of aids around the world, providing a series of interactive maps. WHO also has a range of other statistical reports on sport, recreation and health available at: https://www.who.int/dietphysicalactivity/pa/en/

Next, if the service is developed and run, there is the collection of output data (i.e. primary, quantitative data on the numbers of participants). This data will be an important indicator and a measure of success, which could also be essential in the justification of any public and charity money given. The much harder challenge is to find out how successful the service is in achieving some of the stated outputs. Ideally, what is needed is a proper feedback loop, where people could be interviewed (i.e. primary data) and long-term behaviour tracked, but this is not always a realistic proposition for SDOs with limited resources and time. Using other secondary data indicators, such as the incidence of aids rates, could be a possibility, but it could be difficult to isolate the impact of the sport programme as it is likely to be affected by a web of factors and health initiatives.

Another possibility is to explore a variety of secondary data sources, such as previous research. For example, Maro et al. (2009) conducted research on the value and efficacy of using sport as a mechanism to help educate people about AIDS in poor, remote parts of the world, where formal education and access to media can be more limited. They provided some evidence of the value of using peer coaches within the soccer coaching environment to help educate people about the risks of aids and safe risk practices.

The final key ingredient is the research culture adopted. Syed (2015, p. 188) gives a useful illustrative example of the importance of having open, reflective learning cultures, where data is constantly collected and analysed. He relates the story used by Hartford (2012), in his book about the importance of learning from failures. The story relates to how educational aid projects in the impoverished areas of Busia and Teso in Kenya were compared in the effectiveness of different educational strategies, designed to combat poverty. To improve educational attainment, they initially gave free books to children in a number of schools, because, intuitively, this seemed an obvious way to improve educational performance. When, however, the results were compared with schools that did not receive the free books, they found – to their surprise – no significant difference in educational attainment. Next, they tried to change the teaching methods, but again there was no statistical difference in attainment. In the end, through fresh thinking, they tried a different approach and the action that made the most significant difference to attainment was not books or teaching methods, but worming tablets! The children who received this medication improved their physical and mental health, having less absence and were simply able to work more effective. Syed uses this example to illustrate the importance of using system theory, always looking for small improvements or marginal gains in that system, and always being willing to 'test, learn and fail' (Syed, 2015, p. 189). Themes which are constant refrains in this book.

Discussion
Identify some of the key barriers which may prevent the effectiveness of the educational measures being taken onboard by sport participants?

10.3.1 Why research and consult communities

The reason why it is important to research and consult communities has been frequently touched on in earlier chapters. In Figure 10.2 a simple summary diagram is given about the importance of research.

It should also be appreciated that collecting information and consulting communities is a vital part of the *create*, *maintain* and *improve* elements of service

Figure 10.2 Why Research and Consult Communities.
Source: Author.

operations. Here is a summary of each of the factors, represented in the figure, about the importance of research:

- **Market research**: Throughout this book, it has been stressed the importance of being market orientated, which means designing services that meet individuals and communities' needs and wants. This research process was highlighted as a key part of the design of sport services and programmes, discussed in Chapter 4, which underpins all the other feasibility and implementation processes, such as costing, staffing and risk assessment.
- **Inform decisions**: In addition to collecting market research information, other data may be needed, such as investigating past accidents in sport services, when conducting the risk assessment of an event or programme, which also helps inform the costs and its feasibility.
- **Evaluate performance and achieve outcomes**: In Chapter 2, the importance of asking the question 'how are we doing?' was raised. To do this, data is needed to check if KPI and objectives are on course for being achieved, allowing managers and SDOs to change actions, strategies and policies accordingly.
- **Improve operations**: Intimately tied in with the evaluation is collecting data to look for ways to improve the quality of service (discussed in Chapter 5). Reviewing customer survey data and comments or improving safety is particularly important in this respect.

- **Involve stakeholders**: This process can begin by researching the key stakeholders or communities (discussed in Chapter 7 in relation to producing a stakeholder map). Consulting communities, via a variety of research techniques, can also be a useful for informing participants about future possible services, together with helping them gain a sense of attachment, and commitment to a new sport projects or services.
- **Project justification**: This can be particularly important in relation to winning or maintaining money given by governments or charities. In Chapter 8, it was explained that to win money from public funding sources, such as the UK National Lottery, data is collected which shows there is a need and demand for a new sport facility, project or service.
- **Business environmental analysis**: In Chapters 1, 2 and 9, it was stressed how external factors, beyond the managers or SDOs control, can constantly generate both opportunistic and threatening risks (the O & T of a SWOT analysis), which stem from the internal and external environment (e.g. PESTLE factors), or intermediate environment (e.g. competitors and suppliers of a Porter's Framework).

10.3.2 What data is collected?

The importance of consultation and research should be clear. The next challenge is to consider just what sort of data can be collected? In Figure 10.3, a simple summary is given of the key types of data which can be collected.

When reflecting on the different terms, it should be appreciated that they can overlap, whereby managers and SDOs will usually collect a mix of data. For example, a manager or SDO may collect their own *primary*, *quantifiable* usage

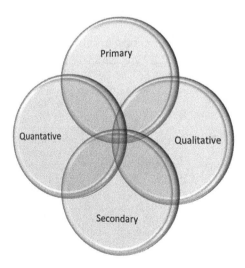

Figure 10.3 What Data is Collected?
Source: Author.

output data, which can be further complemented by some *primary qualitative* customer satisfaction surveys or social media posts. This data can be given further context, by comparing this data with a variety of secondary *quantifiable* and *qualitative* data, as illustrated in both Boxes 10.1 and 10.2. Here is a summary for what the key terms refer to:

- **Primary data**: This is collected first hand, by the manager or SDO, such as interviews, meetings and surveys.
- **Secondary data**: This data and information has already been collected, such as market analysis reports, population data, etc..
- **Quantifiable data**: This is data based on numbers, such as participation rates for a sport.
- **Qualitative data**: This is data which is more descriptive, such as drawing out opinions on the quality of service.

Box 10.2 Using secondary databases to assess demand

Depending on the country operated in, there are a variety of open secondary databases (i.e. free to access) which can be used to gain useful data on the local community, which can then be used to assess recreational needs and wants. For example, in the UK, using the free population census databases, such as the Neighbourhood Statistics and the Nomis link, offers a wealth of invaluable data relating to age profiles, income, employment status or household ownership. For profit-orientated sport service operators, this data can be used to identify affluent communities and potential market gaps (i.e. people have disposable income, but there may be a lack of supply); alternatively, the databases can be used to identify pockets of community deprivation, such as high incidents of unemployment or ageing populations (see also back to Box 10.1 for an example). Below is a simple illustration of the sort of data that can be found, which contrasts one of the richest and poorest communities in the UK.

Location 1 – Jaywick, Essex, St Mary's Ward-One of the Most Deprived Places in Britain (Post Code C013)	Location 2 – Kensington, London, Belgravia Ward – One of the Richest Places in Britain (Post Code SW 7)
Total population: 2,908 (1,403 males: 1,505 females)	Total population:8,417 (4,782 males: 3,635 females)
2,069 are economically active, of which 267 are self-employed and 259 are unemployed	4,116 are economically active, of which 1,036 are self-employed and 169 are unemployed
850 are economically inactive, of which 212 are retired and 138 are students	2,870 are economically inactive, of which 173 are retired and 1,678 are students
The area also has a high number of well-educated people, to degree level or above, 323	The area also has a high number of well-educated people, to degree level or above, 3,363

Source: Nomisweb (2020).

Whilst these two communities have different population sizes, there are some interesting points for comparative analysis. What is immediately obvious is that location 1, Jaywick, has as a proportion to its population, higher rates of unemployment, retired people and a population with a lower educational attainment. Although a smaller population, it can be used for some speculative analysis and discussion of the types of sport and recreational services which *might* be needed. For location 2, this is an affluent part of the City of London, where the market analysis would be the more traditional type for the assessment of the potential for offering profitable sport services, so the focus here might well be more about want satisfaction.

This general UK census database, for England, can be given further refinement by analysing Sport England's invaluable data on sport and recreation segments, available at:

https://segments.sportengland.org/

You are strongly recommended to explore this database, no matter what country you are from, as it gives some important benchmarks of the sort of data it is possible to produce. Using this interactive database and a relevant post code (i.e. the coded letters which give postal areas for the country), it gives some invaluable information on communities, identifying 19 different market segments. Referring back to area 1 and using the area post code, here are examples of just two market segments, from the 19 possible ones, which focus on the retired community and Sport England's description:

'Elsie and Arnold – 19 Retirement Home Singles': 8% of the adult population in Jaywick, who are described as:

> aged 81 and live on their own in warden-controlled accommodation. Their spouses passed away three years ago and they are getting used to life on their own. They can no longer drive, due to their cataracts. Instead, they look forward to a weekly walk to the post office to collect their pension, having a good natter with the lady who works there.
>
> (Sport England, 2020b)

'Frank – Twilight year Gents': 4% of the population, who are described as:

> 69 and lives with his wife in a small bungalow...Frank has a reasonable income and though he can't afford luxuries he enjoys a flutter on the horses, the odd scratch card and spoiling the grandchild.... Frank is not particularly health conscious, enjoying hearty traditional meals and a good pint at his local. He is also likely to smoke.
>
> (Sport England, 2020b)

There is more information available, which gives additional insights into some of their health issues and their interests, which is continued in in Box 10.4.

(continued)

Box 10.2 (continued)

Discussion

For a country of your choosing, search for a variety of secondary open databases, which can be used to profile community segmentations for a selection of city or town.

10.3.3 When is data collected?

The data collection is in fact constant process in operations management. What does vary is the degree of complexity and formality of the data collection methods used. To further help clarify the research and consultation process, it can be useful to reflect what type of data is collected, at the different stages of a sport service or project delivery. In Figure 10.4, a simple summary is given on the key research process stages, whilst Box 10.3 has an example of how to collect data before a service is designed.

Here are some examples of the types of data that might be collected at the different stages of service delivery or project development:

- **Before**: This data relates to conducting market research, such as using quantitative databases on the community, as illustrated in Box 10.2.
- **During**: During the actual running of services, different types of data might be collected. For example, in modern stadiums, they have a variety of surveillance systems which can be used to monitor crowd behaviour, such as scanning for any potential crush zones, where it is even possible to utilise crowd heat maps to spot potential problem areas.
- **After service or project delivery**: This relates to collecting data after the service has been delivered or the project completed. This can involve surveys issued by the service provider, or it can even relate to scrutinising a variety of customer review sites, as illustrated in Chapter 5.

Figure 10.4 When Do You Collect Data.
Source: Author.

Box 10.3 Theoretical modelling

Torkildsen (2005) offers a variety of ways that demand for sport and leisure services can be estimated using a number of different models. One simple and useful technique is the use of the Participation Rate Model. This works as follows:

- Find sport participation rates (many countries around the world will collect this data as part of broader work and lifestyle data) to work out a theoretical demand for a sport service in the community.
- Identify sport supply in a area and the theoretical demand which can be supplied (e.g. number of sport facilities, services offered, hours available).
- Compare theoretical demand with theoretical supply to identify if there is any market gaps or latent demand.

Here's a simple example of how this can apply in practice, using a commissioned report by Rowe (2019, p. 41), which scrutinised sport participation in Scotland. In that report, one of the tables showed the top recreational activities and how it broke down according to the different age segments. This was based on asking what activities people have participated in over the past four weeks and how many times they participated (i.e. the participation rate), and for how long. The following data was identified:

- Most popular activity was 'walking for at least 30 minutes' (70% of the respondents), followed by swimming (18%), then Keep Fit/Aerobic activities (15%). A little further down the list, at 9th, was golf, with a 5% participation rate.
- Keep Fit/Aerobics participation rate broke down into the age profiles of 20% of 16–24 age group; 20% of 25–34 age group; 18% of 35–44 age group; 14% of 45–59 age group; 10% of 60–74 age profile and 5% of 75+ age.
- Golf participation rate broke down into the age profiles of 5% of 16–24 age group; 5% of 25–34 age group; 4% of 35–44 age group; 6% of 45–59 age group; 7% of 60–74 age profile and 5% of 75+ age.

This type of data is invaluable for sport managers and SDOs. Just looking at the examples of Keep Fit, not surprisingly it sees a decline in participation as people age; in contrast golf has a remarkably consistent participation rate, with the peak rate occurring when people are older and retired, which can be explained by a variety of factors, such as some having more disposable income and, if retired, time. The sport manager or SDO could utilise this information by transposing this average participation data to their local communities to identify potential demand. For example, in a fictitious Scottish community of a 1,000 people, using the above data, one could calculate that:

- 700 are likely to walk twice a month
- 180 to demand swimming at least twice a month

(continued)

> Box 10.3 (continued)
>
> - 150 to demand keep-fit activities twice a month
> - 50 to demand playing golf
>
> What a manager or SDO could then do is to audit what sport services can be provided or supplied to calculate if there are any deficiencies in supply, further complemented by collecting other data.
>
> **Discussion**
>
> For a country of your choosing, explore what databases that can be found on sport participation rates and identify the most popular sports. Use this data for a chosen city, town or village, and search to work out the theoretical demand for a selected sport service.

10.3.4 How is data collected?

Clearly, for the manager and SDO there are, in theory, numerous options for collecting data, which vary in their reliability. In Figure 10.5, a summary is given for the variety of techniques which can be used to collect data, with an applied example given in Box 10.4.

Here is a short elaboration of what each of the methods relates to, with a worked example given in Box 10.4:

- **Personal heuristics** – Heuristics refers to people using their own values and experiences to analyse the world which can inform their decisions. More experienced managers and SDOs can have a valuable amount of experience from which to draw upon, but it can also run the risk of them becoming inflexible or blind to market opportunities.
- **Staff meetings and debriefs** – Staff meetings where staff give their views and insights can be invaluable. Having quick post-event 'dust-down' meetings can be particularly useful to help sort out operational issues.
- **Creative thinking exercises** – This relates to using a variety of creative thinking exercises, such as mind-mapping techniques, discussed in Chapters 3 and 5.
- **Competitor analysis** – Scrutinising what others are doing in the industry is important as it can alert the manager or SDO what new services should be considered. There are numerous business tools which can be used here, such as Porter's five forces model.
- **Comparative analysis of previous events** – Scanning the news for new sport service developments and events can be important for generating ideas, adapting practices and learning from good or bad practice (e.g. analysing any accidents).
- **Open secondary databases** – There are large amounts of data that other organisations have collected, some of which can be free, that can relate to

Researching and consulting communities **225**

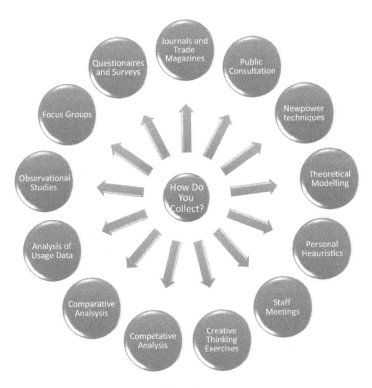

Figure 10.5 Data Collection Techniques Overview.
Source: Author.

more general data and information on populations, or more specific data on sport and recreation participation, as illustrated in Boxes 10.1 and 10.2.

- **Analysis of primary input and output data** – A facility or SDO will generate a lot of data which it can be analysed, as discussed in Chapter 3. This can involve looking at the rhythms of demand in a day, week, month and even a year, as demand can have seasonal fluctuations (e.g. in Europe and America, after the Christmas break, it can often see an increase in gym membership).
- **Observation studies** – This primary data can relate to formal observations, such as counting the number of people using a sport location, or how they move through spaces. This data also relates to the theory of carrying capacity (see Chapter 5). For large-scale events, in many arenas, there is likely to be more systematic video monitoring of crowd behaviour. Sometimes it can be useful to conduct informal observations of the services being delivered.
- **Focus groups** – This is where a group of people are selected then interviewed and discussions held on different issues. The idea is to usually try and ask open-ended questions that initiate and prompt discussion and draw out opinions on various topics and issues, as illustrated in Box 10.4.

- **Questionnaires and surveys** – There are numerous types and variations, which could be a book in themselves, such as using self-completed questionnaires, which can be done online, or questions asked by interviewers whilst users are on site. The questions asked can be open-ended questions (e.g. tell us what you think about...), which gives qualitative data, or closed questions, which ask for simple answers. Alternatively, the person can be asked to give a rating, such as a satisfaction rating based on using a one to five scale. Consideration can also be given to how people are selected, such as using random sampling techniques or quotas.
- **Reading trade journals** – This is a simple tool for scanning the business environment, where opportunities are looked for, such as new trends for services or technologies, or ideas for new services, or how existing ones can be improved.
- **Theoretical modelling** – Torkildsen (2005) gives a variety of ways demand for sport goods and services can be assessed using a different tools, such as: the participation rates method; the need-index approach; or the standards approach. In Box 10.3 a simple illustrative example is given for using the participation rates model.
- **Public consultation** – This simply relates to holding open, community meetings. Sometimes these can be run as public forums, where people ask questions of key figures from the senior management board. In other instances, they can be creative thinking exercises, such as organising the attendees into a series of working group tables, where they come up with designs for new community sport facilities and services.
- **New power approaches** – This is where social media communities and networks can be used to gauge demand and level of interest in services, such as the number of likes given for ideas or services. Having a more formal crowdfunding platform is also a useful way of collecting data, which can be used to reveal potential interest and demand for services, which then can inform decisions and help win money.

Box 10.4 An applied example for researching third age users and their active recreation needs and wants

In the earlier Box 10.2, the population data was explored for a deprived area of the UK. One of the community groups or market segments identified related to the elderly or retired. This group is sometimes described as third age users, which in essence refers to the time after middle age, when people have retired from work. For developed countries around the world, third age users are a growing market segment which needs to be catered for as populations age.

For the community identified in Text Box 10.2, of the 19 market segments identified by the Sport England Market Database, 6 groups can be considered as third age users, which are:

- Roger and Joy – Early Retirement Couples (7% of the community)
- Terry – Local 'Old Boys' (4% of the community)
- Norma – Later Life Ladies (2% of the adult community)
- Ralph and Phyllis – Comfortable retired couples (4% of adult community)
- 'Frank – Twilight year Gents' (4% of adult population)
- 'Elsie and Arnold – Retirement Home Singles' (8% of the adult population)

Source: Sport England (2020b).

Based on this data, over a third of the adult population for Jaywick can be classed as third age users. Although some can be considered as 'economically comfortable', many may be experiencing economic problems and suffer from a variety of health issues. For any managers or SDOs in the area, using this secondary data reveals that there are different potential needs and demands for a variety of recreational services. It also shows a variety of stakeholders and partners who can be worked with to help deliver these services, ranging from health professionals, charities and community groups.

This secondary data is not enough, however. Obviously, the manager will use their own experience or heuristics, perhaps with some creative thinking exercises with staff and other key partners to identify what sport and recreational services may be needed. Yet even with this additional information, it may not be enough to remove all the key barriers for participation (think back to Text Box 10.1 and the story of the education programmes and worming tablets). To give further refinement to the analysis, more data and information can be collected, such as using smaller focus group (8–12 people) discussions, to discern from the direct potential users the challenges they face and the barriers they experience. Using social media and digital technologies may be less useful for this target group, so using more traditional communication tools may be better to inform them of the focus group (e.g. posters and leaflets in local shops, health centres or other community spaces). These interviews should be recorded, with participant consent, with all people encouraged to speak or comment, which predominately asks open questions. The following data should be gathered:

- Identify the different user characteristics (e.g. age, sex, former occupations, etc., which also give a small amount of quantifiable data in an approach which is predominantly qualitative).
- Discuss what sort of recreational activities or sports they currently do/have done in the past, if any?
- Discuss what barriers prevent them from being more active or playing sport?
- Discuss what factors contributed to them stopping sport, if relevant?

(continued)

Box 10.4 (continued)

From similar focus group discussions, here are some examples of issues identified, which helped managers and SDOs adapt the service offered:

- From one focus group session, it was noted that it could be better to use the term 'recreation' rather than 'sport', as sport can carry negative connotations for some, as they have had poor experiences of sport. The term 'active recreation' was therefore considered a more embracing term. The classic meaning of recreation means to *restore health* and, if one considers health in terms of its physical, social and mental dimensions, this creates an important foundation from which to design a service (Torklildsen, 2005, was a keen advocate of this approach).
- A manager of a small community pool, through secondary research, identified a significant group of retired people in the local catchment. The problem was that although they tried to offer various programmes for this target group, such as aquarobics (a light exercise class in the pool), it always suffered a low participation rate, no matter how low the price set. The manager decided to do more research by conducting a number of focus group discussions in sheltered accommodation, where it was revealed that the problem or barrier was not one of price (in fact they were willing to pay more), but transport. What the manager then did was to increase the price slightly, where the additional revenue raised was used to subsidise a mini-bus, used to pick up this group.
- During this focus group conversations, it was also discovered that the physical activity was only part of the attraction, where the opportunity for social interactions and contact was what was really valued. The service was adapted accordingly, whereby tea, cake and biscuits were also offered, but managed by the group members as an additional voluntary activity, so they could talk and socialise after the aquarobics session.
- In another focus group, one of the key barriers identified, which affected participation levels and the quality of the experience, was that the local parking was considered as quite expensive, so it was the cumulative costs of travel and parking that had to be considered, not just the primary cost of paying for the recreational services offered. The impact on the experience was that some of the users often felt under pressure to finish before their parking ran out and they risked a parking penalty.
- In a different focus group, whilst for some users, they longed to be able to play certain sports again, which they played when they were younger. For these particular users, adapted sport activities were developed, such as walking football. These adapted activities have subsequently grown and can be found in a variety of sports, such as walking cricket, basketball, netball and hockey.

Researching and consulting communities **229**

> These examples illustrate the importance of using a variety of data and data collection techniques to fully understand the operational system that customers have to navigate and journey through.
>
> **Discussion**
> For a community of your choice (e.g. children, disabled, women, etc.) outline a research process to collect data on the group, in order to design a service which meets their needs and wants.

10.3.5 How is data analysed and ensuring reliability

In academic research, the concept of validity and reliability is vital in producing research findings and conclusions which can be trusted and believed. These principles of good research should be considered and extended into research for management decision-making, whilst also helping to shape ethical working cultures. For those who have studied research methods as part of an academic course, you may be familiar with the concepts of *validity* and *reliability* (or the looser variant of *trustworthiness*, usually used in social science-based research). As a reminder, they refer to:

- **Reliability**: Reliability of data refers to how consistent the data is collected. For example, if output data is found from a paid-for-service, then there is likely to be more consistency in how this data is collected and recorded; in contrast, if the output data is just found from different people observing and counting the number of users at different times of a day, then this can be less consistent and so potentially less reliable. Issues of bias can also come into play here.
- **Validity**: The reliability of data impacts on the validity, because if you cannot trust the consistency of how the data was collected, or if it is not free from bias (if that is ever possible), then one may question how valid any conclusions made are (i.e. this is sometimes described as the *rubbish in, rubbish out* problem).

There is not the scope to explore all the mechanisms which can be used in research to ensure that data collected and its analysis is valid and reliable, or trustworthy and rigorous. That is better left to more specialist text books, such as in Skinner et al. (2018) or Runciman (2018), or many other books on research. The key point to focus on here is to reiterate the importance of approaching management with integrity and an open, critical reflective culture. It is about having honesty to the critical questions asked about services, particularly when they go wrong, where there is a desire to learn from mistakes, not simply cover them up. This critical, reflective working culture to learn from failures and having a desire to 'find out' and 'learn about' why things work or fail can be particularly important when scrutinising data. There can be a tendency for people to find the data, to fit the theory, opinion or action already established. Borg (2008) cites Bernard Shaw's classic quote to show it is an old problem:

> The moment we want to believe something, we suddenly see all the arguments for it, becoming blind to the arguments against it.

Borg (2008, p. 27) also reminds us about the importance of reflection, saying that 'the unreflective person … goes through life imprisoned in the prejudices derived from common sense'. In turn, this can also lead to the problem of 'narrative fallacies' (Runciman, 2018, p. 147). This is when patterns in data are seen, where none may in fact exist. Critical thinking, reflection and scrutiny can be vital to utilise in these instances. Indeed, some would go further, saying that negative thinking has a place here, as they can encourage the asking of critical questions. Questions, which if it is an open, honest and reflective culture, can be properly explored, not run away from – an important part of De Bono's different thinking hats, discussed in Chapter 3, which is designed to try and ensure a more critical, robust analysis of ideas, which can be brought to focus after the early blue sky thinking stages.

10.4 CONCLUSION

Data collection, research and analysis is an implicit part of operations management. In every chapter, discussed so far, it is always there, where managers and SDOs often engage with the process without thinking. The reason why it has appeared as a separate chapter at the end is to remind managers and SDOs who have studied at university or college, to use the skills and knowledge gained as part of those courses, more systematically.

The practical skills of data collection are relatively easy to learn. The challenge is the development of a working culture which includes the principles of integrity, criticality and a hunger to find out why things work or fail. Too often, managers and SDOs can seek to select data and information that reaffirm opinions and ideas already held, or to support decisions already made. There is also the fallibility that we can all have in times of failure, to apportion blame onto others, or cover up mistakes. One of the themes, therefore, constantly argued in this book, is to approach operations management with honesty and integrity, having feedback loops that allow people to learn from failure. This is not only good for the person's conscious, but can also lay the foundation for protecting the brand of the organisation and maintaining trust, which has consistently emerged as important for Generation Z, who will be the next key group driving sport service operations in the future.

Remember, ethics is doing the right thing, when no one is looking!

References

Davies, B. and Mwaanga, O. (2005). Dunking aids out: Learning about aids through basketball movement games, accessed 22 March 2019, available at: http://www.basketballfordevelopment.org/wp-content/uploads/2015/10/39__dunking_aids_out_learning_about_aids_through_basketball_movement_games.pdf

Cahn, S.K. (1994). *Coming on Strong: Gender and Sexuality in Twentieth-Century Sport*. First Harvard University Press.

Etzioni, A. (1993). *The Spirit of Community: The Reinvention of American Society*. New York: Touchstone Publishers.

Hartford, T. (2012). *Adapt*. London: Abucus.

Masterman, G. (2004). *Strategic Sports Event Management*. London: Elsevier.

Mwaang, O.S. (2005). Kicking aids out: Through movement games and sports activities, available at: https://www.sportanddev.org/sites/default/files/downloads/5_kicking_aids_out.pdf

Nomisweb (2020). 2011 Ward population, accessed 2 February 2020, available at: https://www.nomisweb.co.uk/reports/lmp/ward2011/1140858354/report.aspx?pc=SW7#pop

Putnam, D. (2000). *Bowling Alone: The Collapse and Revival of American Community*.

Rowe, N.F. (2019). Sports participation in Scotland: Trends and future prospects. Report commissioned by the Observatory for Sport in Scotland, accessed 14 April 2020, available at: https://www.oss.scot/wp-content/uploads/2019/06/Final-Revised-participation-report-for-publication28-05-2019.pdf

Runciman, D. (2018). *How Democracies End*. London: First Publishing.

Skinner, J., Edwards, A., and Corbett (2015). *Research Methods for Sport Management*. London, Routledge.

Sport England (2020a). Active population, accessed 8 March 2020, available at: http://www.sportengland.org/research.aspx

Sport England (2020b). Frank-18, accessed 14 April, 2020, available at: https://segments.sportengland.org/pdf/penPortrait-18.pdf

Torkildsen, G. (2005). *Leisure and Recreation Management*, 5th ed. London: Routledge.

WHO (2020). Number of people living with HIV, accessed 2 April 2020, available at: https://apps.who.int/gho/data/view.main.22100?lang=en

INDEX

abuse: coaching 18, 20; mental 19; sexual 19; women 151
action plan 33, 52
administration, sport 1, 2, 14, 28, 77
Africa 157, 200
agent (sport) 57
AIDS 7, 83, 10, 215, 216, 217
American Football 6, 104, 165, 206
Anderson, D. M. 16, 32, 41
athletics 156, 157
attribute listing, 60
Auluck 14
Australia 19, 92, 191, 193
Australian Rugby 38, 39
Australian Sport Commission 36, 37
AWID 108

Barca Foundation 44, 153
Barcelona 23, 37, 45, 155, 165
basketball 215, 216, 228
Benderley, B. 184
Bernstein, B. 207
Bernstein, J. 205
Bernstein, P. 193
Black lives matter 151
Blakey, P. 16, 78, 98
Blinebury, F. 61
Bitner, M. J. 113
Bjarsholm, D. 148
Borg, J. 168, 187, 215, 229, 230
Boston marathon 155, 199
boxing 176, 206
brands 8, 62–63, 146, 207
Bradford, fire 17, 18, 103, 115
Braithwaite, T. W. 117
Branson, R. 37
Buzan Mind Maps 60
business functions 168
business plan 35, 36, 176
Buswell, J. 106
Bryman, A. 47
Byers, T. 34

Canadian 13, 14, 19, 159
care 83
Carlzon, J. 14, 99

carrying capacity 110, 111, 124, 225
causation 18, 21, 52, 57, 99, 196, 197, 204
chaos theory 13, 22, 199
checklists 60, 123, 197, 204, 205, 206, 207
child protection 21, 174
China 22, 61, 62, 63, 102, 178, 179, 181
Clarke, C. 200
Clarkson, M. B. E. 144
coaching xiv, 3, 4, 8, 18, 19, 20, 39, 47, 88, 146, 153, 156, 166, 206
Coalter, F. 4, 6, 32, 45, 47
Coca Cola 176, 177, 178
Collins, M. 5
commercial sector 6
communities 33, 34, 46, 48, 86, 122, 128, 138, 144, 146, 150, 159, 175, 176, 179, 186, 212–221, 221–226
community consultation 88, 213, 217–220
complexity theory xv, 11, 12, 13, 15, 17, 28, 55, 59, 63, 75, 128, 129, 152, 204, 208, 222
consumer 22, 79
Cornell, C. 182
corporate governance 190
Corporate Social Responsibility (CSR) 26, 34, 35, 39, 135, 138, 143, 144, 145–148, 152, 153, 155, 162, 169, 175, 176, 181
Coventry 94, 95
COVID-19 22, 111, 116, 199, 200
cricket 8, 93, 125, 155, 206, 228
crisis 18, 21, 32, 57, 58, 59, 62, 63, 71, 73, 123, 147, 152, 155, 166, 180, 189–210
crisis management 190, 191, 192, 193, 197, 199
crisis recovery plan 204
crowdfunding 151, 167, 170, 175, 182–187, 226
Cunningham, A. 123
cycling 27, 94, 95, 172
customer care xv, 66, 98–109, 111, 113, 116–119

David Lloyd Clubs 94
data analysis 81
data collection 212, 214–215, 222, 225, 229, 230

233

De Bono, E. 60, 61, 230
demand 78–81, 83–84, 87, 88, 89, 92–96, 107, 109, 110, 112, 151, 157, 166, 183, 201, 219, 220, 223–224, 225–227
Deming, W. E. 105
design day 111–112
development, *for* or *as* 121, 132, 134, 139, 144, 151, 154, 160, 161, 164, 183–184, 215–216, 230
disability 9, 47, 85, 160
Doha 157
Drucker, P. E. 100
Dussauge, P. 156
Dynamic Risk Assessment (DRA) 190, 191–192, 204, 209

economy 21, 31, 33, 34, 138, 139, 200
effectiveness 28, 31, 33, 34, 46, 47, 49, 51, 52, 59, 106, 171, 212, 217
efficiency 31, 32, 46, 48–50, 52, 56, 69, 87, 102, 106, 212
equity 10, 31, 46, 47, 87, 165, 166, 167
emotional 16, 19, 24, 26, 28, 40, 104, 143, 159, 168–169, 177, 182, 204, 213
emotional intelligence 160
English Premier league (EPL) 44
ethics 15, 108, 146, 167, 169, 177, 187, 200, 205, 230
Etzioni, A. 213
entrepreneurship 158
Eventbrite 179
event tree analysis 198–199
external business environment 167, 191, 195, 201, 203, 219
externality 6, 166

Facebook 101, 151, 184
Fagel, M. J. 198
Fainara-Wada, M. 206
fault tree analysis 198–199
FIFA 57, 58, 103, 122, 153, 155
Fiji 159
five forces (Porters) 181, 224
Floyd, George 151
football 3, 7, 17, 19, 26, 28, 37, 38, 45, 67, 68, 82, 83, 88, 102, 103, 104, 125, 126, 153, 154, 157, 160, 165, 178, 181, 200, 214, 228
Forbes 165

French, D. 85
funding gap 164, 166, 167, 177

gambling 72, 78, 154
Gantt 122, 133, 134, 135, 136
Gardiner, P. D. 123, 128
Gawande, E. 204
gender 165, 184
Generation Z 152, 167, 209, 230
Germany 79, 157, 178
Gerras, S. J. 13
Gillies, P. 152
goals 4, 7, 26, 31, 35, 38, 41–44, 116, 122, 152, 172, 177, 183
Goodpaster, K. 147
golf 48, 49, 223, 224
González, V. M. 57
government failures 34, 156
grant applications 131, 164, 167, 171, 172, 173, 175, 177, 187

Hamburg 25
Hartford, T. 217
Heizer, J. 11, 133
hockey 125, 153, 228
Homeless World Cup 206; Foundation 135–137
Hong Kong 62
Houston Rockets 62
Highgate Harriers 157
Houlihan, B. 4
HRM 7, 8, 81
Hylton, K. 4

IHRSA 79
incrementalism 14
India 10, 92, 93, 157, 181
Imai, M. 32
inputs 11, 15, 17, 28, 33, 34, 46, 52, 92, 105, 123, 124, 129
IbisWorld 79, 110

Jackie Robinson 195
Japan 19, 23, 126, 138, 158, 159, 181, 193
job tasks 55–61, 63, 65–68, 69, 71, 72, 73, 74, 82, 102, 122, 123, 132, 133, 135, 137, 141
Judo 19

Kaizen 14, 32, 105
Kamaishi 158–159
Kimberly-Clark Worldwide 106

Korea 20, 22, 83, 85, 101, 181
KPIs 35, 36, 41, 42, 44, 45, 46, 62, 74, 124, 132, 135, 218
Kumar, V. 99
Koutrou, N. 156
Krakow 194

labour 162
Lang, M. 20
leadership 5, 7, 20, 27, 38, 45, 68, 73, 75, 108, 132, 141, 160, 205
Leboeuf, M. 32, 99, 100
legacy 121, 124, 125, 137, 140, 141, 172, 185
levels of management xv, 7, 8, 27, 35, 141, 190, 193
leveraging 24, 25, 28, 106, 125, 137, 138, 139, 185, 213, 215
Levitin, D. 63, 72, 73
London Olympics 160

management functions 6, 7, 8, 10, 81, 82, 127
management skills 8, 134, 141
Macht, S. 184
maintenance schedule 116
Manchester arena 113
Manchester United xv, 155, 181
MASTER (objectives) 42
marginal costs 90, 92
marginal gains 13, 14, 52, 98, 101, 102, 104, 105, 217
market failures 34, 156
Market positioning map 94, 95
market research 132, 218, 222
market share 92, 181
marketing mix 79
Maslow, A. H. 78, 214
McNeill, D. 19
McNicol, A. 61
milestone 42, 62, 73, 122, 131, 132, 133, 135, 137, 173, 183
mind mapping 93
mission statements 31, 33, 35, 36, 37, 38, 39, 40, 41, 82
Mitra, A. 104, 105
Mollick, E. 182
monitoring 12, 33, 52, 59, 74, 82, 122, 127, 137, 194, 196, 197, 199, 225
Moore, R. 103, 104, 106

Namibia 159
NBA 61, 62

neo-liberalist 5
netball 125, 176
networks 110, 143, 144, 146, 148, 150, 151, 152, 153, 167, 179, 180, 184, 186, 199, 226
new power theories 28, 146, 150, 151, 161, 162, 164, 167, 170, 169, 193, 201, 226
New York 86, 155
New Zealand 19, 172, 173, 176, 193
NFL 6, 165, 206
Nichols, J. M. 60
Nike 154, 168, 169, 181
Nomisweb 221
NSW 171
nudge theory 25, 26, 27, 28, 106, 108, 109, 112, 168, 169, 197

obesity 27, 78, 148
objectives 9, 10, 34, 35, 36, 37, 39, 41–45, 48, 52, 62, 81, 82, 104, 122, 124, 135, 137, 141, 167, 169, 181, 193, 218
old power 150, 151, 152, 183, 184
Olympics 16, 122, 126, 128, 130, 155, 160, 166
outcomes 2, 7, 16, 24, 33, 45, 47, 49, 56, 82, 123, 125, 129, 137–138, 148, 161, 167, 190
outputs 10, 12, 15, 17, 32, 121, 122, 216

Palmer-Green, D. 44
participation rate 44, 79, 108, 220, 223, 226, 228
participation rates model 223–224
partnerships 9, 61, 62, 110, 143, 144, 146, 147, 150, 152–162, 167, 173, 176, 178, 183, 186
persuasion (theories) 167–170, 175, 177
peak day 111, 112
PESTLE 21, 56, 180, 201, 219
Piekarz, M. 2, 7, 195, 196, 199, 201
planning checklist 60
planning for crisis 73, 197, 198, 206, 209
planning process 127
PMBOK 121, 126
Poland 178, 195
pricing 81, 85, 88–92, 132
pricing calculation form 89, 91
prioritising 63–65
Priority Grid 64
Product Lifecycle (PLC) 79, 80, 93, 96, 108
programming 77, 79, 81, 82, 94, 109, 172
project management: definition 121, 122; process 127–128; system 123; tools 122

promotion 79, 81, 82, 109, 205
Putnam, D. 213
PureGym 94, 95
Pyeong Chang 22

queues 110–113
quality management 14, 98, 102, 104–105, 106, 119
qualitative data 130, 220, 226, 227
quantitative data 216, 222

Recovery rate 46, 49, 63, 92
research methods 215, 229
RFU 44, 206, 207
risk core pillars 191
risk: definition 190, 191, 193; management 122, 189, 190, 191, 193, 194, 195, 197, 209; process 195, 197, 204
Robinson, L. 32, 34, 195
Rowe, N. F. 223
Rugby World Cup 41, 126, 138, 158, 182
Rumelt, R. 35, 39, 41, 70
Runciman, D. 199, 200, 229, 230

satisficing 72, 73
scheduling 62, 128, 132, 133, 135
Schwarz, E. C. 32, 34, 45, 46, 47
segmentation 213, 222
Seoul 84
service design 60, 77, 82, 97
service encounter 104, 107, 108
service quality 102, 105
servicescape 114
Simpson, K. 153, 161
Skildum-Reid, K. 179
Skinner, J. 229
Slack, N. 11, 22, 75, 82, 105, 133
Slater, M. 167
small wins 14
SMART (objectives) 62, 82, 124, 132, 135, 137, 167, 169, 180
social distancing 111, 113, 200
social enterprise 82, 152
social networks 184
social distancing 111, 113, 200
Sogut, E. 57
Sondhi, R. 35
sponsorship 177–182; definitions 177; packs 167; partnerships 153; types 178
Sport and Recreation Alliance 154, 161, 191
sport development definition 3, 4

Sport England 160, 161, 162, 221, 227
sport *for* development 4, 7, 9, 15, 28, 82, 216
Sport Industry Research Centre (SIRC) 45, 47
sportscape 113, 128
Sri Lanka 85
stakeholders 15, 26, 43, 59, 128, 130, 135, 143–148, 160, 168, 193, 196, 205, 212, 219, 227
Statista 165, 167
strategy (classic template) 40
systems theory 11, 12, 14, 17, 57, 59, 84, 98, 105, 107, 123
swimming 19, 66, 80, 84, 85, 86, 94, 223
Swindon 194
SWOT 22, 180, 201, 219

targets 35, 36, 43, 44, 45, 46, 47, 183
Tenner, E. 57
Thaler, R. H. 25
third age 65, 226, 227
third sector 156, 158
throughputs 55, 123, 124
time Management 8, 56, 68–71, 74, 134, 137, 141, 167, 204
to-do lists 59, 65, 69, 70, 71, 72, 73, 74, 138
Torkildsen, G. 2, 32, 34, 47, 56, 59, 75, 77, 78, 127, 223, 226
total quality management (TQM) 105, 115
Tottenham Hotspur 104, 111, 113, 155
triple constraint 112, 122, 125, 126, 131, 133
tsunami 85, 159, 203

Unitied Nations (UN) 5, 83

values (business) 36, 37
VanGrundy, A. B. 59
variability 116
VMOST 35
VUCA 13, 22, 148, 199

Wakefield, K. L. 111, 114
Weber, C. 148
Wooles, A. 14
Worcester Warriors 135
work breakdown structures (WBS) 35, 60, 61, 73, 128, 133, 136
World Rugby 7, 38, 43, 138, 158
Wilson, R. 2, 7, 8, 24, 34, 107

Yoshino, M. 152